My Five Cambridge Friends

MY
FIVE
CAMBRIDGE
FRIENDS

BURGESS, MACLEAN, PHILBY, BLUNT, AND

CAIRNCROSS BY THEIR KGB CONTROLLER

FARRAR STRAUS GIROUX / New York

YURI MODIN

WITH JEAN-CHARLES DENIAU AND AGUIESZKA ZIAREK

Translated by Anthony Roberts

Introduction by David Leitch

Contents

Introduction

by David Leitch

One of the unexpected bonuses of the final years of the twentieth century is the forbidden, almost voyeuristic thrill of seeing inside the battlelines of the 'Other Side', until so recently our most implacable enemy. We can penetrate his old fortifications and even browse incredulously among the archives of his most secret agency, the KGB, inside the guarded corridors of Moscow Centre, otherwise known as the dreaded Lubyanka.

The massive building has a history of arrest and execution going back beyond the seventeenth century: Peter the Great's estranged wife was tortured in these vaulted dungeons specially designed for the arcane requirements of secret policemen. In the nineteenth century people traditionally crossed themselves to ward off evil as they passed the accursed walls, although by then the reason for the curse was forgotten. The Lubyanka had become the central office of an innocent insurance company, who found the enormous cellars useful for storage. In our own century, first Feliks Dzerzhinski, Lenin's secret police boss, and then Lavrenti Pavlovich Beria, who took command by murdering his predecessor Nicolai Ivanovich Yezhov, the so-called 'Bloody Dwarf', restored the building to traditional uses: conspiracy, espionage, foreign and domestic, torture and, ultimately, execution. Once again Muscovites hurried by with averted eyes, as if the very act of looking at the KGB palace invited brutal retribution.

Now, reading Yuri Ivanovich Modin's long-awaited account, we can experience the view from inside the Lubyanka looking out.

For Modin was the professional KGB officer who ran the five

1

Cambridge spies: Philby, Burgess, Maclean, Blunt, Cairncross. They were Modin's agents, and thus 'Friends', in the special sense implied by the spy trade jargon with which John le Carré has made us so familiar.

Modin was initially the Five's deskman in Moscow Centre during World War Two, and after 1948, codenamed Peter, he became the London controller of John Cairncross, aka the Carelian, Guy Burgess, aka Mädchen, and Anthony Blunt, aka Yan. In May 1951, Peter also acted as choreographer of the Burgess and Maclean Great Escape, chivvying them into the sensational defection to Moscow thanks to a tip-off from Kim Philby, aka Söhnchen, in Washington. Officially, Philby served as liaison chief between MI6 and the CIA. In fact, Kim was a Soviet long-term penetration agent, probably the best ever.

Modin's account of his Friends' modus operandi contains some surprises, notably about John Cairncross and Guy Burgess. The latter, chosen as 'duenna' to escort and encourage Maclean on his flight to Moscow, receives an encomium for qualities of man management and leadership which may gratify the ghosts of his expensive mentors at Ludgrove, Eton, Dartmouth and Trinity College, Cambridge. 'Although Philby was the actual founder of the club and found Burgess, Burgess was the man who recruited Blunt, and so on down the line; the real leader was Burgess. He held the group together, infused it with his energy and led it into battle, so to speak . . . He was the moral leader of the group.'

As Modin reveals the Five's interactions in detail, it becomes apparent how much of a club or team they remained, contrary to all KGB (let alone SIS or CIA) precepts. Despite injunctions from Moscow Centre, it was as if they were invisibly and almost incestuously interrelated, a monstrous set of Siamese quins. From the start they were, sometimes literally, in bed with one another.

Burgess and Blunt were homosexual, though with bisexual excursions in their twenties, while Maclean, though ostensibly a somewhat unhappily married man, after an alcoholic breakdown in Cairo underwent psychoanalysis designed to determine whether he might find life rosier with his own sex.

Although Blunt was assuredly in love with Burgess and loyal to him right up to his final statement on the matter in 1979 praising 'Guy's brilliant intellect', Jack Hewit, Guy's lover for thirteen years, and occasional partner of Blunt, often assured me, contrary to what Modin seems to assume, that the affair was platonic. The two were never actual lovers since they both insisted on adopting the active or masculine sexual role. Guy was popularly supposed to have seduced Maclean, and may well have done so, since homosexual seduction was his forte and almost a reflex. 'I never travel by train,' he used to joke in his hoarse Scotch-and-nicotine drawl, 'if I did I'd feel obliged to seduce the driver.'

In the case of Maclean, however, Guy insisted that the conquest was purely intellectual. 'All that white flesh,' he said with revulsion, 'it would be like sleeping with Dame Nellie Melba.'

As people were still sent to jail for homosexual behaviour, and several times Burgess came very close, an entirely clandestine gay society provided excellent practice in conspiracy and leading a double life.

Modin makes us understand what the Five working together contributed to Moscow's wartime survival against Germany, not to mention the parallel intelligence and arms conflict with the USA and Britain, soon known as the Cold War. These likely and oh so bright lads from Cambridge constituted the most influential spy-ring of the first half of the century, and probably all time.

Consider: Modin reveals that at a quite early stage in the war, perhaps the end of 1940, John Cairncross, hitherto regarded as the least significant of the Gang of Five, was the first NKVD (pre-KGB) agent to inform Moscow Centre 'that the Americans and British had been working since late 1940 on the joint manufacture of an atomic bomb'.

Cairncross came from a poor boy's scholarship background, unlike his four privileged comrades, and in 1939 was shifted from the Foreign Office largely because, in the time-honoured phrase repeated snobbishly by Maclean to Modin, 'he didn't seem to fit in'. Instead he was down-graded to the Treasury as private secretary to the power-hungry, workaholic Lord Hankey. As Modin says: 'It was a major piece of luck for us when Lord Hankey was appointed chairman of the British Scientific Consultative Committee...'

Copying 'thousands of different documents on our behalf', Cairncross revealed that the Allies were capable of producing a nuclear device based on uranium 235, and his reports were instrumental in helping Russia to astonish the west by developing and exploding her own bomb.

Here was the central intelligence issue, not only of World War Two, but of the long Cold War that followed it. Cairncross has been at pains to minimize his role, yet the espionage coup Modin reveals probably outstrips even the legendary exploits of his distant comrade in Tokyo, the Soviet agent Richard Sorge. Sorge warned Stalin of Hitler's plans to invade Russia and also, on the eve of his arrest, of the date of an impending Japanese surprise air attack on the US Navy at Pearl Harbor.

The differences between Sorge and Cairncross are instructive. The former suffered an unimaginable two years of interrogation by torture before his Tokyo execution in November 1944. The Russian public knew nothing of this until, twenty years on, Khruschev made tardy amends, and Sorge became a posthumous Hero of the Soviet Union, with his picture on a postage stamp.

Fascinatingly, Stalin disbelieved and disregarded the news of Hitler's imminent invasion, and there is no evidence that he warned President Roosevelt about Pearl Harbor. However, if he did, FDR must have also been a disbeliever. So Sorge, his life's work largely in vain, ended with a hideous martyr's death. Cairncross, contrariwise, survived another decade of intensive espionage, most of it with Modin as either his Moscow case officer or London handler, and was then shuffled off into comfortable, even idyllic, semi-retirement.

Although, after the Burgess and Maclean defection in 1951, Blunt did the 'housework', trying to ensure that the New Bond Street flat Burgess had so hastily fled contained no incriminating material, the art historian, whose mother had been a cousin of the Queen Mother's, overlooked a note Guy had scribbled after receiving information from Cairncross in 1939. Here the Carelian's espionage career ended (though by no means Blunt's). MI5 (to the disgust of the Americans) allowed Cairncross a cash payment in lieu of pension and despatched him into sybaritic exile. He settled in Monte Parioli, the suburb which is Rome's equivalent to Mayfair, and acquired a good job with the UN agency FAO.

The authorities took the view that the suspicions and scraps of circumstantial evidence were not strong enough for an Official Secrets prosecution against him; no doubt they were also profoundly reluctant to publicize his espionage.

4

In Rome Cairncross pursued an agreeable and well-paid second career of nearly twenty years. Since he was finally uncovered (by myself as a matter of fact, with my *Sunday Times* colleague Barry Penrose) at the end of the 1970s, he has led a modest and generally undisturbed exile in agreeable places, Switzerland and, currently, the South of France, where he lives with a younger female companion.

Since writing the story that ended his life in Rome I had always feared that this quiet man had possibly been condemned, as he claimed, for comparatively minor peccadilloes committed at the behest of Burgess. In the end I gave up writing about spies after some fifteen years' involvement in the area. As early as August 1964 I had received permission to interview Philby, then newly declared a Soviet citizen after his defection to Moscow.

This go-ahead had come from the Soviet leader, Nikita Khruschev no less, whom I had interviewed with the then proprietor of *The Sunday Times*, Lord Thomson, in Soviet Central Asia. Before the interview could take place, Khruschev was no more, deposed in a bloodless political coup by Brezhnev. The Iron Curtain now came down with a vengeance. In 1966 I had reported on Philby's first piece of work for the KGB. He had ghosted the highly selective memoirs of Gordon Lonsdale, the so-called Admiralty spy. MI6 let me know the bits they claimed were wrong – and mischievous – and told me Philby had been assigned to Department D of the KGB, which practised the art of 'disinformation', or black propaganda. Later I wrote, with Bruce Page and Phillip Knightley, the ground-breaking book on Philby, which followed what was probably *The Sunday Times*'s most ambitious and exhaustive 'Insight' investigation.

But at that stage we found no trace of Cairncross and were unaware of the exploits that Modin reveals in this book. He tells us that Cairncross was actually awarded one of the Soviet Union's highest honours, the Order of the Red Banner. It's a relief to learn we nailed a copper-bottomed Red Banner holder, and professional spy of great distinction, and not a dilettante idealist trapped by the commitments of a distant youth.

Cairncross achieved this extraordinary position from a humble background in Scotland. Donald Maclean's ancestry was also Scots: Highlanders and distant relatives of the Macmillans, originating from the island of Tiree off the Argyll coast. His father, Sir Donald, was a cabinet minister in Ramsay MacDonald's inglorious National government.

Modin makes an understandable error when he describes the young graduate attending his Foreign Office interview before a board of worthies (one of whom was married to his godmother) and being asked about his – very prominent – Communist Party activities at Cambridge. The Moscow analyst found in the biographical files that, with remarkable sang-froid, the young aspirant replied that 'he still hadn't entirely shed his Communist sympathies, but was working on it'.

The English nuances escaped Modin for what actually happened was that when asked if he was still a Communist he answered 'Yes, of course'. Since this issue was the first all his friends asked him about when he came out of the interview, the correct version was well remembered when I originally worked on the story. Donald was gleeful at the result and told his chums, 'They thought I was being ironic': the 1930s equivalent of being cool.

In 1944, scarcely a decade after that amiable examination board, the young Communist, perhaps the most rigidly ideological of the Five, was assigned a top-secret Foreign Office mission to Washington, co-ordinating the American atomic bomb project with the British equivalent, known as Tube Alloys. Still on the nepotist course, he got this incredibly responsible job for a man not much over thirty, thanks not least to his father's close friendship with Lord Halifax, the ambassador to Washington.

So Moscow Centre had two of the Five, who scarcely knew and felt little affection for each other, working in tandem, one in London, the other in Washington, to provide espionage on the greatest contemporary political issue by far. This miraculous access to the command centres of what both Americans and British believed was the tightest secret in world history was complemented by the purely scientific material arriving at Moscow Centre from 'Fuchs, Pontecorvo and Greenglass'. Here again the Cambridge Old Firm was right in the middle. As his wife Melinda was pregnant again, and so lived with her mother and stepfather in their apartment in Manhattan, Maclean had cast-iron cover for visits every weekend. He gave his handler in New York oceans of scientific secrets and microfilms, as well as his own priceless political intelligence.

Modin, meanwhile, on the receiving end, was in the Lubyanka, working eighteen-hour shifts, month in, month out, for 'every day brought its fresh harvest of intelligence to the Lubyanka, and it was all intelligence that we had ordered, like a suit made to measure.'

Another member of the club was also having a good run. In 1944, when Modin took desk responsibility in Moscow for the 'Cambridge Five', as they were known, Kim Philby, whose alias had now changed from Söhnchen to Stanley, was 'the rising star within the British Secret Service [and] canvassing for the top post in Section IX, the anti-communist department'. Thanks to some vicious office politics and patronage from an old friend of his father Harry St John, who had served in the Indian Civil Service, Philby was able to get the job by bypassing his immediate superior, a former Indian Army officer called Felix Cowgill, who later resigned from the service in disgust. Henry, Kim's handler, was wild with delight: his man had brought off a masterstroke. Stanley (Philby), a Soviet agent, had become head of the section within British Intelligence whose sole mission was to do battle with the KGB and thwart the spread of Communism worldwide.

Philby, aided by looks, charm and a stammer he learnt to use as a defence, seems to have found deceit and trickery came to him as naturally as to Kipling's boy spy hero and virtuoso of *The Great Game*, for whom he had been named at birth (in Amballah, India, in 1912).

Even so, it was not quite as straightforward as Modin makes out. There had been a blonde NKVD officer called Elena Modrzhinskaya working in the Moscow Centre who found the Cambridge information too good to be true. How could agents carry documents out in such bulk without being detected? How could SIS recruit and promote Söhnchen/Stanley, the rising star Kim Philby, so assiduously while his biography rang alarm bells in any conscientious State secret policeman's ears? Surely they could not be such fools (Elena's words) as not to check on available documents, like his marriage certificate, which indicated he was still married to (though separated from) a well-known Communist activist? Nowadays, what's more, Litzi was also an ardent Zionist. As such she was a sworn enemy of British policy in Palestine and, moreover, of Churchill, the wartime leader.

Elena's suspicions became more aroused the more she examined the files. In due course she succeeded in spreading her 'Revolutionary vigilance' to some other colleagues.

According to a forthcoming book discussing another collection of Philby's wartime files, transcribed by the Russian TV literary figure Genrikh Borovik, and edited by Phillip Knightley, there was actually a short period when Moscow Centre became convinced that the Cambridge spies were double agents, 'plants' by SIS from way back!

However, in 1944 the suspicious lady Elena was moved on. The 'anti' faction evaporated with her and so highly were the Five regarded towards the end of the war that in the spring of 1945 Moscow Centre decided to offer them a reward for their services, a large sum of money or 'a life pension'; all refused.

They were the purest converts and ideologists, and preferred it that way, apart from the security issues raised by any dramatic improvement in their material circumstances. At least one of them, Guy Burgess, did nonetheless receive 'small' sums, reported as 'twenty-five/thirty pounds', although in the light of Guy's legendary extravagance on food and, ever increasingly, drink, this could well have been suggested as a weekly cash float. From time to time even a Soviet spy needed to have dinner at the Ritz.

When Modin, his wife Anna and their baby daughter left the Soviet Union for the first time in the summer of 1947, they sound like babes in the wood. 'Anna and I were hopelessly young and naive . . .' he remembers. In Paris, bedazzled by the chic of Parisians – they had been educated to expect capitalist penury – the very young couple were lodged in the Grand Hôtel de la Paix, hard by the Opéra. They were 'struck dumb', in Modin's words, by the grandeur of it all.

As he frankly says, the KGB was reluctant to allow its employees out of the country at this time for fear they would defect. His status as cipher clerk was lowly. As 'cover' it was necessary for him to dissemble his knowledge of English, and also arrive at the same time as two other (genuine) cipher clerks.

Yet Modin seems never to have considered or perhaps conceived of defection. At twenty-five, a highly disciplined and conscientious intelligence officer, he was lost without the tunnel vision of his trade. In postwar London he felt 'in disarray'.

When the time came to meet the men he knew so well via their reports, disarray accelerates to something approaching chaos. First was the Super Spy Cairncross, who, in the flesh, turned out to be a spy from the Ealing comedies so popular at the time.

For all his Red Banner and brilliant Cambridge degree (what was the Leningrad Naval Academy to Cambridge? Modin humbly asks himself), the spy conducted himself like Charlie Chaplin. He had 'an appalling memory', which became 'a grave handicap to our work together'. And how. For their second meeting Cairncross was thirty minutes late, and it was downhill from then on. Cairncross could not remember the times of the meetings, the complicated back-up procedures, whether they had decided Richmond Park or Wandsworth. On further acquaintance he proved even more vague and unpunctual, and totally bereft of mechanical ability. He could not take photographs, or learn to, and when they gave him a Vauxhall car to improve security months passed before he learned to drive the thing. When he did, he managed to stall it next to a traffic policeman at a major junction and poor Modin thought his moment of exposure had come.

If he was, as he says, 'driven mad' by his agent's vagaries, then Cairncross was plain terrified. 'He agonized about getting caught and talked about it whenever we met.'

Here is a portrait of a burnt-out spy if ever there was one. Add to it the fact that Cairncross proved deaf in one ear . . . The young KGB officer could not believe the absence of proper discipline and procedures. He was also disappointed by Cairncross's shabby appearance. To his mind, a Super Spy should have had his shoes polished occasionally.

Guy Burgess's shoes proved, if anything, too polished (because he always had them done at the Reform Club, in fact), but on closer acquaintance, 'even though his clothes came from the best tailor in London, they often tended to be stained and wrinkled'. This Burgessian trait was observed by many others besides the tyro KGB handler. I have heard of champagne, red wine, whisky, cigar and cigarette ash, food and even semen stains on areas of Burgess's clothing from friends or acquaintances of the time. But Guy was impeccably punctual and practical to a fault. He suggested that the best cover of all was to pretend to be lovers looking for somewhere to find a bed. 'I changed the subject hastily,' Modin says.

Burgess and Modin were soon meeting regularly, and as an

agent/analyst/contact man Burgess proved unequalled. On a personal basis he was, well, Burgessian, and I commend to the reader the hilarious account Modin provides of the world's most eccentric and preposterous spy since Mata Hari.

Again, there is the high farce of postwar espionage: suitcases full of FO documents, one exploding all over the floor of a pub, another having to be shown to two suspicious policemen. They were immediately very respectful – Burgess kindly explained afterwards that they had been suspected of being burglars!

Burgess was no man for the suburbs, he claimed he did not know where they were, and Modin fought many a battle to arrange meetings outside Mayfair, Whitehall, Chelsea, the seedy clandestine gay bars and night-clubs of sleaziest Soho – the Burgess animal's preferred habitat. Characteristically, the Burgess reaction to Moscow Centre's suggestion about buying a car was sublimely different from Cairncross's response.

No Vauxhall for Burgess: 'I made my painful way to Acton, where I only had to wait a few seconds on the pavement before Burgess made his appearance – it was a Rolls-Royce. The money I had produced wasn't enough to buy a new one, he said, so he had picked up a powerful second-hand two-seater model with a folding top, the colour of old gold.'

Burgess's famous driving style caused Modin's body 'to go numb', not surprising since there is a persistent rumour that Guy had once actually run down and killed a man in Dublin during the war.

Modin, now perhaps twenty-six, was already a survivor. 'Never again did I get into a car with Guy Burgess.'

Burgess and motor cars made a deep impression on Modin. He describes another much later incident in the USA, probably acquired from Moscow Centre files once he himself had returned home safely after the Burgess and Maclean defection. Why such an impassioned anti-American as Burgess was ever posted to Washington is still unexplained; neither the KGB, whose own long-term plans for Philby the move ultimately ruined, nor anyone on the British side has ever made sense of it. I have heard people formerly in both services conclude that the only explanation was the anonymous black joke of an enemy Burgess had made as he wended his picaresque way through the Foreign Office corridors.

At his chaotic farewell party in New Bond Street, where naturally the police were called, Hector McNeil, Guy's direct boss as Under Secretary of State at the FO, reiterated a set of warnings Guy had been given in numerous briefings before departure.

'For God's sake, Guy,' McNeil warned, 'remember three things in America. Don't be too aggressively left-wing, don't get involved in race relations, and, above all, no homosexual incidents.'

'I understand, Hector. You mean I mustn't make a pass at Paul Robeson.'

The famous black singer was at that time prevented from performing in the USA because of his well-known admiration of the Soviet Communist system. No wonder Guy's departure was regarded with foreboding, by Modin as well as people at the Foreign Office.

In any case, on 28 February 1951, driving the Lincoln which now replaced the old gold Rolls, Burgess set off for a rather high-toned private military academy called the Citadel in Charleston, South Carolina, to represent Great Britain at a conference on international affairs. There were many dignitaries attending and, more to Guy's taste, the Citadel cadets themselves. Modin fails to report the Burgess response to this scintillating array of American military manhood but, as he may surmise, the FBI agents working for J. Edgar Hoover charged with the Great Defection inquest filed reports by the hundred. After the Freedom of Information legislation of the 1970s I was privileged to read of Guy's Citadel adventure in elaborate and appalling detail.

Needless to say, even the journey of some 560 miles proved eventful, with Burgess flagged down three times for speeding.

At the conference, either through mistake or mischief on Guy's part, many of those present took him to be the British ambassador. He delivered a rambling but eloquent address, which many regarded as an insult to the American flag. He was particularly critical of American policy in South-east Asia, made inflammatory remarks about 'adventurist and imperialist' US policies in Korea – this was of course wartime – and poured scorn on State Department policies regarding the fledgling People's Republic of China, long one of his special hobby-horses. Reports say he kept asking, rhetorically: 'How Red is the Yellow Peril, tell me that?'

In a sense this was to be Burgess's finest hour, for he had comprehensively achieved his first objective, to get himself expelled from Washington. This was the only plausible scheme he and Kim

Philby could devise as a way of warning and supporting Donald Maclean, back in London, around whom the net was closing daily. The evidence turned on a complex code-breaking operation without computer assistance which could not be hurried at this time. J. Edgar Hoover at the FBI had long been positively baying for blood.

Meanwhile, Burgess had enjoyed himself immensely, drunk at least two bottles of Bourbon, and picked up two hitchhikers (male, naturally), as the FBI files show. Hitchhiker number two even proved to have a criminal record.

Guy had done as he pleased, said what he thought, and got away virtually scot-free. It was the story of his life so far. He had also, incidentally, managed to offend nearly a thousand Americans of the period's most politically correct kind all at one sitting.

He travelled home luxuriously on the *Queen Mary* and, need it be said, found a companion, a young American academic called Miller. In due course, on the eve of defection with Maclean, Guy was to go to a lot of trouble to concoct a cover story involving Miller, pretending he had originally bought the cross-channel tickets with Miller in mind, claiming they might go and stay with the poet Wystan Auden in Ischia, laying all kinds of confusion around his tracks. This, so he thought, would give him leverage when on his return he needed to fend off interrogation from MI5. But Modin's account makes it more likely that he really believed, with heavy KGB prompting, that the trip would be as comparatively harmless an escapade as the outing to the Citadel. Burgess would see the extravagantly burnt-out Maclean to Prague, keep him steady and reasonably sober and then, hey presto, back to Whitehall and, thanks to the usual friends in the right places, all would be forgiven and forgotten.

Following a suggestion from Anthony Blunt, Burgess and Maclean had chosen to escape by ship via Jersey to St-Malo because the passport requirements were negligible on this route and, with an investigation ready to begin at any moment, they feared a Stop order. At almost exactly midnight the two men stood aboard the SS *Falaise* at Southampton pulling away from shore. An indignant sailor down on the dock called to complain about their car, this time an Austin A70, the best Guy had been able to hire at short notice. True to form, he had left it parked in the most convenient place for him and the least for anyone else. It was virtually at the foot of the passenger gangplank; the men had arrived at the very last minute.

'Back on Monday,' Guy had called insouciantly. There is now little doubt he believed it, and indeed went on believing it in a sense until his death twelve years later, exiled in a Moscow he loathed. He had not even liked it much on his only previous visit, in 1934, when he had reportedly been arrested for urinating in a public – or People's – park.

Nor had Anthony Blunt, who, rather than flee with the other two, chose, in an Old Boy reflex identical to Guy's, to gamble on friends in high places – even when it came to friends in Buckingham Palace. Surely the authorities, he argued, even if they could muster sufficient proof, would back off at the prospect of naming a relation of the Royal family as a Soviet spy? As we know, it was a reasonable assumption. The bet held for twenty-eight years or so. Had it not been for Mrs Thatcher's personal outrage in 1979, insisting he must be named and stripped of the knighthood he had acquired along the line, he might have scraped by unscathed. His Nemesis was a second blue-eyed lady, one far more powerful than Elena at Moscow Centre, but with similar strong views and a nose for something smelling wrong about the files.

Of Burgess, Modin says, 'This brilliant, difficult character could not adapt to Soviet conditions,' an understatement if you have seen the exiled spy's desperate letters home. British friends might, conceivably, forgive and forget, but the American cousins never would. Lyman B. Kirkpatrick, who became inspector-general of the CIA shortly after the defection, and later rose to comptroller and number three in the hierarchy, confirmed to me in the 1970s that even ten years after the defection there had been feasibility studies made about assassinating Burgess, Maclean and later Philby in Moscow.

James Jesus Angleton, who had worked with Philby in the OSS in Rome after the war, was another senior figure who never forgave. In Washington they had lunched together weekly, and Philby had, after all, in the old days of Allied co-operation been almost a partner in setting up the CIA. There would never be any partnership, or pretence of it, again. The Cambridge spies had destroyed all trace of the positive sentiment that survived from the great wartime alliance. There was henceforth no special relationship between the intelligence communities. Over the years diplomacy followed suit. When in 1994 President Clinton's peace initiatives in Northern Ireland looked to Dublin, the IRA and local Belfast loyalist politicians for a solution, bypassing Whitehall altogether, it might be seen as the culmination of an ineluctable process of distrust and alienation which the spies had so destructively triggered off in mid-century. The destruction of much that had worked well in Anglo-American relations was their own version of the atom bomb.

The Lubyanka, incidentally, which knew all about assassinations, regarded the threat as serious for a long time. The KGB were also, remembering the vigilant Elena, not at all sure what to make of their defectors, and, as the years passed and personnel changed, probably Modin was the only person who really understood them.

Having read Modin's enthralling view from Moscow Centre, one can envisage a revisionist historian making claims for the Five in terms of having helped to preserve an often desperately precarious weapons balance between East and West during the most dangerous years of the century. In 1950 the conspirators, in common with Joseph Stalin, all said how they feared – and anticipated – World War Three. Such a historian might make a case in their defence along the lines of that offered by Georges Paques, the French NATO spy who claimed at his trial in 1963 that he had supplied material to Moscow largely to defuse international tension.

Khruschev, he claimed, had said NATO secrets supplied by Paques had enabled him to treat the Berlin crisis of 1961 with moderation. Paques, then aged fifty, was nonetheless sentenced to life (later reduced to twenty years) for treason.

Modin seems to see the Cambridge Five as patriots, Russian or maybe Soviet ones, and Philby certainly wished to underline that view by insisting so fiercely on being buried on Russian soil. There is no escaping that if you accept Modin's view, then you must also describe them as traitors in the fullest sense.

As we read in the first words describing Judas in the Acts of the Apostles: 'For he was numbered with us...'

Modin has survived a threatened posting to Siberia, and much worse. In old age he emerges as an amiable figure. He is chairman of an association designed to help former KGB officers and one can imagine all the flushed faces and ample waistlines – do they wear their medals, one wonders – at commemorative dinners. Perhaps because of his Cambridge Friends there is an element of outdated Englishness about his views – a spy should be fit, he should be smartly turned out, he should have a sound mind in a clean body. He should not drink too much – although, inevitably, we know he will.

It is as if there is an affinity of nostalgia to past glories and empires long ago – except it was the middle of this one. I do not know whether, mindful of a surviving Moscow Centre file advocating a study of *Mowgli* (*The Jungle Book*'s Russian name), he has gone so far as to read Kipling 'to get a better knowledge of the agent's psychology'. Easy to see him raising copious vodka toasts to the glory days in the Big Four, and later Big Two, when the Great Game seemed won – with a little help from his Cambridge friends.

David Leitch is the co-author (with Phillip Knightley and Bruce Page and a preface by John Le Carré) of Philby: The Spy Who Betrayed a Generation.

Chapter 1

LONDON: FEBRUARY 1948

It was well past midnight before I was certain I had committed to memory everything the KGB[1] knew about John Cairncross.

I was in London and it was February, the bleakest month of the year. In the days that followed, I double-checked details with Nicolai Borisovich Rodin, alias Korovin, my official superior and the resident KGB chief in the British capital. I wanted to know about the life and character of this man named Cairncross, the first operative agent I was to meet, face to face, in my career. I aimed to establish a psychological portrait of him – clearly the best way to predict how he would react to any situation that might arise.

As we talked unhurriedly on about Cairncross, Korovin warned me that this agent had two serious drawbacks: he had a tendency to be vague, and he was almost never on time. In the light of these facts I made my arrangements.

I gave considerable thought, first of all, to the place I would select for our meetings after the first contact – which would be arranged not by me but by Milovzorov, Cairncross's current handler,[2] who would introduce me to him before bowing out. I spent several days selecting a spot in London that would be both convenient for me and easily identifiable for the Carelian – Cairncross's KGB code name, derived from the name for the people of Carelia, a region straddling the Finnish border and what was the northwestern USSR. In other words, it had to be an address he could easily memorize and get to without danger.

Next I settled on the route I would take to this rendezvous. The itinerary had to include a spell on foot, followed by a long, meandering trip on the Underground and several halts and doublings-back to be sure there were no pursuers.

The plotting of these itineraries was always a protracted affair, but the care I took over them had the advantage of keeping me 'clean', as we say in our profession, meaning unshadowed. Unfortunately, not all our handlers took the same precautions. After two or three meetings had passed without incident, they tended to feel more at ease; then they would lower their guard and neglect elementary security measures, thereby inviting all kinds of trouble. It didn't take me long to work out that Korovin, who as an active agent had evolved a thoroughly practical system for shaking off potential followers, did not himself respect the very rules he imposed so strictly on other people. His negligence eventually resulted in the loss of several agents.

The evening before my first encounter with Cairncross I had a final interview with Korovin, at his request. We had nothing to discuss, but I went all the same.

I found him in his office. He got up portentously, lumbered round his desk and sank into a chair beside me.

'Yuri Ivanovich,' he began, in the donnish tone I had come to loathe, 'as you may well imagine, Moscow sets a lot of store by the Carelian, especially the military. Look how quickly the Centre[3] took Milovzorov off the case when he had a few problems with the man. If you follow Milovzorov's example, you'll undoubtedly wreck your career.' Looking pleased, Korovin paused for a moment to consider this possibility.

'As a matter of interest, what do you plan to use as your own code name – I assume you've given the matter some thought?'

Of course I had given it no thought at all; a code name was the least of my worries at that point. For two days my mind had been running on something far more basic: would I be equal to the job?

'Yes, of course. If it's all the same to you, I'll take the code name Peter.'

I could just as easily have said Max, Harry or Jim. But I settled on Peter, perhaps because of a film I had seen as a child – *Sous les Toits de Paris* – in which Peter is the name of the hero.

Peter was the first of a long series of pseudonyms. My colleagues, for example, all knew me under different names. I used these names in my contacts with agents, or at the KGB London residence to sign certain telegrams or documents addressed to Moscow. I was Peter to some agents, George to others, and so on. Each group of operatives knew me under a separate alias.

As he saw me out of his office, Korovin reverted to his usual blank, expressionless self. 'Now you're on your own, Yuri Ivanovich,' he murmured, as he closed the door.

The night before my first sortie into enemy territory I slept soundly. I already knew one thing about myself: the worse the danger, the cooler I became. I had taken a lot of care to work out exactly what I needed to ask my future agent; nevertheless, I told myself, the most important thing at this stage was to set up the right atmosphere between us from the word go. There would be time enough later on for detailed questions.

I was afraid of losing face, of allowing myself to be overawed by this man Cairncross, who was so much older and more experienced than I. Yet at the same time I felt a kind of secret exultation, which seemed to well up from my inner being. The mere foretaste of the risk I was about to run gave me intense pleasure. I told myself I had done right in opting out of my job as a KGB intelligence bureaucrat, a nonentity in the bowels of Moscow Centre.

In February 1948, London was miserably damp and cold. That morning I left my flat early and made my way to the Soviet Embassy in the usual way. As I passed the white-faced Londoners hurrying to work, I told myself I was capable now of blending inconspicuously into these surroundings. I could go unnoticed in the street among these English people, these ordinary working people and employees.

In the embassy I went about my work as usual. At noon, I lunched alone in the canteen, something I had never done before. I don't know quite why, but for some reason I had no wish to talk to my colleagues. I concentrated instead on the coming rendezvous, which in the event was hardly a crucial one. I had no particular message for the Carelian, and he had nothing much to tell me, either. It was no more than a first meeting, and anyway we wouldn't even be alone together – Milovzorov would be on hand. Nevertheless it was my first foray into London on active service.

In the afternoon I went to see a film. When I slipped out of the theatre at about 6 p.m., night had already fallen. There was an icy drizzle. I raised the collar of my raincoat and jammed my hat down tight over my ears, the picture of a conspirator. I had the eerie sensation that every figure on the street knew I was a spy. In reality, the hunched Londoners hurrying home through that vile drizzle weren't remotely interested in Yuri Ivanovich Modin, junior KGB officer, on the way to his first contact with a British agent.

I followed the tortuous route I had devised, taking a full two hours about it. I crossed several residential areas, streets and squares in which it would have been child's play to spot a pursuer, had there been one. One of my ruses was to favour streets with only one pavement. This I would march down, then suddenly turn on my heel half-way and retrace my steps. Anyone tailing me would thus be presented with three choices. They could abruptly cross the street to nowhere, making themselves conspicuous. They could meet me head on. Or else they could opt for the third choice, the most discreet, which was to make a wide detour and try to find me later – but this would give me all the time in the world to lose them.

I walked, took the Underground, then continued on foot in broad concentric circles, obliquely approaching the place we had chosen for our rendezvous, a popular pub in West London. It was a pub I didn't know; but as soon as I saw the door, the windows with their little square panes, and the cosy, brightly lit interior, it occurred to me with some force that I didn't care for it one bit. We would be too visible here. The establishment had been selected by Milovzorov, who doubtless saw this meeting as a final chance to spend some time in a nice pub at the expense of the State.

At eight o'clock, after an initial reconnoitre, I was still pacing warily round the neighbouring streets. By now I was sure no one had followed me. It was safe to enter the pub. When I did so my suspicions were confirmed: meeting agents in places like this was a thoroughly risky exercise. The fact is, London public bars are largely clubs where the majority of the patrons know one another by sight. I might go unnoticed in the street, but in the bar it was a different matter. Several faces turned in my direction. My awkwardness was painfully obvious; it couldn't have been more clear that I was a foreigner, totally unused to places like this. In what may have been a paranoid reaction – I'll never know unless one day I gain access to the British intelligence file that certainly exists on me – I felt the hostile scrutiny of everyone in the room. It was a deeply uncomfortable sensation.

I wasn't any too confident I'd recognize Cairncross, though Korovin had shown me a photograph of him. I looked for the darkest, smokiest corner in the pub, and on my way to it ordered a beer at the bar. No sooner had I sat down than I saw Milovzorov appear in the wake of a man of about thirty-five wearing an old raincoat, whom I took to be our agent. They sat down at a table and I went over to join them.

It was clear that the two men had little use for each other. Milovzorov, a glum, ill-tempered lout at the best of times, seemed surlier than ever. He avoided my eyes and spoke only to Cairncross.

'This is Peter,' he said. 'He will be your contact from now on. You'll find him efficient – and punctual. I wish you both the best of luck.'

With this he took his glass, drained it, rose and shambled out of the pub, leaving the two of us awkwardly face to face.

For the few minutes we were together I observed my man closely. John Cairncross, code name the Carelian, was very much the typical Scot, with a tallish frame, a bony face and darting eyes. In my experience well-bred men invariably have one or two distinctive traits which set them apart from the crowd: for example, their shoes tend to be freshly polished; their shirts may be frayed, but the collars will be stiff and starched; their trousers, even if they are dirty, will always have a discernible crease. Cairncross displayed not one of these tell-tale characteristics. Moreover, I noticed right away he was short-sighted, though he wore no spectacles.

I suppressed the impulse to ask questions, knowing this was neither the time nor the place. We both drank several glasses of beer for form's sake, and made futile small talk like ordinary well-mannered people meeting for the first time who have nothing in particular to say to one another.

The conversation took no professional turn because I could find no way of broaching the subject, even though it was our only reason for being here. There are certain things one can't bring oneself to say to people one doesn't quite know, a bit like a man and a woman meeting on a blind date, both of whom have the same thing on their minds but can't find the words to express it. Cairncross was entirely calm and so was I; I felt his quick eyes appraising me with professional skill. I was by no means the first KGB handler he had dealt with. At least three or four others had gone before. He seemed to be comparing me to these. I felt like a novice under his scrutiny, though our ages differed by only nine years. Above all he seemed much more experienced than I was.

I thought it best to make our encounter as brief as possible. There was little point in lingering in an establishment where at any moment we might be spotted by some acquaintance. Despite my professional calm, I was boiling with inner rage at being placed in so conspicuous a position and made a mental note never again to rendezvous with agents in pubs. The way I was dressed had nothing to do with it: I could have worn a kilt, but still nobody would have mistaken me for a Scotsman. Cairncross and I set down our glasses in unison. Before we parted I set the time and place of our next contact, 8 p.m. at Hammersmith Grove, on 12 March 1948.

A month in advance I already knew the exact itinerary I would use to reach this tryst by dint of rehearsing it over and over after my interview with Korovin. My first concern was to minimize the risks of our agent's falling victim to his own principal weaknesses, namely his absent-mindedness and lack of punctuality. These were constant bugbears throughout our association, and I knew only too well that at any moment they could have disastrous consequences for both of us. So I decided from the start that we should try to meet (a) in places that were not too hard to find and (b) always at the same hour, eight in the evening.

So this was my first experience as a handler of spies in the field. The work was completely new to me, and I confess I wasn't fully prepared for it. I should point out right away that I was never a spy to the manner born, nor was I remotely a James Bond figure or even a character out of John le Carré. I confess that in the matter of spy novels I have always preferred the type described by Eric Ambler, who paints truer, more subtle portraits of the profession than either Fleming or le Carré.

I am a completely ordinary person, with no exceptional talents and certainly not above-average brains. I was always a good learner, from secondary school right through Naval Academy, but I never had any specific gift for what is usually called espionage. Films, books and newspapers tend to portray spies as brilliant supermen; I've seen a lot of spies in my time and nothing could be further from the truth. In general their intellectual level leaves a lot to be desired, and this is no bad thing. I know from experience that a high IQ should never be the main criterion for recruiting the average secret agent, who is really another kind of soldier.

On the other hand, certain other qualities that soldiers don't have are absolutely essential for a spy. For example, he should have a childish, gleeful, mischievous side to his nature. It's hard to believe, but it's so. This childishness will help him bear up under the steady pressure of danger and fear that is so much a part of the work. When an agent loses this extra quality he becomes no more than a man of action, hard, austere and pitiless, analysing events coldly and methodically like any other functionary. Function he will; but he will command no respect in his profession, because he will possess none of the enthusiasm, intuition and delight in his job which will allow him to see what the ordinary run of people cannot see.

I also believe that a good intelligence agent should have strong political awareness. If he doesn't, he will never be any use, because he will never ask the right questions at the right moment. Nor will he be able to glean the information he needs. I respect people who have this kind of highly developed awareness. I feel relaxed in my dealings with them, and this in turn makes my work easier. An effective agent should, in my view, be as capable of analysing political problems as an experienced politician. If he wants the information he sends back to the Centre to be of any service, he must not dispatch it in bulk just as he receives it, but should classify it, sifting out the items that may help to anticipate or predict coming events. The agent should be able to predict today what his superiors will be requiring of him tomorrow. If he waits for orders, time will be wasted and the risks he has taken to gather intelligence will be fruitless, because the intelligence will be obsolete. Far too many of our own KGB agents were apt to keep repeating that they were 'awaiting orders'.

It is an article of faith with me, one that I later took care to teach my pupils at the KGB intelligence school, that every agent should keep a close eye on the political news if he wants to stay ahead of the game. The agent who is a poor hand at politics will never produce anything like satisfactory results. Likewise, the agent who thinks he's James Bond has no place at all in a real intelligence service. There are those who try to ape Ian Fleming's fictional spy, bristling with gadgets, sexually voracious, intrepid and constantly involved in battles of one kind or another. I've known a few like that, and none of them ever went very far.

A good secret agent should also possess physical and moral strength, a healthy mind in a healthy body. Being in good physical shape will help him stand up to all kinds of peculiarly nasty pressures; moreover, it will help him to view problems with complete clarity, whether they are soluble or not. What I say here may seem banal, but the dreary, anxious grind of the agent's work, with its secret contacts and constant vigilance, leaves deep scars on a man. A secret agent is necessarily much more fragile and highly strung than other men, whose professions do not subject them to such constant tension.

From the day of my first clandestine meeting with an agent abroad, I realized the importance of physical fitness. If he trains regularly, a spy gives himself an added advantage which may one day save his skin.

A gulf has always existed in the world of espionage between what may seem useful to the agent in the field and what his superiors deem important. This is true of all intelligence services, whether Soviet, American, French or British. There are often discrepancies, even direct contradictions, between what the hierarchy wants and what the agent judges to be correct on the spur of the moment. The good agent should know how to construct a shell of icy self-control around himself which enables him to do the things his employers need him to do; these are often things that he, if left to himself, would not dream of doing.

And the pressure is sometimes unbearable. Your stomach is permanently in knots. Day and night you have to be prepared for the worst; you worry about failure, about losing control of yourself.

You drink too much. Not that all agents are alcoholics; it's just that the need to relieve the pressure is sometimes overwhelming. Some have profound feelings of guilt, others have weird relationships with women, still others gamble insanely. If he is somehow to decompress, an agent needs some kind of pastime. We Russians are particularly fond of the soil, and many of us are passionate gardeners. We dig, plant and generally take care of the small plots around our dachas with love and reverence. Other people spend their leisure hours decorating and beautifying their apartments, often unnecessarily. What we all look for is some way of freeing ourselves, of cleansing ourselves, of relaxing. When the body is relaxed, the mind becomes calmer and clearer. My personal hobby is my vegetable garden in the

country, where I grow aubergines, courgettes and broccoli, in addition to the usual Russian staples. Vegetables are my passion.

What I say here may seem to have little to do with what one reads in spy novels, in which the protagonists never seem to have psychological problems of any kind; nevertheless, that's how it is.

[1] For convenience' sake, the Soviet state security organization will be referred to in this book as the NKVD (1922–43) and the KGB (from 1943 onwards). In reality the organization has changed its name on many different occasions in the course of its history: December 1917, Cheka; February 1922, GPU (NKVD); July 1923, OGPU; July 1934, NKVD; February 1941, NKGB; July 1941, NKVD; April 1943, NKGB; March 1946, MGB; March 1953, MVD; March 1954 onwards, KGB.

[2] The KGB handling officer's duty is to maintain contact with the agent in the field.

[3] The Centre, in KGB jargon, is the organization's headquarters in Moscow.

Chapter 2

JOINING THE KGB

I had no predisposition to be a spy. My parents had nothing whatever to do with the secret service; indeed, they were completely apolitical. Moreover, I came from Suzdal, an old and deeply conservative Russian town isolated from the rest of the world because of its lack of a railway station. All roads into Suzdal were terrible. We were only 130 miles from Moscow, on the road taken by the convicts on their way to Siberia, but the people of my home town still lived much as they had in the last century. Most of the houses were of wood and the usual means of transport across town was by horse and cart. It was rather quaint and beautiful; the eternal Russia of children's storybooks.

In 1922, the year I was born, there were still many churches in Suzdal. I remember the hundreds of babushkas who went to the services each Sunday. The streets around the churches vibrated with the psalms of the old women and the deep-voiced priests. I was not given a religious education, but still I was thoroughly imbued with the ambience of belief. There were two very large monasteries at Suzdal which attracted quantities of pilgrims every year.

Revolution had come to Russia, but still the religious fervour of our small town, with its 11,000 inhabitants, remained largely unaltered. Suzdal was the closest holy place to Moscow after Zagorsk.

My family background was fairly mixed. My grandfather on my mother's side was a rich shopkeeper who married a woman from a poor family. He died of tuberculosis while he was still a young man, and the situation for my mother and grandmother looked dire. But thanks to the city authorities my mother was enabled to continue her studies, and eventually she went on to secondary school with a State grant. When she left school in 1917, she spoke English and German fluently. Her education was complete.

My father was a professional soldier, and this meant that as a family we travelled widely. In my own ten years of schooling, I changed schools no fewer than ten times in different cities. This nomadic existence of the Russian military family, constantly moving from one barracks to the next, left a deep mark on my life. It left me with the ability to make immediate contact with other people, and above all with a sense of ease and confidence, whatever the situation.

I was particularly good at English, which my mother taught me at home, though German remained a problem throughout my school years. I don't speak a word of German today; my mother is partly to blame for this, because she usually did my homework in that language while I went out to play.

My secondary education came to an end at Lipetsk, south of Moscow. This was a smallish town with a flying school that specialized in retraining pilots. Following an intergovernmental agreement between Russia and Germany, the Germans, who had been barred by the Treaty of Versailles from training pilots on their own territory, came *en masse* to this school. Hermann Goering, for example, received his flight training here. Later, when the Nazis overran the region, Lipetsk was the only town left standing. Goering himself gave the order that it should not be damaged, for sentimental reasons.

It was in Lipetsk that in 1938 I became a member of the Komsomol (Communist Youth), against the advice of my father, who wanted me to stay out of the limelight. Under the circumstances then prevailing, he thought I should stay aloof from this organization, at least for a while. The Soviet Union was in the throes of the Yezhovshchina, a Stalinist terror of unprecedented ferocity, 'named after Nikolai Ivanovich Yezhov, head of the NKVD from 1936 to 1938.' The Bolshevik old guard had been annihilated, the Central Committee decimated. The purge spread to the provinces, where large numbers of functionaries and even Communist Youth members were liquidated. But the main target of the purgers was the army. Marshal

Tukhachevsky, a hero of the war with Poland, was shot, along with seven other prominent military leaders. In 1938 came the turn of the lower-ranking officers.

Problems had already begun to surface in my father's life the year before. On the orders of Klimient Voroshilov and Semion Boudieny, the two leaders of the purge, he was first banned from the barracks, then relieved of his duties. At any moment he expected to be arrested without warning and summarily shot.

Nevertheless, all through this time he continued to receive his officer's salary. At the end of each month the regimental paymaster would appear at the door; I would see my father sign the papers and receive a wad of roubles, which he stuffed into his jacket pocket. This period of anguish lasted for a full year, from which by extraordinary good fortune my father emerged unscathed. We never knew why. Since he had been demoted in the meantime, he knew that his military career was effectively finished. He found work as a teacher in Lipetsk. We were all deeply relieved; though he was never a thoroughgoing, convinced Communist, my father had never been actively against the regime either. He fought on the Bolshevik side in the civil war and was wounded at Petrograd, before being sent to the Caucasus as a commissar, a rank which carried the responsibility for political instruction of the troops.

Despite my father's misgivings, I went ahead and became an active member of the Communist Youth and was soon elected to my school's Komsomol Committee. By comparison with others of my age, I had a lively interest in politics, though my ideas were not at that stage fully formed. I had a somewhat childish faith in Communism. As a member of my school's Komsomol Committee, I represented it on a number of occasions and participated in meeting after meeting. I found this rather stimulating: it gave me the self-satisfied impression that I was carrying out my duty as a Soviet citizen.

When my secondary studies came to an end, at seventeen, I began to address the problem of what to do next. Although I am a countryman at heart, I was attracted at that time by the sea, which promised adventure, wide horizons and voyages to far places. We had entered the last months of 1939 and war had just broken out in Europe. Despite the Molotov–Ribbentrop non-aggression pact, we knew that we would eventually be drawn into the conflict. As a consequence, many young people sought places in specialist schools, which would allow them to play for time and avoid military conscription, fixed at eighteen by a recent law. Naturally, the candidates for such schools were very numerous and the competition for places intense.

My mother was desperately worried, convinced as she was that I would be killed immediately if I was called up for military service. My father had noticed my skill as a handyman – as a child I loved making things with my hands and I have always admired people who build their own houses – and he wisely advised me to sit an especially difficult exam for the Leningrad Naval Academy, where public works engineers were trained.

My father warned me that there were many candidates for a very few places in this prestigious establishment. Nevertheless, he said, 'since you seem to think you're cleverer than the others, here's your chance to prove it. I know your mother thinks you can, but she may be wrong. There's no shortage of mothers in the Soviet Union who believe their sons are a cut above everyone else.'

There were forty candidates for each place, even after many more applicants had been rejected on the basis of their school records. These weren't even allowed to sit the exam.

My own school record was excellent, so I got through this stage. Several people then tried to discourage me, saying I was only a provincial and the Naval Academy was heavily biased in favour of Muscovites and Leningraders. Since I came from wretched little Lipetsk, they said, my chances of admission were exceedingly slim. 'And even if you manage to get out of this dump, they'll always find a way to bury you . . .'

Other similar establishments, rather easier to get into, were suggested, but I thought them all a great deal too military. I never had the slightest urge to be a navy captain.

I sat the exam – and passed. The only hitch was my maths paper, which was no more than 'adequate'. There were many Leningraders and Jews among the students; I've always counted plenty of Jews among my friends and they were always a good deal better at maths than I was. My mark was the lowest one – but still I had earned my place at the academy and that was enough for me.

For a boy with no inclination for a military career, my situation was hardly ideal. The first thing they did was shave our heads. We lived under iron disciplinary conditions, for Marshal Timoshenko, then

Minister of Defence, was a fervent promoter of discipline, both in official military barracks and in semi-military academies like ours.

We would be put in confinement at the slightest provocation. Locked into tiny punishment cells, culprits were allowed to lie down only between midnight and six in the morning. The rest of the time the bed would be chained on its end against the wall. The stench was appalling.

I was put in the punishment cell only once, but that was quite enough. I had been delegated to keep order in the kitchen; the food was ultra-frugal and the other cadets emptied their plates within seconds. Four tablespoons of kasha, or cracked wheat, is nothing like enough to satisfy an eighteen-year-old. The din was deafening. Some of the boys were already yelling for more before others had had their first helping. In my attempts to stop the clamour I totally forgot to have someone fetch the principal's dinner. Retribution for this crime was swift and savage: the duty officer appeared with a couple of uniformed cadets and told me I was under arrest.

I finished my first year with considerable credit, but by the time we had completed our cycle of exams in June 1941, war had broken out and the Nazi invasion had begun.

As future military engineers, many of my fellow students were called up to the lines defending Leningrad, though I myself was deemed too young for this role. When the city was encircled and cut off, we all went to the siege area, where we were issued with rifles as student-soldiers. Our job was to patrol the streets in the evenings and by night. Leningrad was infested with German agents who routinely sent up flares in the darkness to guide the bombers of the Luftwaffe circling above the city. The principal targets were the headquarters of the NKVD, and Smolny, where the Leningrad Party Committee was based. Unfortunately, our academy was exactly half-way between these two buildings.

By October 1941, we were patrolling every night. We were still in fairly good shape, slightly thinner perhaps, but by no means starving. One wet, foggy night we were just completing our patrol, dropping with cold and fatigue, when a flare went up from a building barely a hundred yards away. It soared high into the sky and plummeted towards the Neva.

For a few moments everything around us was as clear as day, as we marked the partially bombed-out building from which the rocket had originated. Along with the NKVD agent commanding our three-man patrol, we raced across and climbed to the top floor of the building four steps at a time. The stairs were cluttered with beams, boxes and rubbish of all kinds. The NKVD man, who was pretty old, couldn't climb as fast as we did; I could hear him puffing and blowing two floors below. At the top landing we blocked the way into the attic and waited. The NKVD agent caught up with us and without taking the time to wipe the sweat from his face he ordered us straight down again. We were amazed that he wanted to be alone at this critical moment, but he cut us short. 'It's no job for youngsters like you to liquidate spies,' he said. 'That's up to me.'

We turned and left him to his horrible duty. Back in the street we heard a single gunshot; a few minutes later he appeared in the doorway. Without a word we made our way back to the cantonment. Much the same thing was to recur several times in the course of those months.

Fuel was desperately short in Leningrad. On a peninsula separating the German lines from ours, there was a huge stock of coal; this no man's land was known as Coal Bay. We were given orders to slip over there in the night hours to scavenge as much coal and coke as possible. I took part in several of these surreptitious expeditions: we filled up our jute sacks, most of the time by hand so as to make as little noise as possible, and then dragged them back to the boats. The operation seemed much more perilous than it was, because in fact the Germans had little chance of seeing us in the dark. Sometimes they would open sporadic fire for form's sake, without much hope of hitting us. Personally I have never fired a shot at a German, but I can tell you they've often enough tried as hard as they could to shoot me. Nevertheless I am still rated a front-line veteran, maybe because I nearly died of hunger like everyone else in Leningrad.

In December, people began dying of starvation. The academy's supervisors concluded that we should be evacuated. We were not yet suffering acutely from lack of food, and since engineers were desperately needed at the front, we should be moved from Leningrad to a more secure area of the Soviet Union. The hardest part was getting out of the besieged city. It was decided that soldiers would escort us across the ice-covered Lake Ladoga, along the route that was later to be known as the Survival Trail.

We were the first to attempt the crossing of the lake in the direction of Bolshaya Zemlya, the Great Steppe. We had to cover thirty miles on foot, and the cold was bitter enough to freeze vodka solid. We dressed as warmly as possible, cramming on every sweater and jacket we could find. Each carrying his bundle of possessions, we made our way one by one on to the ice, and started our long march through the night. We could see nothing but a tiny light far ahead, a beacon specially lit to guide us. We were told to head directly for it and on no account to stop. The Germans quickly understood that a column was attempting to escape across the lake. This time they could hit us and they knew it; we had been walking for barely an hour when the first mortar shell exploded beside us on the ice. Curiously enough, we had been hungry for so long and we were so debilitated that we forgot to be frightened.

I called out to my friends. What were we to do? Should we group ourselves together more closely, or should we disperse? We chose the second option, moving along at forty-yard intervals. I felt very alone. The time lapses between the mortar shells shortened significantly; muffled booms echoed beneath the shuddering ice and the air was filled with the shriek of flying shrapnel. At any moment the surface might dissolve beneath our feet. Through the gloom, I saw a glimmering pool of light not far away from me, a great hole gouged out by a mortar shell. I warned the others and we gave it a wide berth. Thereafter we watched our step: there were scores of similar sinkholes along the way. The lake's surface was one vast labyrinth, through which we had to thread our way, with mile upon mile of detours. And all the time the mortars kept raining down, aimed at random, landing sometimes within a stone's throw, sometimes at the far end of the lake. The Germans had settled on a diabolical tactic: since they couldn't see where we were, they were attempting to create a kind of trench across the ice with mortar bombs. In this way they hoped to cut us off from our goal on the far bank. Those of us who lost their sense of direction were as good as dead. Some did, but most made it to the far side.

In 1985, I went back to Leningrad to commemorate this strange episode in my life. I recognized the spot where we began our march across the ice, I looked long and hard at the lake . . . I think I shall never go there again.

When we came at last to the far bank, we were utterly exhausted. Yet there was no question of stopping for a rest, because the academy principal had given us strict orders to strike out for the railway line and if possible carry on by train to a rendezvous at Tikhvin. With three other boys I plodded on and on through empty fields covered in deep snow. The going was appallingly difficult. I fell flat on my face in the snow again and again. Worst of all, when we reached the outskirts of Tikhvin we found the town already overrun by the enemy. We made a long detour, groping our way slowly because we didn't know this area and we might at any moment blunder into a German patrol.

That winter was unbelievably bitter, and to this day I still don't know how we survived. We ate nothing for days. I teamed up with Yuri Proskuriakov, a boy of my own age, and eventually we staggered into a shepherd's hut deep in the countryside. The people inside received us warmly: they clearly hadn't much to eat, but they gave us a few potatoes to keep us going. On several occasions during our wanderings in the Leningrad region we were fed by country people. I owe my life to them.

Finally, in the last stages of exhaustion, we found our way to a station – I cannot remember the name of it. We collapsed on a pile of straw in a stock waggon and slept like logs until the train rumbled into Yaroslavl. There we found the majority of our schoolmates, along with our teachers. The local soviet, or elected council, decided to put us up, placing a kind of barracks at our disposal, and fed us liberally with kasha. It had been so long since any of us had eaten our fill that we leapt on the food like wild animals. We knew we would be horribly ill as a result but we couldn't restrain ourselves. Hunger is exquisite agony.

We stayed at Yaroslavl till July 1942. At this time my comrades suggested I should join the Party. I refused, saying I was far too young. Our living conditions had improved to some extent, though supplies were very erratic, with certain staples like butter and oil being almost totally unobtainable. We were all anaemic and listless. Above all, our morale had reached rock bottom, and of this the academy hierarchy was only too aware.

It was at this juncture, in the wake of a disastrous incident, that I found myself directly involved for the first time with the NKVD.

It happened that I was once again overseeing the kitchen – my section head liked me to do this because I was good at sharing out the food equally. Just as I came on duty, Dementiev, a fifth-year student whom I was relieving, told me that one of the cupboards in the kitchen was locked and might contain stolen food. 'I couldn't get it open,' he said. 'You do it, it's your watch.'

The kitchen staff, obviously very uncomfortable, told me the key was with the cook, who had gone home. The duty officer was called in; he sent for a crowbar and broke the lock himself. Inside, packed in a newspaper, was a kilogram of yellow butter.

It was June 1942, and Stalin had recently decreed that any soldier caught stealing food in the army should face a firing squad. If a thief was taken red-handed he was to be shot right then and there. It was a radical solution to what had become a serious problem at the front.

I had heard about this decree, but it was not until that moment that I realized what I had done. Some officers of the NKVD came to arrest the butter thief, who was, of course, the cook. An inquiry was opened and I was summoned to give evidence.

I confess I was terrified. Everyone at that time lived in mortal fear of the NKVD. In an empty room, a security officer sat me down on a chair in front of a table. On it lay a sheet of paper and a pencil.

We talked. He wanted to know if I had suspected the thief previously, if I knew he was storing butter in the cupboard, if I had carried out an investigation of my own to entrap him, if I had meant to catch him in the act, if I had acted out of patriotism or from some other motive. I explained that I didn't know the cook from Adam; I told him the story exactly as I remembered it. All this time the officer was scribbling away, and when he no longer had any questions to ask me he wrote in large letters at the top of the first page: RECORD OF INTERROGATION. For a moment I wondered vaguely 'What interrogation?' Then it hit me.

A few days later all the pupils were summoned to the main courtyard, a highly unusual event. I still expected the thief to get a dressing down and a few weeks' confinement. The security officer stepped forward and read a report of his enquiry. The cook had pleaded guilty. Finally, without missing a beat, the officer pronounced sentence: 'The culprit is condemned to be shot by firing squad tomorrow at dawn.'

We dispersed in stunned silence. I was stupefied by what I had done, but I did my best to show no sign of it. Not one of my fellow students made the least comment but nevertheless I felt acutely unhappy. The thief was duly executed; there was no appeal. I was shattered by this episode.

I have often thought about this awful moment in my life, both during the war and after it was over. I felt no guilt. I knew as well as everyone else that only the most savage discipline in our armed forces made it possible for us to resist the invaders, to defend our territory house by house and yard by yard, as we did. The slightest wavering could have proved catastrophic, not only to the conduct of the fighting, but also to the morale of our troops.

At that time the situation at the front was desperate. The Germans were advancing in the Ukraine, along the Don and in the direction of Stalingrad. On Stalin's orders, half of the navy's personnel were drafted to the land army. We were among these. No one was particularly worried – we had no way of knowing then that Stalingrad would prove the bloodiest battle of the Second World War, and that the 190-day siege would change the course of the war and ultimately bring Germany to her knees.

We received orders to head for Stalingrad by way of the Volga, a simple matter by comparison with the trials we had endured on our way to Yaroslavl. At Kostroma the principal of the local school for engineers where we were staying managed to convince our instructors that it was folly to send us to the front without the slightest training, and furthermore that it was plain stupid to make cannon fodder of trained engineers in whom the State had invested so much time and money. Our instructors and our military overseers therefore took the decision to leave us at Kostroma for a month or so, to learn how to operate and maintain electrical power sources for the *katyushas* (light rocket batteries). My own destiny was finally decided at Kostroma shortly thereafter.

We knew that the Germans had reached Stalingrad. We also knew that this industrial city of about half a million inhabitants possessed neither fortifications nor a remotely defensible site. On the contrary, it lay sprawled along the right bank of the Volga and was to all intents and purposes impossible to defend.

Like everyone else, I was deeply depressed at the prospect of going to Stalingrad. It was at this moment that one of my fellow students came to see me and offered me the chance to enlist in the VKPB, as the Communist Party was then known.

At first I refused, feeling I was still too young for so drastic a decision. A few days later I was asked again; apparently a major propaganda offensive was under way in the wake of the German advance on Stalingrad, and I could be of real use.

This tipped the balance and I duly became a member of the Communist Party at Kostroma on the banks of the Volga, the homeland of the Romanov family and their ancestors. I was barely twenty years old.

A second event was to have even greater significance for my career. One day, I was summoned by an officer of the NKVD.

The officer began by describing events at the front, the horrors of the war and the outrages committed by the Nazis. Then he came to the point.

'Yuri,' he said, 'has it occurred to you that you can be just as useful to your country without going to the front at all? We have a proposal for you. Work with us, and after the war is over we will make it possible for you to complete your studies.'

I didn't know what to say. I suspected that the butter incident might have something to do with this interview, and I was afraid the officer was trying to turn me into a professional informer. Then the officer added firmly, 'You can be an active member of SMERSH, our military counter-espionage service.' The meaning of the words represented by the acronym was, literally, 'death to spies'.

This relieved my mind considerably. I wasn't being asked to inform. I asked for a few minutes to think it over, then accepted his offer unconditionally.

In my heart of hearts I was glad to have been chosen for this role, and I had no moral scruples about it. Until the end of the war, it seemed to me completely right and normal that we should do battle against the spies of Germany; to work in a counter-espionage service in wartime seemed a completely honourable occupation. I wasn't the only one to choose this course.

Shortly after, in October 1942, I found myself on a train to Moscow with a few of my fellow cadets. We were detailed to attend a one-month intensive course in the Novye Doma district. In theory, we were to learn the rudiments of counter-espionage, in other words how to track down, arrest and interrogate enemy spies, and how to retrieve documents from them before they had time to destroy them.

Some people believe that the NKVD confined its activities to arresting spies and summarily shooting them. This is far from the truth. Every case had to be duly recorded, investigated and painstakingly pursued to its conclusion according to accepted legal procedures. During our training period, we were given real cases to work on, matters dealt with in the recent past which we were told to analyse. Much of the course was devoted to what *not* to do. This was vital for us, given that we were so young and so completely inexperienced. If the truth be told, we were still hardly better than schoolboys.

But this course of study, like my training as an engineer, was destined to be interrupted. When my superiors found out that I spoke fluent English, I was sent straight to an annexe of the NKVD headquarters at the Lubyanka on Dzerzhinski Square to perfect my knowledge of that language.

At that time there was a shortage of translators, which had become acute since Stalin's *rapprochement* with the British and the Americans. By invading the Soviet Union, Hitler had made this *rapprochement* inevitable. In June 1942, we signed a twenty-year agreement with Britain asserting our common aim of 'working together for victory and establishing a lasting peace'. We also subscribed to the Atlantic Charter devised by Roosevelt and Churchill in August 1941. Among other things, the charter proclaimed that all people had an intrinsic right to liberty, self-determination and equal economic opportunity. This somewhat Utopian programme was more than acceptable to the authorities ruling the Soviet Union.

Thus for the time being we found ourselves in the same boat with the great nations of the West. We shared the same goal, which was the destruction of Fascism.

Our diplomatic and military contacts with our new friends suddenly burgeoned. Translators were desperately needed both in Moscow and the major ports, when British and American supplies began to flow in. A constant succession of convoys carried arms and munitions between Britain's naval bases and the ports of Murmansk and Archangel in the north; British officers began to be a common sight in the streets of these cities. In the meantime American war supplies reached us by way of Iran and Baku. To keep abreast of all this, intensive language courses were arranged within the army and the NKVD.

Nearly all our young men who could speak a foreign language were at the front, so the NKVD was obliged to recruit women in their stead. This was how I came to meet my future wife, who happened to be in the same group as I was in the English section. There were four or five of us in the group. Later, she went to work for the KGB's translation department.

Our services were so badly needed that we studied nothing but English all day long. Courses in Marxism-Leninism, required in all Soviet schools, were dropped from our programme of study. Apparently, when the list of subjects we were supposed to be taught was presented to Lavrenti Pavlovich Beria, the head of the NKVD, he crossed out everything except languages. The instruction was in depth and totally intensive – seventeen hours a day. By night, in the barracks dormitory, I heard the other students dreaming in English, French, Turkish and Italian. I worked like a demon for ten months solid, but once again I was doomed never to finish my course.

In December 1943, I was transferred without warning to the KGB's principal foreign intelligence unit. Nobody bothered to enquire what I thought about this, but it hardly mattered – we were so short of English translators that I could hardly have refused. The opportunity given to me to work in the most prestigious section of the secret service might have been flattering at any other time but I knew full well that I had been selected not because of my exceptional abilities, but because there was simply no one else available for the job.

The British section of the KGB consisted of seven people and the American section of five; all the other officers either were at the front or had been killed in action. Nevertheless we were receiving a steady flow of information, mostly in the form of microfilms which arrived at Murmansk on the ships. Intelligence of the highest importance was accumulating steadily, with nobody to analyse it. The seven individuals who worked day and night at the Lubyanka would dip more or less at random into the pile, translate what they could of it, and file the rest away 'to be read later'. This was a euphemism for forgetting about a good proportion of the information gathered by our agents in England. Yet these men and women sometimes took the most stupendous risks to get at intelligence and send it through to us. What would they have thought if they had known that their telegrams and reports had barely a fifty per cent chance of being read? The situation was all the more ludicrous because much information of the highest importance had no doubt already been shuffled aside for ever.

At least the heads of the KGB were fully aware of the problem. They knew that for lack of people the State was unable to make the most of the advantages furnished by its network of agents abroad.

This was the only reason why I found myself working in this section. My superiors at first directed me to investigate the files at random and to file documents that had yet to be translated.

Confronted with the mountain of paper dumped on my desk by the filing clerk, I summoned up what courage I possessed, then plunged doggedly into the first of the bulging folders neatly bound with cotton ribbons. I read through several pages. Was this sufficiently interesting to warrant a full translation? What should my criteria be for deciding this? I put the first folder aside and attacked the next and the next. After I had seen about ten, I stopped, reflected and finally established a hierarchy of what I deemed vital and what unimportant.

I had to go on with this arduous task for several weeks before I was given my first translation. It was a report from one of our agents in London; I forget what it was about, since my work consisted of translating on and on like an automaton. I've no idea what the information signified. Most of the time I was assigned to technical texts. I filled in a docket which was then signed by my superior, because at that stage my own signature was worthless. Then I went down to the archive rooms to ferret out the document requested and translated it on behalf of the head of the English section. This mechanical, purely administrative drudgery was dull beyond belief.

Later, as my superiors' confidence in me grew, I was set to classifying freshly arrived documents from our London residence and reading their contents before passing them on to their next destination. I quickly learned to spot items deserving full priority; these I communicated to my immediate superior only. We treated as highly sensitive everything that had to do with the internal and foreign policy of Great Britain, atomic research, the war economy and Britain's relations with other countries. All these matters were of special importance to Stalin, who knew quite well that the British Prime Minister, Winston Churchill, was lying when he complained at their meetings that the Allies were desperately short of men and supplies. He knew as well as Churchill did what resources were available to the Anglo-American alliance, and he could also gauge more or less exactly what help the Allies could realistically offer him. My first analyses and translations of sensitive texts were judged fully relevant by my superiors, who began to repose more and more confidence in me.

In effect, I had the fortunate privilege of learning the art of intelligence not in a school, not in theory, but in the field, under exceptional circumstances. That was really how I learned my trade and acquired a genuine taste for it. While I profited to some extent from the advice and instruction of all the men I worked under, I confess I owe the most to my first boss, Josifovich Koghen, a man some ten years older than I who had formerly worked as a diplomat and who was thoroughly competent, methodical, cautious and above all humane.

I came from the provinces, it should be remembered. I had no contacts in Moscow and at first I lived in the barracks, from which I was quickly expelled on the grounds that the rooms there were reserved for students. I was no longer a student, because I had a full-time job. I wasn't keen to lodge in a workers' hostel, which appeared to be the only alternative; fortunately, I was rescued by Koghen, who offered to put me up himself. With this simple act of kindness he completely won me over, subsequently taking me under his wing at work and teaching me the basics of my job as an operational agent. Through him I gained greater and greater confidence in my own abilities. In particular he taught me that all information should be carefully examined, even though it may seem unimportant on the first reading. Thanks to Koghen I discovered how to write with clarity, brevity and precision, so that the person receiving my message could understand immediately what I was driving at. Often he would check the texts I produced and hint politely that I had omitted some crucial nugget of information.

I can't say we were really friends; the difference in our backgrounds was too great for that. He belonged to a family of intellectuals, while I was from the 'working intelligentsia', as they call it in Russia. We had differing points of view on a wide range of subjects, but all the same I am sure that without Koghen I could never have become an intelligence officer of high rank.

Reading over the reports of our agents, I began to get to know them intimately, if at second remove. I grasped their qualities and their faults, understood their fears, anxieties and nervous obsessions. Eventually I found myself endowing them with physical features in my imagination. When I read some of their microfilmed reports and the synopses they sent, I could pinpoint exactly when an agent was lying, when he meant to shuffle off responsibility, or even take credit for recruiting some other individual. In South Africa, for example, we had a hard-working, thoroughly active agent who recruited tirelessly. He showered us with useless information about the relations between blacks and Afrikaners, and between the various native tribes. He knew everything there was to know about the nationalist groups who financed them and on whose behalf they operated. This was all quite useless to us in our struggle against the Germans, but we let him continue as he wished. Studying his reports, I sensed that they were his sole *raison d'être*, the most important thing in his life.

In general, my career as a bureaucrat in that time of desperate struggle, when other men of my age were fighting at the front, was none too agreeable. But it didn't take me long to work out that it was now within my power to render great services to my country.

Chapter 3

THE PICK OF THE LITTER

The only travelling I did was by proxy. I received information from England, Australia, New Zealand, India, South Africa, Canada and the British colonies, but in the summer of 1944 most of my time was taken up by the batches of photographic negatives that filtered in from London.

We were inundated with work, so much that it was physically impossible to process everything. We had a number of highly effective agents operating in the United Kingdom, all of them Britons who worked for us 'on an ideological basis', as we used to say. Here again I classified incoming documents on a scale of importance and sent on those that seemed to be the most interesting to my superiors, some of whom were specialists in British affairs. When I had any spare time – a rare occurrence – I turned my attention to the material I had set aside as being of lesser significance.

We developed a highly efficient procedure. All of our thirty-odd agents in London were directed to work on a single given subject; they would then send in whatever they could find, which was subsequently analysed. Gradually, by comparing each agent's contribution, we were able to establish a kind of hierarchy among them. Five names stood out from the rest, of men who quickly showed themselves to be the most valuable spies. The information passed on by the other twenty-five was paltry by comparison.

Years later, when I was teaching at the KGB training centre, I tried to explain how we operated at that time. I suggested that my pupils imagine a cooking pot, which the cook fills with the various ingredients of a stew. After an hour's slow cooking, only the essence remains. That was how we dealt with our London agents.

The 'Cambridge Five' – this was our internal KGB name for them – were the essence. They were by no means a tightly knit group; each was radically different in character, though they were nearly all acquainted. The information they produced was so dense and concise that our superiors eventually assigned a single translator to concentrate on nothing else but the documents the five produced.

That translator was I. It was early 1944, and I was still only twenty-two years old.

For some time I remained in the dark about who these five intelligence stars could be; I wasn't even told what their pseudonyms were. All I knew was that the documents I was translating into Russian came from them. There was no indication as to who had provided what. After two or three months of working in this way, I was given access to their pseudonyms: the KGB knew them as Stuart, Söhnchen, Mädchen, Johnson and X; *Söhnchen* means 'sonny', and *Mädchen* 'girl', in German.

At this point I began to take a much more serious interest in the five agents, casting my memory back over the various documents that had already crossed my desk. At that time the KGB did not keep the original coded telegrams it received, for fear of spies within the service. We preferred that no written trace of our collaboration with foreign agents should survive. Before the assistants took away the telegrams to be destroyed, it was our role to write résumés of what they contained in our own handwriting. These were then passed on to specially assigned colleagues, who filed them away in the dossiers of each agent in ultra-secret archives. To begin with I wasn't allowed to consult these dossiers, so I made a special point of committing to memory whatever I read of the intelligence yielded by Stuart, Söhnchen and the rest.

In June 1944, I learned for the first time – and in a very strange way – exactly who these mysterious Britons were.

In recognition of their excellent services, the heads of the KGB decided to assign life pensions to our five principal agents in Britain, to be paid to them discreetly every month, every three months or every year by our London residence. The sums were fairly large by contemporary standards. This offer was made to them by their handling officer. They did not respond immediately, but eventually each agent wrote his own letter to the KGB containing his answer. First of all they thanked us for the gesture, which they appreciated; then they set out the motives for their involvement with the Soviet Union in fighting Fascism and promoting world revolution. In conclusion, they declared to a man that it had never entered their heads to carry out this work for money and that there could be no question of degrading their commitment by accepting the smallest payment.

As a supreme gesture of his confidence in me, the head of our English section asked me to translate these five letters into Russian. One of them, signed by a certain Guy Burgess, contained a passage which I have never forgotten: 'I cannot see how any self-respecting individual could live in my country and not work for the Party.'

At last I was able to put a name to each pseudonym and to form my first clear idea of these agents, by whom I was now thoroughly fascinated. The one we first knew as Söhnchen, then Tom and Stanley, had the real name of Kim Philby. Mädchen or Hicks was Guy Burgess. Johnson, Tony and later Yan was Anthony Blunt. Stuart, Wise, Lyric or Homer was Donald Maclean. As to the fifth agent, I shall describe him later.

I received the agents' microfilms, filed them, translated them with infinite care and produced for each one a résumé to accompany my translation. In dealing with the various problems linked to their work, I found myself expressing my own views more and more frequently in the presence of my immediate superior. Obviously he could take account of what I said, or ignore it, as the case might be. Nevertheless, my rise from the status of an ordinary clerk to a fully fledged intelligence officer began at this time.

Over a period of three years, from 1944 to 1947, my daily existence was entirely consumed by my work with these men, about whose lives I knew by then practically everything there was to know. When I was given clearance to consult the archives, I first of all set about reading each man's file from start to finish. The files contained highly detailed biographical notes, including names and dates, in addition to the information the subjects themselves had provided as to the chronological order of events in their lives. I was allowed to consult another astonishing file which detailed the final recipient of each document received from the five agents. The names of Stalin, Molotov and Beria were repeatedly mentioned.

Today, journalists and historians are sorting through the so-called archives of the KGB with the tireless energy of ants; but the fact is that they will find nothing of real interest concerning intelligence matters, apart from a few résumés and notes.

Above all, there are no original texts. Most of the files on the Cambridge ring were destroyed in 1953. This I can categorically assert: nearly all of the documents that served to keep the Kremlin informed are no longer in existence.

I think that had the KGB employees of the time been more alert, they would have appreciated the real value of what was under their eyes, in which case they would have preserved the papers and today's historians might have an easier task in piecing together what really happened in that far-off time.

Obviously it was strictly forbidden for me to take notes when I was working in the archives. For this reason I spent hours reading and rereading the various files, making certain I knew them by heart.

The first folder I opened was that of Söhnchen or Stanley, real name Harold 'Kim' Philby. From 1944, the Centre had placed inordinate value on this agent because he had brought off what was quite simply a masterstroke. He had managed to get himself appointed chief of Section IX of the British Secret Service.

Our interest in this gentleman stemmed from the fact that Section IX's mission was to study the intelligence activities of the Soviet Union and of other Communist parties around the world. In effect the British Secret Service had just named a Russian agent as head of the branch whose specific task was to spearhead the battle against Russian spies. This made Philby the most important operative we had anywhere in the world.

Over the years I pieced together a portrait of Philby, who had fascinated me from the start. This is what I found out about him.

Harold Adrian Russell Philby was born in India on 1 January 1912 in Ambala, the capital of the Punjab. His father, Harry St John Bridger Philby, was a remarkable character, a Cambridge graduate who spoke eight languages fluently, including Farsi, Baluchi and Afghan. Harry St John Philby made his base at Jedda, became a convert to Islam, took the name of Abdullah and married, as his second wife, a Saudi slave girl with whom he had two sons, Farid and Khalid, Kim's half-brothers. As a close friend of Ibn Saud, he furnished that great Saudi monarch with confidential information from the British intelligence services, before being forced into an early retirement by His Majesty's Government.

Despite the distance between them – Kim lived in England with his mother, Dora – Harry St John Philby remained deeply attached to his son and was very attentive to him whenever he came to England. Observing his son at play and in the company of adults, noting his love of life, enthusiasm and child's perseverance, St John compared him to the eponymous hero of Rudyard Kipling's novel *Kim*. He often told the boy he was a carbon copy of Kim and as 'obstinate as a mule'.

I have read *Kim*, and I think Harry St John Philby was quite right. So Harold became 'Kim' to his family and his friends. He was barely six when his first name was altered, along with a small corner of his identity. Little did anyone dream that this first pseudonym would be followed by a long series of double lives and double games.

In his outlook, Kim closely resembled his father, who was an adventurer and a rebel, firmly opposed to his country's colonial policies, above all a brave man who never shrank from seeing his passions through to their logical conclusion. Kim admired and imitated his father. Both were stubborn, resolute and quixotic; difficult men to fathom. For example, the British never understood how Harry St John Philby, a prominent official, an aristocrat and a man of wealth, could champion the cause of an insignificant desert emir – and even marry a Muslim woman. Later they were to be just as baffled by Kim.

Other traits of his father's character rubbed off on Kim, notably his way of tackling problems. St John took an unbearably long time to make even the smallest decision, but once he had done so, no power on earth could move him. His views remained set in stone until the end of his life, despite the intense pressures brought to bear on him by his social caste. In the same way his son Kim chose his own great purpose for living, the struggle against Fascism, and remained faithful to it till the day of his death. In his last years, I remember someone asking him in my presence, 'Kim, when you die, do you want to be buried in England, like Burgess and Maclean?'

Kim snapped, 'Certainly not. Put me in Russian earth!'

His wish was granted. Kim Philby lies buried at Kuntsevo, in the cemetery compound reserved for generals.

After an uneventful time at Westminster School, Kim went up to

Trinity College, Cambridge, in 1929. In his first year, he read history and signed up almost immediately as a member of the CUSS (Cambridge University Socialist Society), an undergraduate organization.

The Great Depression, triggered by the New York stock market crash, was about to overwhelm Europe. The Labour Party victory in the 1929 general election, and the resumption of diplomatic relations between Great Britain and the USSR, provoked an immense wave of sympathy for Communist Russia. 'The Russian Experiment', as people called it then, mesmerized many Britons, both in the working classes and among the intelligentsia.

The crisis became acute in June 1931, when unemployment figures in Great Britain reached 2,665,000. The British Left, whose ideals were shared by large numbers of students from the middle and upper classes, appeared to have lost control of the situation. The government didn't know how to react to the hunger marches organized by the miners and unemployed people the length and breadth of the country. At the same time, idealistic students believed that the first Soviet Five-Year Plan was a success, and that it would accelerate the country's transformation. They saw the new society being built in Russia as the natural enemy of arrogant, inhuman capitalism, which callously permitted millions to drown in a morass of poverty. Above all, the Soviet model was profoundly seductive to young intellectuals, who were always alert to any pretext for rebellion against their families and social class.

Kim Philby was much drawn to Socialist ideas, though Communism rather scared him, as it did other young men of his generation. His militant posture took a while to develop. Initially he did little more than attend the meetings of CUSS; he had a certain natural authority, but he was by no means a raucous militant clamouring to lead demonstrations and harangue the crowds at rallies. At the end of his first year at university, he became the treasurer of CUSS; at the beginning of the university year, in October 1931, he abandoned history to study economics. This shift in direction was motivated by the political context of the time: Kim felt that a knowledge of economics would prove useful to him in the political fray. At this time, also, he became friends with Maurice Dobb, one of the economics dons teaching him at Cambridge. Dobb's gifts as a political speaker intrigued Philby; he was also one of the first British intellectuals to become a card-carrying Communist. Philby gradually absorbed more and more of Dobb's ideas, but made the error of talking about his views so that his teachers became aware of his political convictions, which caused him a mort of trouble a bit later.

A notorious Communist sympathizer, Kim Philby was nevertheless invited to join the Apostles – a mixture of dining club and top-secret society at Cambridge – in 1932. Though never a full member of the Apostles, he met two other students who were members, Anthony Blunt and Guy Burgess, with whom he quickly became friends. Kim took his degree in economics in 1933. By now he was a convinced Communist, and he informed Maurice Dobb that he planned to go abroad, to Austria or Germany, to improve his German. Dobb strongly approved of this idea. He added, 'I've no further advice to give you; however, if you feel like doing something useful for our cause while you're on your travels, I can give you the address of some French comrades, who may be able to help.'

The contacts in question were activists belonging to Willi Münzenberg's World Committee for the Assistance of Victims of German Fascism. Münzenberg was an individual who played a major part as a voluntary NKVD recruiting agent between 1930 and 1935. After a leftist youth, he formed his committee in Paris – at a time when the Nazis were on the rise in Germany – with the purpose of thwarting Nazi propaganda by every means. Although he recruited for the NKVD, he was never a Soviet agent.

In Paris, the committee members took the young Philby to their hearts. Dobb had written to them praising his sincerity and reliability. They also knew Kim had been treasurer for a group of Socialist students at Cambridge, and they provided him with several contacts in Vienna. One of these addresses was that of the International Organization for Aid to Revolutionaries (IOAR), currently short of a treasurer and looking for a volunteer to fill the post. They suggested that Philby might like to take it for a few months.

I myself knew the IOAR well: while I was studying at Lipetsk, I was a member of its Russian branch, the MOPR, and paid a few kopeks a month towards a fund to help the workers.

At that time, every industry, school and government department had its MOPR cell. The money these cells collected was distributed to the families of workers in prison in the capitalist countries, and was even used to pay their lawyers.

49

The second address given to Philby by the French committee was that of the Kohlmans, a family of Polish Jews who had emigrated to Austria before the First World War. Israel Kohlman, the father, was an accountant who spent most of his time working with his wife to assist Jews in Vienna. The Kohlmans had a daughter, Alice, nicknamed Litzi. Litzi was small but extraordinarily pretty. She had already been married once, at eighteen, to a certain Karl Friedman, but had divorced him almost immediately. She and Philby were attracted to one another at once; Philby became temporary treasurer of the local IOAR cell, a job in which he showed a notable lack of zeal, being a good deal more interested in Litzi, to whom he devoted every moment of his spare time.

Litzi was a convinced Communist who remained loyal to Socialist ideals as long as she lived. She had a decisive influence on Philby, for it was she who gave him his first real initiation to the cause.

In the autumn of 1933, the political situation in Vienna was explosive. Chancellor Dollfuss, who had been in power for just over a year, had installed an authoritarian regime, banning all public demonstrations, refusing Hitler's proposed Anschluss, dissolving the Austrian Parliament and banning the National Socialist and Communist Parties. The Social Democrats then called a general uprising, which was put down violently by Dollfuss's 35,000-strong police force. It is estimated that 1,500 died and 5,000 were injured.

Throughout those months Philby and Litzi were immersed in a passionate love affair, while around them martial law was declared and people were executed daily. Finally, in February 1934, civil strife broke out in earnest. Kim Philby, though a British subject with no need to become involved, showed real courage and devotion in the workers' cause. Encouraged by Litzi, he joined a network that was helping hunted Communist militants to get out of Austria. He collected clothes for the fugitives, found places for them to hide and made arrangements for them to escape abroad.

He married Litzi in February 1934, thereby making her a British subject and saving her from certain arrest. She was a well-known Communist and spent most of her time working for the Party. Despite their extraordinarily difficult circumstances, Kim showed himself an attentive husband. Litzi's undercover work had brought her to the edge of nervous collapse; Kim, realizing this, insisted when she came home each day that they should go for long walks together around the town, or in the countryside. This steadied and calmed her. Another trait in Philby's character had come to the surface: all his life thereafter he was unfailingly tender and gentle with women, though frequently unfaithful to them.

This episode in Kim's life was very important, a turning point. I believe the massacres of Socialists and trade unionists by government forces that he witnessed in Vienna were a decisive factor in his engagement as a Communist: in Austria, he was able to see Communism as a deadly serious reality. The events in Vienna marked him indelibly. Moreover, his active involvement with Communism in Vienna was a direct repudiation of the ideas of his father, who was an avowed Fascist and a fervent admirer of Hitler.

In later years Kim often told me that the Soviet intelligence services had shown considerable interest in him during his time in Vienna. This seems to me unlikely, although he must have had his reasons for saying so. What I can say with some certainty is that the decisive influence in persuading him to become a Soviet agent came not from his friends but from Litzi. Neither Theodor Maly, an NKVD agent, nor anyone else recruited him. He was won over by his wife – not directly, of course, and not on behalf of the NKVD (she was not a member), but in the name of the Comintern, the international Soviet Communist organization (also called the Third International), whose purpose was to promote world revolution, for which she was an agent. She told her superiors in that organization that she had come to know somebody highly interesting who might prove very useful to the cause.

Of course, the NKVD was not unaware of Philby's presence in Vienna: he had been spotted at once, but in all sincerity I don't believe the young man was approached by us at that time. Years later Philby and I often spoke of his wife Litzi. I don't know why, but in conversation he systematically minimized her influence on him.

For over thirty years now, journalists, writers and self-proclaimed experts have speculated about how Philby was originally recruited. A dense fog of disinformation cloaks the entire episode. At least five men, over the years, have claimed that it was they who found the spy of the century. I myself have read reports by several different intelligence officers who swore that they alone had accomplished the exploit. This is any intelligence officer's dream, of course. But it was all nonsense. I don't want to sound pretentious, but each time I could tell they were lying. The times, places and individuals they cited were hopelessly mixed up. The reality is as plain as day: the NKVD was not involved and there was no John le Carré plot. Kim Philby, deeply moved and outraged by the atrocities he had witnessed in Vienna, simply went along with Litzi. Neither their political convictions nor their engagement with Communism was the prime mover; they were just a young couple in love, who shared a bitter loathing of Fascism. From 1934 to 1940, the Soviet secret service was the very last thing on their minds. Instead their youth, their courage, their intelligence and their energy were committed to the struggle against Fascism in Germany, Italy, England and anywhere it raised its head.

Though Theodor Maly did not recruit Philby, he had a powerful hold on him. Maly was one of the NKVD's best 'illegal' agents in the West before the war; illegals are secret agents sent abroad under a foreign identity. A former priest and artilleryman in the Austro-Hungarian Army, he exchanged religion for a belief in Communism early on. He had left Russia to work first in Germany and then, when Hitler came to power, in Vienna, where he was living when Philby arrived.

At the meetings in Vienna attended by Kim and Litzi, Maly forcefully explained that the war against Nazism had to be waged outside Germany, and that everything possible should be done to crush the Nazi tentacles groping into neighbouring countries. Maly's charisma was immense, and the two young people listened raptly.

Kim Philby returned to England in May 1934, taking his wife to live with his mother, Dora, in Hampstead. It is a cliché that mothers and daughters-in-law don't get on; this was certainly not the case with Dora and Litzi, who immediately became close friends and allies.

As soon as she arrived in London, Litzi made contact with the local Communists, notably Edith Tudor-Hart. The Philbys went on to meet several Communist militants, some of them NKVD agents. The Centre was quickly made aware that the young man who had shown himself so active during the Vienna uprising was now back in England and still a likely target.

It must be stressed that, contrary to received opinion, it was neither Burgess nor one of our own Russian agents who lured Philby into the toils of the Soviet espionage apparatus. Again, it was Litzi. Through her friend Edith she brought Kim into contact with Arnold Deutsch, who had recently moved to London. Kim had known since Vienna that he had aroused the interest of a secret anti-Fascist organization within the framework of the Comintern. At the instigation of Deutsch, he began his clandestine work in the belief that he was working for a Comintern cell.

Deutsch was, like Maly, an NKVD illegal operative. An Austrian Jew, he was vastly interested in psychoanalysis, and later became involved in the Viennese psychoanalyst Wilhelm Reich's campaign against political and sexual repression. Deutsch met Maly in the early 1920s, joined the Communist Party in 1924 and in 1933 was trained, with his wife, as an illegal agent by the NKVD. Later he worked in Paris, whence he was sent to England under his real name, posing as an Austrian scientist. In the course of 1934, Arnold Deutsch met Philby on several occasions; but Deutsch was not the man ultimately delegated by the Centre to direct Kim's work. I never learned the name of the NKVD officer in question.

Kim Philby now set about his first mission, which was to recruit one or two other agents to form an embryonic network. He travelled up to Cambridge during the month of May. There he met Guy Burgess, told him what he had done and seen that winter in Vienna and thus convinced him to join his fledgeling group. It has been said that Burgess was recruited by a Soviet agent; this is entirely untrue. He was taken on by Philby in May 1934. Before he set out, Philby discussed his friend Burgess at length with his handling officer and with Arnold Deutsch, then known to us by the code name of Otto. An encounter between Burgess and Deutsch took place several weeks later in a London pub.

In the meantime the group received a third recruit. Philby had asked Burgess to forage among his friends, and Burgess came up with Anthony Blunt.

In addition to seeking out new talent, Philby was directed by his handling officer to join the British civil service, with a view to assessing any Fascist elements by which it might have been infiltrated. Philby duly compiled an application, and to increase his chances of success he enlisted the support of one of his former economics dons, Dennis Robertson, and a friend of his father (who bore the same surname but was not related), Donald Robertson. He visited the two men in turn, and both agreed to sponsor him. But shortly afterwards they abruptly distanced themselves from his application; only after a month had gone by did Kim receive a letter from Dennis Robertson, who with classic British understatement explained that Kim's hypersensitivity to political injustice might render him unsuitable for the work of a civil servant.

Kim Philby understood immediately that his past as a Communist sympathizer had come back to haunt him. He did not insist; he merely withdrew his application and for the moment abandoned the idea of joining the civil service. At the same time he officially and very methodically repudiated all ties with the Communist Party. He made it known to everyone he spoke to that as far as he was concerned, Communism was a dead letter. From now on, his much more frivolous objective was to enter society in London.

It was at this point that his handler told him who his real masters were. Curiously enough, Philby was unfazed; I think he had probably suspected as much for some time. The officer then asked him to focus his work on Germany, and to go there in search of intelligence which might be used against the Nazi regime.

In spite of his Cambridge degree, Kim Philby had considerable trouble landing a job. He wanted to try journalism, and to that end became an occasional contributor to the *Review of Reviews*, a London journal. He was aware that this job was unlikely to yield much in the way of ammunition against the Fascists; but all the same he contrived, through his father's connections, to penetrate Lady Astor's group of Nazi sympathizers, to join the Anglo-German Fellowship, and to meet Joachim von Ribbentrop, Hitler's ambassador in London and the future Foreign Affairs Minister of the Third Reich. Their relationship was cordial, even friendly; Ribbentrop took a shine to Philby, and he recommended him to Joseph Goebbels, the Propaganda Minister, with a view to finding work for him in Berlin. Philby duly travelled to Germany and met Goebbels. Their interview led to nothing concrete, but Kim was undeterred: his father had just introduced him to Professor Haushofer, editor of the German political magazine *Geopolitik*, an intelligent, well-produced review dedicated to disseminating Hitler's ideas for a new world order.

Thus it was that Philby's work began to bear fruit. The first information he passed on to his handler was a list, covering several pages, of the names of Nazi sympathizers in the upper echelons of government, in the political classes, and among the aristocracy of Britain. Attached to this list was an analysis of the opinions of sundry aristocrats, business leaders and politicians about National Socialism and about Hitler himself. This list seemed rather insignificant until the outbreak of war.

In mid-1935, Kim Philby began working systematically with Otto (Deutsch). In early 1936, Deutsch was joined by Theodor Maly, who arrived posing as a respectable banker by the name of Paul Hardt. Maly's mission was to take overall control of our clandestine operations on British territory. During his brief spell in England, he used a number of covers, some genuine, others not at all. For several months he was officially employed on the staff of the Soviet Embassy. The British Secret Service never even noticed him.

Maly and Deutsch were both highly professional agents, and to give them their due, they were not out for information at any price. They knew Kim Philby was a star recruit. Their approach was to give him all the time he needed to establish his contacts, learn the ropes and take his place in the sector of British society where he could be of most use to Soviet intelligence later on.

So Philby set about finding himself a job that would not only earn him a living but also tap him into sources of information about Germany. He went to Berlin in 1936 to activate the contacts he had made in Nazi milieux; while there, he heard the news of the outbreak of the Spanish Civil War. On his return to London he was asked by Otto to turn his attention to Spain, in whose affairs the Soviets were soon to become closely involved, and to infiltrate Franco's entourage if he could.

This was a delicate task, given that General Franco, known as the Caudillo, or leader, was extraordinarily suspicious of Western countries, particularly Britain and France. Every Briton or Frenchman was for him a potential member of the International Brigades, and his policy was therefore to allow into Spain a strict minimum of journalists from the two countries. Philby had therefore to conduct a carefully planned campaign to obtain accreditation. Again he applied to his father, swearing that he had given up his flirtation with Communism and was now set on becoming an international reporter.

Harry St John swallowed this and used his influence to obtain a visa for Kim. One of his close Spanish friends was the Duke of Alba, who represented Franco in England; the Duke intervened on Kim's behalf, and in February 1937 he was granted a visa to enter the territory controlled by Franco's Nationalist forces.

In Spain, Philby was in his element. He wrote several excellent freelance pieces; these were noticed by the editor of *The Times*, who promptly engaged him as a war correspondent.

Years later Philby told me his career as a spy was very nearly brought to a premature close in Spain. He arrived at a small town, omitting to register his presence with the local police, and was routed out of bed by the Guardia Civil in the middle of the night. In his trouser pocket was a small piece of notepaper bearing his codes for communicating with the NKVD. He was hustled to the police station under close escort, racking his brains all the while for a way to unload this highly compromising document before it was discovered. While he was being searched, he tossed his wallet on to the table in such a way that it slid off the edge and fell to the floor. The policemen pounced on it and he took advantage of their momentary inattention to swallow the fatal slip of paper.

A second incident in Spain earned Philby the confidence of Franco himself – counterbalancing, for a while at least, his youthful flirtation with Communism. While he was making his way to the front with three other journalists, their car was hit by a shell. One journalist was killed instantly and Philby's other two colleagues died later of their wounds. Philby himself escaped with a few scratches. The incident made him a kind of hero to the Nationalists, and Franco personally awarded him the Red Cross of Military Merit. This decoration proved of immense importance in his later work, because it gave him privileged access to the highest echelons of the Nationalist movement in Spain.

This piece of luck yielded invaluable information on the exact scale of Italian and German assistance to the Spanish Nationalists. The Italians were quietly sending aid in the form of infantry, and the Germans were providing massive air support.

At one point in his tour of duty in Spain, Philby proposed to the NKVD that he should personally assassinate Franco. I don't know what the Centre's initial reaction to this idea may have been; probably the project was vetoed because the NKVD's priorities suddenly altered at about this time. The Soviet Union had decided to attack the extreme left, in particular the Trotskyists and militants of the Workers' Unification Party, before liquidating Franco.

Meanwhile Philby made the acquaintance of Frances Lindsay-Hogg, nicknamed 'Bunny', the wife of an English baronet, who had lived in Spain for some years and moved in Francoist and Monarchist circles. Bunny became Philby's mistress and an unwitting assistant in his secret work.

At the same time she wrecked his marriage. Kim, who frequently travelled to and fro between Spain and Portugal to deliver his information, would sometimes meet his wife in the Portuguese capital, Lisbon, where she had come especially to see him. The intuitive Litzi soon guessed that he was being unfaithful to her.

When Philby returned to London, there were no fights: the two remained friends, but they could no longer be lovers. Kim continued to work for *The Times*, though his position was less brilliant now that he was back in England. His earlier spate of published articles dried to a trickle. Moreover, he was at loose ends because Theodor Maly and Arnold Deutsch had been recalled to Moscow. Stalin's purges were at their height and both men knew what probably awaited them – a secret trial and a firing squad – but they nonetheless obeyed orders. Many other agents acted in the same fashion.

A few ignored the Centre's summons and fled elsewhere; among these were Lev Lazarevich Feldbin (alias Aleksandr Orlov, alias Nikolski). When Orlov, the former head of the NKVD in Spain, was recalled from there at the beginning of July 1938, he sensed that the wind had changed and embarked for Canada with his wife, daughter, and 22,000 US dollars in cash from the residency's coffers, afterwards settling in the United States.

Orlov, whose nickname in Moscow was Chved (the Swede), was an important figure in the NKVD, with access to much vital information. He was resident in Spain in 1936 during the Civil War, setting up guerrilla units to fight behind the Francoist lines and organizing the counter-espionage operations of the Republicans. In 1937, on Stalin's orders, he was one of the principal figures in the liquidation of the Trotskyist opposition.

To save his skin, Orlov sent a letter to an American lawyer which contained a list of about a hundred names of Soviet agents around the world. The lawyer was instructed not to open the letter except in the event of Orlov's violent death.

Orlov's next move was to let the NKVD know exactly what he had done – and this saved his life. Later he collaborated in a small way with the American intelligence services but he gave them no names of any importance. The names he knew, after all, were his life insurance.

Although Orlov certainly knew the code names of Philby, Burgess, Maclean, Blunt and X, he didn't know – any more than anyone else in the NKVD in 1938 knew – that these five young individuals would soon form the KGB's most successful espionage network; at that time they had not yet provided any very significant intelligence.

Kim Philby had to wait till the outbreak of the Second World War in September 1939 before he again found himself in an interesting job. At that time he was attached to the British Expeditionary Force headquarters at Arras, France, as war correspondent for *The Times*. Here he remained till June 1940; after Dunkirk he returned to London, where he continued to work for *The Times* while waiting to be called up. His friend Guy Burgess, who had joined the British Secret Service permanently in 1939, offered him some good advice: 'Find yourself a decent job quickly,' he said, 'otherwise before you know it you'll be at the front, God knows where, and perfectly useless to the rest of us.' When Burgess talked about 'a decent job', Philby didn't have to have a crystal ball to guess what he meant.

Before long Kim had applied to join the Government Code and Cypher School, known as the GC and CS, at Bletchley Park, twenty-five miles from Oxford. He was interviewed by the school's recruiting officer, a former Cambridge professor, and was offered a place; but he refused this on the grounds that the salary was too low. Time was short, and the risk of Kim's being mobilized was growing daily; the army sent him a summons for a medical examination. At this point Burgess again stepped in and suggested his friend try his luck with the service he himself was in, Section D of MI6, which ran a propaganda, sabotage and subversion training school. He thought Philby might teach politics there, politics being his special interest. Like the shrewd diplomat he was, Burgess did not propose Philby to his superiors point blank; instead he went to the school's chief of staff, Marjorie Maxse, and suggested that a specialized instructor in German politics and propaganda was badly needed to instruct the trainee agents. Some time later he suggested the name of someone he had heard about – a former *Times* correspondent who had covered Spain during the civil war, and who knew the methods of the German propaganda machine from having seen them applied in that country. Burgess moved his pawns forward with the utmost care, behaving as if he in no way intended to influence Miss Maxse's decision. Naturally, Kim Philby's application was considered and he was invited to a melodramatic secret rendezvous, in an empty house with boarded-up doors and windows. In a tiny attic room he was interviewed by the chief of staff – a woman who was highly professional and knew the workings of her country's secret services inside out, he told me later. Philby met her twice, the second time with Burgess present.

With his class, his charm and his cultivated manner, he easily won over Maxse, who took him on as an instructor in the celebrated spy school at Brickendonbury Hall, near Hertford. As a teacher of politics Philby was a success; he worked hard and quickly earned a solid reputation. The students at the school were hardly intellectuals, tending to be straightforward individuals training as field agents. Philby's job was to teach them to hate Fascism and the German military, but above all to counteract Nazi propaganda. He knew how to influence his listeners.

Penetration of the British Secret Service in this manner did not satisfy the NKVD. What the Centre still dreamed of was access to Bletchley Park; but this was far from simple: even Burgess was unable to help. Burgess did what he could to promote Philby, praising him to his highly placed friends in the Special Intelligence Service (SIS), but without success.

Nevertheless Kim's first assignment had brought him within the charmed circle of the secret service and had made it possible for him to get to know a number of agents, notably his fellow instructors at Brickendonbury Hall and later at the Beaulieu training school in Hampshire, to which he was transferred after the amalgamation of Section D with the brand-new Special Operations Executive (SOE).

Philby knew how to gain people's confidence. He would drink and exercise with his colleagues, enlarging more and more on his views. During this period there occurred an incident that was to have incalculable consequences for Anglo–Soviet relations in the future: the secret flight to Scotland carried out by Rudolf Hess on 10 May 1941. Hess's purpose was to negotiate a separate peace between Britain and Germany. Whether he did so on the orders of higher authority we shall probably never know, but the embarrassment of the British Government was so genuine that the Soviets became deeply suspicious.

The Hess affair was horrifying to the Kremlin because an alliance between Britain and Germany would have meant the demise of the Soviet Union. The behaviour of the British, seen from Russia, was clumsy and strange in the extreme. The Soviets concluded that their allies were indeed negotiating with Hess and were seriously considering his proposals, even though they had made a public announcement of his arrest and claimed that he was mentally ill. Philby made superhuman efforts to get at the details of the affair but failed to do so.

Among the people Philby worked with at Brickendonbury was a certain Tommy Harris, an MI6 agent, with whom he became fast friends. In civilian life Harris was a wealthy dealer in pictures and antiques. When Philby was in Moscow during the 1970s, Harris sent him a magnificent marquetry table, a real jewel. Philby showed it to me with considerable pride; Harris bore him no grudge, even though it was he who had helped get a promotion for Philby within the British secret service. This had been in July 1941, a month after German forces had launched the massive surprise attack on the Soviet Union that became known as Operation Barbarossa.

Philby, under mounting pressure from his new handler, Henry (the code name of Anatoli Borisovich Gorsky), moved heaven and earth to have himself transferred to the holy of holies at Bletchley Park, or else to a section where more important information would be made available to him.

He had plenty of potential to become an efficient agent of MI6 and, once inside the organization, to rise through its ranks. Among other things he spoke several foreign languages fluently and he knew France, Spain and Germany well. When Harris recommended Philby to MI5's head of personnel, he happened to mention that Kim's father was a friend of Valentine Vivian, one of the heads of Section V (counter-espionage). Vivian was a highly intelligent and competent officer, and a great expert on counter-espionage. He had served in India, where he had known Philby Senior well. When he heard that the recruiting section was considering the candidacy of someone named Philby, he took an immediate interest in the question, and as soon as he established that Kim was Harry St John's son, he called him in. The two men liked each other and Philby was offered a job.

At that time Kim was having a passionate love affair with Aileen

Furse, who worked in the MI5 archive department. He had been frank with Valentine Vivian about his separation from Litzi; in fact, Litzi was by now living somewhere on the Continent, where she was fulfilling her role as a militant Communist. Philby claimed to have been out of touch with Litzi for several years, and openly announced that he planned to marry Aileen Furse as soon as his divorce went through. After the birth of their first child, Kim and Aileen did indeed decide to get married, but Philby, who had no desire to commit bigamy, wanted to wait till the end of the war before making his separation from Litzi official. He appeared to be very happy with Aileen, but even in his most intimate private life he never forgot his goals as an agent. Aileen had access to all the archives, and Philby contrived with unbelievable subtlety to read the files on an assortment of British agents working all over the world. In the course of time his list of them arrived on a desk at the Lubyanka – a coup of immense significance. This time we were seriously impressed.

I should add that there were no names in Philby's files. Each individual was identified by five ciphers containing his country of residence and his number as an agent. There was no way that any of these individuals could be immediately identified; but by slow deduction it was possible for us to uncover certain identities because opposite the five ciphers, in a separate column, there were a substantial number of clues. Such information as the official jobs occupied by the agents, the names of the towns and other places where they stayed, and detailed biographical data enabled our experts to pinpoint many of them with absolute certainty. We were at war, and I have to say frankly that we were primarily interested in the British spies operating at that time within the Soviet Union. As to those in South America, Africa, etc., we didn't have time to follow up on them.

The information Philby supplied was never exploited as fully as it should have been, and by the time the war was over, it was too late to dig it up again. The rumours that have circulated recently that his list was mere disinformation have no foundation. At that time, thanks to Kim Philby, we possessed a nearly complete list of British agents operating throughout the world.

When Kim Philby joined MI6 at the beginning of 1942, the secret service hierarchy wondered how he could best be put to use. Should they send him into occupied Europe, France for example, or should they have him work directly on German and Italian affairs from London? Harris, his MI6 friend, offered a further alternative. Why not attach Philby to the Spanish section? There was nobody in the service who knew Spain better than he did. Philby himself was writhing in anticipation. Before long he was working as assistant to Felix Cowgill, the head of Section V and director of the European section handling Spain.

Kim set about his new job with considerable energy and almost immediately began to produce results. His service did serious damage to the German spy networks which had adopted Spain as a bridgehead for their intelligence operations against Great Britain. Philby and his colleagues in the European section received the decoded intercepts of the Abwehr's communications. It goes without saying that Philby (or Stanley, as we knew him in the KGB) did not keep all this information to himself. He kept Henry, his handler, abreast of everything he discovered about Spain, Portugal and the activities of the German secret services. In this way his group intercepted a message announcing the impending visit to Spain of the head of the Abwehr, Admiral Wilhelm Canaris. The document listed every detail of Canaris's itinerary with dates, hours, the names of the hotels in which he was to stay and the names of the people he was scheduled to meet.

Philby knew one of the hotels, the Parador at Manzanares between Madrid and Seville, very well. Manzanares was then a small, fairly remote village, but quite easy to reach. Philby therefore suggested to his superiors that an attempt should be made there on Canaris's life.

His plan was carefully prepared: there was every chance that it would succeed, given that the British knew the exact date of the visit, the layout of the Parador and ways to escape once the assassination had been carried out. The only element lacking was the number of the admiral's bedroom, but this could easily be obtained on the spot. Philby even arranged a hideout where the killers could lie low after the attack.

This was highly acceptable to Kim's immediate superiors, particularly Felix Cowgill. All that was needed was the assent of the head of MI6, Stewart Menzies. His reply came back instantly, a categorical negative. The idea was anathema to him.

'I forbid you to lay a finger on Canaris,' he said. 'Don't even think about it! Leave the man alone!'

This stupefied everyone in the Spanish section. Why on earth should they abandon such a golden opportunity to get rid of a highly placed Nazi? Why did Menzies insist on sparing Canaris, his bitterest enemy, whom he had never met? Some of the officers in Section V speculated that Menzies was afraid of meeting the same fate, given that Canaris was his exact opposite number, but this seemed unlikely in the extreme.

Philby offered a different interpretation. He suspected that there might have been some kind of collusion between MI6 and the German secret services. He had no proof whatever, but in his report to us he drew the NKVD's attention to the possibility. The Centre took this warning very seriously and ordered a detailed investigation of Canaris's youth, career and friendships. We deduced from this that the Nazi admiral had always had close ties with the British, knew them well and had many English affinities. Nobody had imagined it before, but after analysing all the facts we concluded that contacts between Canaris and MI6 were perfectly possible, even probable. This was another very good reason to be on our guard against our so-called allies, the British. Philby's vigilance appeared to have paid off – though in hindsight it is clear that Canaris, who was hanged for his suspected part in the attempt to assassinate the Führer in July 1944, was an easy mark, and that the British Secret Service was dealing with him behind Hitler's back.

The attempts of different Nazi officials to obtain a separate peace with the British and the Americans, leading to a reversal of alliances whereby the Germans would fight side by side with them against the USSR, were a source of deep disquiet to our leaders. Towards the end of the war, in 1944, we received information – later confirmed – that the British and the Americans had actually negotiated with the Germans to this effect. The Americans did so openly, while the British operated secretly by way of Sweden. This example shows once again that Philby had been perfectly correct in his judgement.

In his Spanish subsection, Philby showed himself conscientious and hard-working beyond the call of duty, and his subsequent success was largely due to this. The others hurried home after work, but Kim stayed on in his office till late at night. He did this not only because he had plenty on his plate, but also because he genuinely loved his work. His capacity for concentrated hard toil produced a very favourable impression not only on the British, but also on us. Later, when he was in Russia, he carried out every task we gave him rapidly and professionally, in just the same manner.

He was commended by his superiors. He was the kind of man who knew exactly how to please his entourage. For example, Valentine Vivian, deputy chief of MI5, said of him, 'In our service I would say that Philby is the only man who has no enemies at all. Everyone else has one or two, people who are jealous or envious of them. Philby has no enemies of that kind.'

Valentine Vivian was highly respected and his views carried great force. A veteran of many years' service for the Indian police, he would later become deputy head of SIS. He is thought to have known the secret agents of Britain better than anyone else, along with the work they did and their way of thinking.

Among other things, Vivian gave much time and thought to projects anticipating the immediate post-war period. A number of reports had been prepared under his aegis, all of which concluded that when hostilities against Germany ceased, the Soviet Union would become Western Europe's number one adversary. Vivian's suggestion was that the British Government should immediately initiate measures to counter the Soviet Union's expansionist ambitions, and generally engage in a more active struggle against the Communist movement in Europe and the rest of the world. To this end he proposed the creation of a special anti-Communist section. He even worked out the structure of this organism, which would naturally be a part of SIS. In his reports Vivian outlined in some detail the methods that could be used against the Soviet secret services, as well as those that should be adopted in the struggle against the spread of Communism around the world. He proposed technical ways and means of infiltrating, provoking and disorganizing the different parties. All this work, which was intended to be submitted to the British Government for its approval, was kept in a special file. Naturally, this file was an object of deep fascination for us and we asked Philby whether he could get his hands on it; he said he would try. He succeeded far beyond our expectations without, as he said, taking the slightest risk.

Back at the Lubyanka, it was very hard for me to read these documents because they were always on the desk of one or other of the departmental heads, but eventually I got hold of them for an hour or two and studied them greedily. At that time I was still very young, lacking the experience to make an objective analysis of what was under my eyes, but when I think back on it today I have to acknowledge that Vivian's report was an extraordinary piece of work, a sharp and dispassionate analysis formulated by a superb intelligence professional.

In general I have a very high opinion of the British Secret Service, which I have always rated among the finest in the world. This dossier, one of their best products, became known in our offices as the 'Vivian Folder', and was cherished as a kind of trophy, a perfect testimonial to the brilliance of Kim Philby's work. It is still jealously preserved in the archives of the KGB.

A year after he entered the Spanish subsection, Philby's responsibilities were doubled. He remained deputy to the subsection's head, but his field of activity was broadened to include North Africa and Italy. Then came the creation of the anti-Communist group proposed by Vivian, which was named Section IX.

All of this represents more or less all I knew about Kim Philby prior to the moment when I myself was delegated to handle the intelligence that he and his fellow agents obtained for us.

The next two files I took an interest in were those of Guy Burgess and Anthony Blunt. Guy Burgess was the son of an officer in the Royal Navy; his mother, who was wealthy in her own right, survived well into the 1960s. Born in 1910, Guy came from a long line of generals and admirals and was initially drawn to a naval career, entering the Royal Naval College at Dartmouth at an early age.

Guy was a bright student, but at the end of his second year he abruptly left Dartmouth. There are two versions of what happened: one has it that the school doctors found he had problems with his eyesight and let him know he would never become an officer in the service. (Personally I never noticed the slightest defect in his vision – and I worked closely with him for many years.) The other and more likely explanation was that he loathed Dartmouth and despite his extreme youth was sufficiently independent and tough-minded to tell his parents that it would be too great an honour for the Royal Navy to receive Guy Burgess into its ranks.

His family therefore transferred him to Eton, where he had a brilliant career and won both the Rosebery and the Gladstone prizes for history. At Eton he was taught by G. M. Trevelyan, the author of

English Social History, who instantly recognized the boy's great potential as a researcher.

At the end of his time at Eton, Burgess won a scholarship to Trinity College, Cambridge, and went up to the university in October 1930. By this time his father had died and his mother had remarried, to a man of whom Guy was very fond.

He quickly became a popular figure at Cambridge; his charm, his devastating sense of humour and his deep culture were equally attractive to both dons and fellow undergraduates. Moreover, he was extremely good-looking; and this, coupled with self-confidence and a natural ease of bearing in any company, made him very much the man of the moment. His friendship was coveted.

Among Guy's more fervent admirers was Anthony Blunt, a graduate three years his senior who had already assembled a formidable array of degrees in mathematics, French and German. Blunt was an austere young man, the son of a Church of England cleric and a highly educated, pious, kindly mother, a cousin of the Earl of Strathmore, whose daughter, Lady Elizabeth Bowes Lyon, married George VI and is the mother of Queen Elizabeth II. Thus Anthony Blunt was related to the royal family, and although he never boasted of this connection he was nonetheless rather proud of it. He was reserved, to say the least, with his fellow students.

Arthur Vaughan Stanley Blunt, his father, was a man of great discretion, much respected in church circles. He was chaplain of the English Church in Paris for ten years, hence Anthony's perfect mastery of French. The elder Blunt gave his son a strict education and passed on to him many of his own qualities of dignity and austerity in regard to things and people. Anthony lived in the French capital until the age of fifteen, a fact which was to have a considerable effect on the course of his future life. He then went to Marlborough, where he received a solid English education – and something more, because it was here that his homosexual predilections began to emerge, predilections that were to be confirmed at Cambridge. He wasn't even eighteen when his father died, an event that brought him still closer to his mother. He was a bookish young man, an aesthete who affected disdain for middle-class conventions, while not being specially attracted to politics, which he thought rather vulgar.

Blunt's interest in art, above all in the history of painting, showed itself early; but at that time the history of art was not taught at English schools and universities. As a matter of course he earned a scholarship to Trinity, Cambridge, in 1926, though, curiously enough, he opted to study neither literature nor languages, but mathematics, in which he received second-class honours after his first year. He next decided to change to languages, which suited him well because he already spoke excellent French and German. He obtained a first in French and an upper second in German for the first part of his degree.

During his first years at Cambridge his homosexuality, which had been latent ever since his school years, was suddenly fully awakened. He had a number of affairs, but tended to keep them very quiet. This discretion was in strong contrast to the behaviour of Guy Burgess, whom he met around this time. The two men were strongly attracted to one another, both physically and intellectually.

Blunt never betrayed his friendship with Burgess. In an interview given to *The Times* in 1979, just after Margaret Thatcher officially revealed that Blunt had worked as a Soviet agent, he defended his friend. 'Guy Burgess was one of the most intelligent men I have ever met,' he said. 'But it's quite true that even then he tended to get on people's nerves.'

Guy Burgess, affectionately known to his friends as Jim, was a very complicated individual. He was extraordinarily cultured, and his mind was subtle enough to grasp the most difficult concepts. His views were invariably pertinent, original and interesting.

Despite his habitual neglect of his studies, Burgess received top honours in the first part of his history degree course in 1932, having made up for his lack of organization and of hard work by a virtuoso display of eclectic knowledge. His penchant for the bottle and his homosexuality now began to be noticed, and it was also at this time that his friend Blunt co-opted him into the highly secret society of the Apostles. Here he caught the attention of Maurice Dobb, the economics don at Pembroke College, an avowed propagandist of Marxist ideology and one of the first university professors in Britain to join the British Communist Party. It was Dobb who introduced Guy to a young and brilliant undergraduate by the name of Harold 'Kim' Philby.

Maurice Dobb could scarcely have imagined that he was to be instrumental in creating the most effective spy ring of the twentieth century.

Despite his aristocratic manner and élitist attitudes, Guy Burgess sympathized deeply with the masses. During his third year (1932–33) at Cambridge, he championed the cause of the employees at Trinity, who had to live on nothing during the vacations because the university would pay them only during term time. He was one of a small group of students who organized a successful strike on their behalf, enabling the Cambridge college staffs to receive paid holidays well in advance of the rest of the nation. Moreover, Burgess was among those few Cambridge undergraduates who was militant outside the university, not only taking part in demonstrations but also organizing meetings and strikes – on behalf of the city's bus drivers, for example. He also joined a group of striking sewage workers who were demanding better working conditions.

Many Cambridge students, fired by the ideas of Maurice Dobb and by his exhortations to join the struggle against Fascism, were content to talk and do nothing. Guy Burgess matched his words to deeds.

Though born into the upper class, Burgess found lovers in every social category. He had a strong preference for lorry drivers and other working men, whom he habitually paid for sex. He liked their company and would cross-examine them mercilessly about how they were coping with the Depression.

Indeed, the social and political conditions of the Depression overshadowed his third year at Cambridge, which he completed somewhat ingloriously. I don't think he even took his final exams, because he was very ill throughout his last term. This did not prevent him from beginning the year 1933–34 by settling on 'Bourgeois Revolution in Seventeenth-Century England' as a title for his PhD thesis. But in the end he abandoned it. In that year he had affairs with a number of students and dons. As a rule his liaisons seldom lasted long, but Guy had a way of making his temporary lovers into lasting friends.

He was above all a brilliant talker, completely at home in high society. His sheer intellectual ability enthralled people. Goronwy Rees, a close university friend, used to say that Burgess was the most brilliant undergraduate of his time at Cambridge. Yet he was also an authoritarian young man, perfectly capable of bending others to his will and of dominating them, even as he remained tolerant and understanding of their difficulties.

Looking back on his life, I have always found it hard to understand how this remarkable student could have sacrificed a future as a high official, man of the world and diplomat to join our side in what was after all a doubtful, dangerous, thankless endeavour, offering no personal reward other than that of advancing the cause of revolution in the world.

Anthony Blunt and Guy Burgess were very close at Cambridge. Blunt was madly in love, lost in admiration for Guy's brilliant intellect and dancing wit. In return Guy tried to initiate Anthony Blunt and turn him into a convinced Communist.

He was assisted in this task of conversion by another under-graduate member of the Apostles, Alistair Watson. Their first attempt on Blunt was not a success. They failed to convince him, though he appeared interested. They talked for nights on end in their favourite club, the Pitt, but Blunt was unwavering. He refused to take part in meetings and demonstrations, and there was no question whatever of his expressing any leftist convictions. But many years later, scholars analysing his writings of the period have found that even then his ideas carried a Marxist overlay.

It took Guy Burgess a while, but eventually he succeeded in winning over Anthony Blunt and recruiting him into his group of anti-Fascist activists. The decisive moment came during a visit to Rome in 1933. Blunt was writing a thesis on the history and theory of French and Italian painting between 1400 and 1700, and he spent a lot of time in Italy, where he worked with Ellis Waterhouse, the librarian at the British School of Rome. Burgess, Blunt and Waterhouse went out together, visited museums, frequented bars and went for long, rambling walks around the city. None of them talked politics except Burgess, who from time to time brought up Marxist views. Waterhouse noticed at the time that Burgess seemed to have gained an ascendancy over Blunt.

At that point there was still no question for Guy Burgess of the NKVD, the secret service, or espionage. His mind was set on the struggle against Fascism. But Blunt's support even here was tentative at best, and in contrast to his Cambridge friends Burgess, Maclean and Philby, he was no more than an active sympathizer with the cause.

So Blunt's interest in Marxism did not come naturally. Burgess, and Burgess alone, was at the root of it. Furthermore, I cannot imagine that he was entirely in agreement with all of Guy's views, though Guy had contrived in one way or another to make him rethink certain aspects of art history and its relevance to society. As far as I know, Marx never considered the question, but this didn't prevent Burgess from convincing his friend to study Marxism in this light.

Now that he himself was an art lover of sorts, Guy won over his friend by advancing an argument that was very much in vogue in leftist circles at that time: namely, that art was doomed to wither away in the climate of bourgeois society. The bourgeois does not invest his money in art. He may build up a private collection, but only a few people will be privileged to see it. The bourgeois, who is selfish by definition, does not contribute to the development of culture in every social milieu. Only Socialist states can be true patrons of the arts in the twentieth century; capitalist states slowly asphyxiate culture.

This reasoning, which Burgess expounded to me in person on several occasions, may be summed up in a few assertions, all of them naïve. But Burgess clung to them tenaciously. 'The Renaissance,' he said, 'was a great period, I agree; but at that time there were patrons whose money was used to develop the arts. They didn't worry then about the growth of workers' productivity. As long as they supported art with money, art was alive. But when the patrons vanished, the quality of artistic production fell dramatically. Today art is more than ever dependent on money, yet the bourgeois state does nothing to develop it. Only a totalitarian state can assume the role of patron to encourage all the disciplines of art.' It appears that this argument was enough to convince Blunt, forming the eventual basis of his political beliefs.

Impelled as he was by the force of Guy's conviction, there is no doubt that Blunt began to take an interest in Communism in a more serious manner than that of a detached schoolboy studying a theory of political philosophy. Yet the fact is that we still don't know for certain whether or not Blunt really was a Communist through and through. Having known him myself, I think that in his heart of hearts he wasn't, even though he shared certain Marxist opinions. He never advertised his beliefs. It is true that the occasional Marxist aside crept into the articles he wrote at that time. When I mentioned this to him, he said: 'I haven't a clue whether or not that approach is Marxist or anything else. It just happens to be *my* approach.'

It is true that the theories he had at that time were anything but conservative. For him, art was inseparable from society. For example, it was one of his maxims that works of art cannot be understood historically in any other terms than human ones – meaning, in the last analysis, in social terms.

This reasoning led him to the conclusion that the state really should protect and nourish culture and the arts. He often told me in later years that in his view neither television nor the cinema was an art form. As far as he was concerned, these disciplines would always be minor ones, 'because they give nothing back to people'.

'Where,' he used to say, 'are the Sun Kings and the Medicis of today?'

Another of his concerns was how to save art from prostituting itself for money. He felt that the Americans had invaded Europe with dollars, bringing with them a form of culture that he was incapable of comprehending. He thought modern art was a gigantic hoax. In his eyes only Picasso was worth a damn, and he proclaimed that *Guernica* was a masterpiece on a par with the greatest classical works.

Blunt's ideas on this subject were close to Marxism, then, but I think that in all other respects the doctrines of *Das Kapital* held no interest for him whatever. Very few people had any reason to suspect him of closet Communist sympathies, and nothing on earth could have induced Anthony Blunt to show himself in the street brandishing a placard.

A few weeks before his trip to Rome, Burgess in his role of talent scout had supposedly roped in yet another choice recruit. He had seduced intellectually – and, it has been said, physically too – a promising Cambridge undergraduate by the name of Donald Maclean, who henceforth became a trusted member of his cell of activists.

At the beginning of 1934, this cell numbered several members, all of them prepared to enter the struggle against Fascism and change the world along Marxist lines. These men were Burgess himself, Blunt and Maclean. Philby had graduated from Trinity in June the previous year.

Guy Burgess's anti-Fascist preoccupations had their effect on his studies, because he soon abandoned his PhD thesis on the bourgeois revolution in England in favour of a monograph on the Indian Mutiny of 1857–58.

In May 1934, Kim Philby travelled up to Cambridge to see Burgess.

For once it was not Philby who was bewitched by Burgess, but the other way round. Guy was enthralled by his friend's tales of the horrors he had seen in Austria and his derring-do on behalf of workers hunted down by the regime.

The first stage of the recruitment of Burgess and his group into the Soviet secret service had begun. With a minimum of prodding, Burgess agreed to come to London to meet Arnold Deutsch (Otto), who had just moved to England.

At the suggestion of Deutsch, Burgess spent part of his 1934 summer vacation in Germany, perfecting his political training in the field. This visit occurred at a crucial juncture in the history of Nazism. He was in Berlin on 30 June 1934, the 'Night of the Long Knives' when Hitler liquidated about eighty of his adversaries in a bloody coup. When he left Germany, Burgess joined a group of four students, among them Anthony Blunt, on a trip to the USSR. This voyage, which was also arranged by Deutsch, had a very precise objective: to provide the pair with an alibi, in that on their return they could shout from the rooftops that the scales had fallen from their eyes, that they had seen the ugly reality of the Soviet Union, despised it and consequently renounced their former Communism. In effect they knew before they left Britain exactly what they had to say on their return. They went to Leningrad by ship, then on to Moscow by train, where they were received by Ossip Piatnitski, a member of the Western bureau of the Comintern known by the initials OMS, and by Nicolai Ivanovich Bukharin, the Party ideologist, whose charm, intelligence and conviction delighted Guy Burgess. Bukharin was able to strengthen the young Englishman's belief that only violent struggle in alliance with the Comintern could smash the forces of Fascism.

For Anthony Blunt, the aim of the visit was largely cultural. He wanted to see the art collections at the Hermitage in Leningrad and the Kremlin in Moscow. The Hermitage in particular he found breathtaking, a confirmation of his ideal of Marxism as protective of the arts. For him Russia was culturally beautiful and passionate, but doomed. He used to tell me that this tragic side of my country shone through everywhere, in its landscapes, its people, its way of life and most of all in its art.

On the group's return to London, all of its members confessed, truly or falsely, that their experience of the hard realities of the USSR had left them disappointed. They had seen our living conditions for themselves and they now knew that the Soviet Union was not for them. It may well have been as a direct consequence of this trip that Blunt, for one, decided never again to set foot in the USSR. I think the others may have agreed with him in their heart of hearts. Everything was so different – the political pressures and the standard of living, in particular. Not one of the group was remotely suited to life in the Soviet Union.

Shaken by what he had seen in Germany and convinced by his interlocutors in Moscow, Burgess had no second thoughts about Deutsch's proposal that he should adopt a clandestine existence while officially renouncing his earlier Communist convictions. This he accomplished with his usual brilliance and strength of will. To his university friends, to his professors and to anybody else who had heard him propounding Marxist ideals, he announced that he had decided to break with Communism. This he did in gradual stages, with such subtlety that nobody suspected the reality of the change. With all the humour and irony that he could muster, he passed the message to everyone who would listen that Communism had disappointed him, and that he no longer believed in it.

Then he went on to speak of Germany, and declared that the future of Fascism looked remarkably bright.

Burgess had no trouble persuading his friend Maclean to follow him underground and to act out the same farce of breaking with the Communist Party. At the same time he was constantly on the lookout for new agents. He approached another undergraduate friend, Goronwy Rees, on whom he practised the tried and true argument that the best way to combat Fascism was to do everything possible to assist the Russians. Rees, himself of humble origins, was intrigued by the intelligence and personality of Guy and considered the proposal a signal honour. All the same, he turned it down and never mentioned it to anyone – until 1951, when he was interviewed by MI5 and asserted that he had tried to persuade Burgess to abandon his contacts with the NKVD and indeed had tried to stop the British Secret Service from employing him, knowing full well that his friend would pass on all useful information to the Soviets.

As a committed agent, Burgess had it in mind to create a hermetic organization in the service of the NKVD. But he failed to win Deutsch over to this viewpoint, because the latter correctly preferred to deal with his agents individually, for obvious security reasons. This Burgess could never quite accept, and he continued to the end to consider himself as one of a team with his friends.

At the close of 1934, Guy abandoned his second thesis and left Cambridge to begin his working life, spurning the offers of postgraduate positions made to him by Trinity College. The reason for his departure was that the NKVD had directed him to find employment that would allow him to work against Fascism and penetrate pro-Nazi groups in England. So Guy Burgess went to London.

After his visit to the USSR, Anthony Blunt stayed in regular contact with Arnold Deutsch, to whom he had been introduced by Burgess. No doubt he already suspected that he was to work for Soviet intelligence, fronted by the Comintern, though he asked no questions about it. Both for him and for the others, the struggle to defeat Fascism was the first priority. He didn't need to act out Burgess's comedy of breaking with the Communist Party; he merely continued to affect complete indifference to politics in any shape or form.

In the two years prior to leaving Cambridge, Blunt (known to the NKVD as Tony) recruited or tried to recruit several Marxist-leaning students at the behest of Burgess. His task was that of a talent spotter for people who could be of service to the Comintern. The cause attracted a number of young men who wanted to join the fight against the rising tide of Fascism. Secret work was not mentioned, merely the noble cause of standing firm against Hitler, Mussolini and their minions around Europe.

As a supervisor at the university, Anthony Blunt routinely came into contact with scores of students. His job as a recruiting agent suited him very well because he had every quality needed for success. In the course of time he was able to put Burgess on the track of an undergraduate named John Cairncross, who was his pupil in French literature. Blunt and Cairncross were to some extent allergic to one another: by Blunt's account, Cairncross was neither particularly nice nor particularly distinguished, though his knowledge of French was well-nigh perfect. Blunt's reservations did not prevent Arnold Deutsch from recruiting Cairncross ... but that's another story, which will be detailed later.

Blunt's second candidate was Leo Long, a young Communist who arrived at Cambridge to read French in October 1935. Long was deeply sensitive to social injustice, having seen his father, a carpenter in North London, suffering through long spells of unemployment. He immediately became an enthusiastic member of the Communist Party cell within Trinity College, making every effort to convert his other friends. Blunt, who was his tutor in French, had no difficulty at all persuading Long to work for the Comintern.

Rather less successful was Blunt's attempt to subvert an American economics student, Michael Straight, the son of a millionaire who took no pains at all to conceal his leftist sympathies, which, in any case, were widely shared at that time.

In February 1937, Blunt and Burgess, who both now knew quite well who they were really working for, decided to recruit Straight without telling the Centre in advance. First they won him over to the cause of ideological struggle against Fascism, which was not difficult; of course, there was no question yet of working for the USSR. Little by little, they nudged the young American in that direction. A major hurdle was cleared when Straight acknowledged the rightness of the Soviet struggle, and that the time had come to take the field against Fascism. Then came the moment when he agreed to work for the USSR, as the only country then capable of defeating the Nazi menace.

To begin with, Michael Straight wanted to acquire British nationality and become a Member of Parliament. But Blunt convinced him to try a different tack and go back to the United States for a career in the banking sector; Blunt's idea was that Straight should infiltrate Wall Street as a Soviet mole, a project that seemed entirely feasible given that his father was a major shareholder in the Morgan bank.

Straight dug in his heels at this point. Anthony Blunt sought a compromise, abandoning the banking idea in favour of simply assisting the Comintern. He flattered his friend by telling him that his recruitment was viewed favourably at the highest levels within the Kremlin. But still the American vacillated. Ultimately, I don't believe he ever really wanted to serve the Soviet Union.

Just before Michael Straight left England, Anthony Blunt tore an invitation card in two before his eyes and gave him half of it, telling him that some day in the future he might be visited by a special emissary who would produce the other piece as a guarantee of trust.

Back in the United States, Michael Straight worked as a volunteer in the State Department, where he compiled reports on the financing of the German National Socialist Party. Before long an 'illegal' agent of the NKVD, Michael Green, made contact with him. The two men met on several occasions, but Straight was suspicious because the second half of Blunt's invitation card was not forthcoming. He gave Green some titbits of information; they were unimportant, but this didn't matter to Blunt and Burgess, who saw Straight in the light of a long-term investment.

At this point, in November 1939, the Russo–Finnish War broke out, completely neutralizing all Blunt and Burgess's propaganda work. The Soviet attack on Finland provoked furious outrage in all the Western countries: Stalin, seeing that this small country was doggedly resisting all peaceful pressure to shrink its frontiers to the advantage of the Soviet Union, had simply invaded without warning. Michael Straight viewed the event as a betrayal by the fatherland of Socialism. He supported the Finns one hundred per cent and resolved to reduce his contacts with the Soviets to a minimum.

While he was still working for the US Government and writing outlines of speeches for President Roosevelt and members of Congress, Straight saw Green from time to time; but in 1942 he decided to make a clean break. He relayed this decision to his handler, though at the same time he gave his word to keep secret the small amount of work he had done for the Russians. Green did not object.

We never spoke to Straight again, and he kept his side of the bargain scrupulously. He never uttered a word to anyone about Burgess or Blunt. In my opinion he was scared of them. He must have believed that if he denounced Blunt and his friends they would find some way to exact revenge. Only after Burgess's death in 1963 did Michael Straight confess. He made the whole affair public by writing a completely truthful book about his flirtation with the Soviet secret service. The only thing he omitted to say was that his thirty-year silence was motivated above all by his fear of the KGB; nor did he ever accept a post within the US administration, though he was offered several by Franklin D. Roosevelt and later by John F. Kennedy.

Guy Burgess found his first job soon after leaving Cambridge. He was

76

employed as a financial adviser to the mother of one of his friends at Trinity, Victor Rothschild. For a salary of one hundred pounds per month he provided this lady with information on investments – for, as she herself said, 'in my family everybody is a financier but nobody knows where to invest their money.'

Burgess did his work thoroughly and conscientiously. He invested Lady Rothschild's money remarkably well, and she had plenty. In short, he operated like a born capitalist.

Naturally, Guy wanted to make a living, but he also had plans of his own. His project was to use his contacts with the Rothschild family to penetrate the corridors of power and above all the British Secret Service. Through the Rothschilds he was able to meet the head of MI6, Stewart Menzies, and Dick White, head of MI5's B Division. He also made the acquaintance of Robert Vansittart, a permanent under-secretary at the Foreign Office who acted as MI6's watchdog. Vansittart, though strongly anti-Nazi, maintained excellent contacts at the highest level of the German regime. At the beginning of the war he was named head of propaganda, which among other things involved putting out radio broadcasts eulogizing democracy. When Churchill came to power he appointed Vansittart as his diplomatic adviser. Guy Burgess then met Winston Churchill himself, who was delighted by his intelligence and subtlety.

The Rothschilds also put Burgess in touch with influential members of the Conservative Party, notably Joseph Ball, an MI5 agent but also the founder of the Conservative Research Department (the Party's private intelligence service).

Without undue exertion, in 1935 Guy managed to become parliamentary assistant to a young extreme right-wing Conservative MP named MacNamara. Jack MacNamara was a homosexual; he was also a member of the Anglo–German Fellowship, a friendship association which included among its devotees a number of highly placed Nazi sympathizers (in addition to a certain Kim Philby). Guy and Jack got along so well that before long they were happily organizing sexual forays to Germany, where MacNamara had scores of friends in the Hitler Youth. Burgess's address book was steadily filling with the names of people living all over Europe. In Paris he met Édouard Pfeiffer, a flamboyant homosexual and the principal aide to Édouard Daladier, the Minister of War. Among other things, Pfeiffer was an agent of the French Deuxième Bureau (Secret

Service) and incidentally of MI6 – though not of the NKVD as well. MacNamara, Burgess and Pfeiffer threw a series of orgiastic parties in Pfeiffer's apartment on the Avenue Henri Martin, and were frequently to be seen in Paris's foremost homosexual nightclubs.

At the close of 1936, Burgess left MacNamara to join the BBC, where he concentrated on domestic politics and reportage. His programme 'The Week at Westminster' quickly acquired a wide audience. Burgess made commentaries on the debates in Parliament and discussed topical issues with a panel of guests.

His interviews soon took on a specific colour, mostly involving personalities with present or past links to the secret services. Among these was David Footman, a man who Burgess was sure was a member of SIS but of whose exact function he was unsure. He had noticed that Footman was interested in the Narodniki, a late-nineteenth-century revolutionary movement within Russia which advocated assassination and terrorism to gain its ends. Burgess telephoned Footman and asked him if he would like to come on his radio programme and explain his views about the Narodniki. Footman agreed. Before long Burgess had ascertained that his guest was none other than the assistant director of MI6's Political Intelligence Department, Section I. Naturally, he did everything in his power to obtain prime air time for Footman, who proved to be exceptionally erudite; for his own part, Footman was intrigued by the breadth of Burgess's knowledge of international politics and by the acuteness of his analyses.

Burgess's manoeuvres finally bore rich fruit at the beginning of 1938, when he became the first of the Cambridge Five to enter MI6 as an agent for a trial period.

Even before Burgess was officially accepted for a post, Footman asked him to use his contacts in the international homosexual milieu to open a discreet line of communication between the British Prime Minister, Neville Chamberlain, and the new Premier of France, Édouard Daladier, who had replaced Léon Blum on 10 April. Chamberlain was unhappy with the open hostility to the Nazis of some members of his government, notably high officials of the Foreign Office like Robert Vansittart, whom he had just fired.

In the same spring of 1938, the nations of the West were deeply anxious about the behaviour of Hitler, who, having put himself at the head of the armies of the Reich, had annexed Austria without firing a shot. They now knew all too well that Hitler would not be content with this single success. Tension was rising in Czechoslovakia, where the German majority population in the Sudetenland, supported by the Nazi Party, was demanding unification of that region with the Reich. Some members of the ruling classes on both sides of the English Channel would have been only too happy to see the dictator's aggressive onslaught continue in an eastward direction, towards the Soviet Union; nevertheless, this policy was risky in the extreme because public opinion in Britain and France remained undecided. Some were prepared to acquiesce in Germany's eastern expansion, while others were fiercely opposed to it. Whatever their position, the British and French leaders had one thing in common: they were terrified of backing the wrong horse.

Hence the ultra-secret nature of the negotiations between Daladier and Chamberlain. The members of the British and French parliaments were not to get wind of what was happening, any more than were the ministers of the two governments. If Hitler concentrated his offensive on the USSR and eastwards, the Western nations would be freed (for a while at least) from the Nazi menace. Moreover, the defeat of Russia, which at the time seemed inevitable, would destroy the Communist threat for ever, while seriously weakening Hitler. Thus Britain and France would kill two birds with one stone. This, in essence, was the policy that certain members of the Chamberlain and Daladier governments were secretly attempting to put in place.

During these delicate negotiations Burgess served as a vital intermediary. Contacts between the two heads of government were effected in writing, and on the British side these documents were delivered by Guy Burgess to his friend Édouard Pfeiffer, in whom he had total confidence. For his own part he informed the NKVD in the summer of 1938 that Daladier had just sent Pfeiffer and Fernand de Brinon (founder of the France–Allemagne committee and a future member of the Vichy government) to negotiate secretly with the Nazis.

This highly equivocal policy of appeasement led to the Munich agreement of September 1938 – when Chamberlain and Daladier caved in and allowed Hitler to annex the Sudetenland – and was followed in December by a Franco–German friendship pact. In later years, the USSR frequently and stubbornly claimed that the West's deliberate intention from 1938 onwards was to lure Germany into an attack on Russia. This claim was neither propaganda nor disinformation but the unvarnished truth, proven by the documents obtained for us by Burgess. Because of these documents, the Soviet leaders knew the real motives of the British and the French. They understood only too well that sooner or later the West's main preoccupation would be the struggle against Communism; and that, in anticipation of this, the West was prepared to consort with the Devil, otherwise known as Adolf Hitler.

At that time the information gathered by Burgess was no longer transmitted via our London residence, because Arnold Deutsch (Otto) and Theodor Maly (Hardt) had been recalled to Moscow. Instead Burgess took advantage of his frequent trips to France to deliver documents to the NKVD residence in Paris.

He also served as a courier for our few remaining agents in Great Britain. Apropos of this, it is hard to imagine that in the years immediately preceding the Second World War, at a time when the secret services of all the major nations were engaged in frantic activity, the USSR repatriated practically all the intelligence officers operating abroad on its behalf. The lunacy of Stalin's purges took precedence over all other considerations. Hence the promising network of agents created by our representatives in Cambridge was for a while left entirely to its own devices.

Guy Burgess continued to work methodically for the cause. He knew how to screen the various government offices and set up contacts that might be useful for his career and, incidentally, for us. With his usual patience he nurtured his relationship with Dick White, to whom he had been introduced by the Rothschilds.

The second mission assigned to him – by Lawrence Grand, the head of a new section (Section D) with responsibility for covert operations – was intended to provoke a split within the Zionist movement. Nobody really expected Burgess to manage this, but against all odds he succeeded.

British counter-espionage had concocted a scheme to divide the Zionists into warring camps, as an offshoot of British policy in Palestine and of the Balfour Declaration. I know nothing of the details, but I believe the plan was to create an effective opposition to Chaim Weizmann, the Zionist leader.

Guy began by working on Victor Rothschild. With the extraordinary confidence that was by now his trademark, he succeeded in proving to his friend that the Zionist movement could no longer continue as it had done hitherto, that Chaim Weizmann had gone off the rails and that true Zionists could no longer trust him as their leader. The thoroughly shaken Victor then brought his own influence to bear on his father, Lord Rothschild. He managed to discredit Weizmann so comprehensively that Lord Rothschild actually launched a short-lived Zionist opposition movement.

Burgess accomplished this mission to perfection. The NKVD had nothing to do with the business, which was entirely engineered by the British counter-espionage service.

In January 1939, recommended by his friend David Footman, Guy Burgess formally joined Section D and was immediately assigned to create a subversive radio station to counter Nazi propaganda and sap German morale. The scheme involved broadcasting from clandestine transmitters on various parts of the Continent. Thanks to his international contacts and his own boundless energy, Guy quickly found sites for the transmitters; the radio station began broadcasting the following spring.

The NKVD, which prided itself on its unrivalled expertise in manipulation, propaganda and phoney broadcasting, derived much quiet pleasure from the spectacle of the British finally breaking into the field of what was known in secret service parlance as 'active measures'.

Anthony Blunt left Cambridge at the close of the 1937 university year. He joined the Warburg Institute in London as an art teacher. In 1939, to everyone's astonishment, he suddenly forsook his job to join the army. His motives were patriotic: he knew that war was imminent and he wanted to serve his country in some way. For my own part I am quite certain that had our NKVD officer been able to make contact with Blunt at that time he would have strongly advised him against this move.

On 23 August 1939, the news broke that a non-aggression pact had been signed between the USSR and Nazi Germany. Article 4 of this agreement, signed in Moscow by Foreign Ministers Ribbentrop and Molotov in the presence of Stalin, stipulated that neither of the signatories would on any account participate in any alliance directed against the other.

This had the effect of a bombshell on our London network, all of whose members had focused their energies on the struggle against Nazism. Blunt and Burgess, who were on holiday together in France, decided to return to England immediately. Burgess was so upset that he left his beloved automobile, the most precious thing he possessed, in a car park at Calais because it was too late to load it on the ferry. He came back to fetch it three days later, but the fact that he abandoned it at all was a measure of how seriously he took this development.

The group hastily organized a meeting in London, with Philby present. They analysed the pact with precision, considering its articles one by one and gauging its probable consequences. The discussion was calm but uncompromising. After several hours of argument they concluded that the pact was no more than an episode in the march of world revolution; that in the circumstances it might easily be justified; and that in any event it did not constitute sufficient pretext for a break with the Soviet Union. In short, they decided that as far as they were concerned the battle against Fascism would continue.

We in Russia only heard about this meeting many years later; at the time not one member of the group registered the slightest change in attitude towards us.

After several months of ordinary military service, Anthony Blunt made use of the influence of his brother Christopher to enter the Minley Manor school in Hampshire for five weeks of counter-espionage training. His career with the secret service came close to being cut short after a few days when he was summoned to the War Ministry in London. A report had revealed his past links with Communist militants; he was not the only one by any means. He apparently managed to convince the authorities that there was no problem, because the head of military intelligence sent him straight back to Minley Manor. When the training course was completed he returned to London with the rank of captain, and was immediately sent to join the British Expeditionary Force in France. Thereafter Blunt had a difficult time in command of a campaign police detachment – a kind of military police outfit detailed to catch deserters – and was very unhappy with his garrison life. During the phoney war he was stationed on the Belgian border. His duties had nothing whatever to do with the real work of an intelligence agent;

instead his time was spent organizing patrols, keeping an eye on seedy bars and nightclubs and arresting soldiers who were drunk or absent without leave.

Despite his patriotic motivation, Blunt found the atmosphere unbearable because he had nothing in common with the other soldiers. His constant contact with working-class people whose main interest was in their daily life was in stark contrast to the artistic circles in which he usually moved.

Blunt found life so wretched in Belgium that he wrote to his friends Victor Rothschild and Guy Burgess, asking them to get him home. Burgess quickly obliged, and before long Blunt was back in London, living at Guy's flat in Bentinck Street, rented to him by Victor Rothschild. The love affair between Blunt and Burgess may have been over by then, but they were still very close friends; they even shared lovers on occasion, one of the most regular being a young soldier by the name of Jack Hewitt, who came to stay with the pair every time he was on leave from the army.

I have to say that I never paid much attention to this side of their lives. I never raised the subject with either man, and they never spoke of it to me; nor was it mentioned in our reports and this was all to the good. Although he was a homosexual, Blunt had many women friends, and indeed had affairs with certain women who afterwards remained loyal to him. In 1930, he had been briefly engaged to an aristocratic young woman who later married Philip Dunn, son of the industrialist Sir James Dunn. Anthony Blunt was also a close friend of Teresa (Tess) Mayor, the future wife of Victor Rothschild, who lived round the corner from his flat in Bentinck Street during the war. Burgess, too, had occasional liaisons with women.

Having completed his various missions entirely to David Footman's satisfaction, Guy Burgess was free for further work. Footman was highly complimentary about his new man the next time he saw Valentine Vivian, the head of Section V of MI6. He was also perfectly open about the fact that Guy had had close contacts with the Communists, and that he knew the history of the movement as well as having an excellent understanding of Marxist theory.

By June 1940, Valentine Vivian was convinced that Guy Burgess might yield spectacular results if he went to work at the British Embassy in Moscow under diplomatic cover.

Burgess couldn't refuse the position, though he was no happier with this idea than was the NKVD. From the Centre's point of view, the best place for Burgess was London. Furthermore, from the little he knew of Moscow he was sure it was no place for him: the British capital in wartime was positively convivial by comparison. He told me later that he had always loathed travelling, and had a healthy dislike of foreign capitals, especially Paris. He was prepared to go to Tangier or Spain at a pinch, but only for short holidays.

Making the best of a bad job, he packed his bags and left London with Isaiah Berlin, a Foreign Office functionary who had been assigned the post of press attaché at the embassy. Berlin wondered gloomily if there would be any work for him at all in Moscow, given that all communication was so effectively stifled there.

Since it was impossible to reach Moscow direct, the pair were scheduled to travel by way of Washington, Japan and the Trans-Siberian railway to the Soviet capital. Two days after their arrival in the United States, they received an urgent telegram from England ordering them to come straight home. Apparently the ambassador to Moscow, Sir Stafford Cripps, objected very strongly to the Foreign Office's posting new people to his embassy without consulting him.

Vivian's next project was to use Burgess as an *agent provocateur* within the British Communist Party. He had Footman approach Burgess with the suggestion that he infiltrate the Party with a view to destabilizing it from the inside, aided and abetted by British intelligence. Guy received this offer without turning a hair, made no immediate response, played for time – and finally refused. The disappointed Footman then tried a different tack: why not mount a few trouble-making operations against the Soviet Embassy in London? Burgess's reaction was exactly the same – he stalled, then refused. As a convinced Communist, he could not accept work that might compromise his position.

Long afterwards I saw a letter he sent to one of his friends at this period, when the war was in its early stages. 'What torments me most,' he wrote frankly, 'is the fact that my former comrades, the people I worked with in the Communist Party, believe I've betrayed the cause. They think I've forsaken militant Communism for my work as a civil servant.'

These reservations were nothing new in Burgess's record. I read in his Moscow file the following remark about him, penned in 1937 by the NKVD's London resident: 'It wounds Burgess that his friends, who knew him as a Communist, now believe he has abandoned them.'

However, the important thing was that the secret service hierarchy in England accepted his refusal to work against Communism without difficulty. Instead he was appointed instructor at the subversion training centre at Brickendonbury near Hertford. This job, which might have been a dead end for a lesser man, suited Burgess very well. He promptly set about using his connections to get his friend Philby appointed to the same school.

There followed a period when Philby and Burgess saw a great deal of one another. Together they devised special teaching methods for the centre. They discussed politics often, though they rarely mentioned their work for the NKVD, which was anyway fairly barren at that point because neither man had access to any information of real interest. Philby never meddled in his friend's private life; nor did he ever allude to Burgess's homosexual affairs. He once told me that he viewed Guy's homosexual tastes as a sickness – and none of his business. I myself soon concluded that this was a subject one didn't discuss with Burgess, and I never made the smallest allusion to it, either with him or with Blunt. I behaved as if I had noticed nothing whatever out of the ordinary. I think this was the right course: the matter may have formed an unspoken gulf between us, but in most respects I believe our relationship was made easier by our avoiding any reference to it.

Also at this time Anatoli Borisovich Gorsky, alias Henry, arrived to replace Otto and Hardt as the go-between for the Cambridge ring.

As soon as Gorsky arrived he sent a report to Moscow, complaining that the British agents he was running failed to respect the most elementary rules of security. He was especially horrified by the fact that Burgess and Blunt were living together in the same flat on Bentinck Street. He did his best to convince them to separate – or at least to live in different flats – but neither man took the least notice of him. He was made to understand that all the reports in the world were powerless to make the slightest difference. Burgess and Blunt were adamant.

In the early autumn of 1940, following a reorganization of the secret services, Section D was absorbed into the Special Operations

Executive (SOE), a new organization which among other things was assigned to promote subversion in Germany and in the territories occupied by the Nazis. Though Philby was able to continue working within the new framework, Burgess's name did not feature among its operatives. We never knew quite why he was dropped, but I would speculate that it had something to do with his overt homosexuality.

Burgess therefore returned to the BBC in the first weeks of 1941 and was rehired by an old Cambridge friend, George Barnes, then in charge of the BBC's discussion section. He resumed his work as a journalist energetically, organizing debates and interviews with politicians and other influential figures. For his own programme he requested an interview with Winston Churchill himself. The Prime Minister called him in to discuss the idea, and the two deliberated at length – to no avail, as it turned out, because for technical reasons the interview never took place. Nevertheless, Churchill (who had already met Burgess once before) seems to have enjoyed the meeting; afterwards he was heard to ask why so few of the younger sort of British politicians were like Guy Burgess, clever chaps whose judgement could be relied on.

Thereafter Burgess kept his head down till June 1941, when the German invasion of the Soviet Union supplied him with a pretext to launch a series of reportages and broadcasts about Russia, Britain's new ally. On the wireless he expatiated on subjects as diverse as literature, economics, painting and science. He even put forward Anthony Blunt's name as a commentator on artistic matters, gleefully adding that 'Dr Blunt will make an eminently acceptable spokesman on art, *not being a Communist.*'

Guy was assisted in his work of pro-Soviet propaganda within the BBC by a British journalist of Austrian extraction named Peter Smollett, who was also an NKVD agent. Smollett, who had met Philby in Austria in 1934, kept up an intermittent relationship with the Cambridge group. He succeeded in penetrating the Ministry of Information in 1940, and when his friend Brendan Bracken took over the ministry under the Churchill coalition in June 1941, he secured the post of head of the Russian department. For almost the entire duration of the war, Smollett continued to promote Soviet interests in every area, be it economic, cultural, political or military. He organized demonstrations and travelling exhibitions throughout

Britain, and naturally the BBC was among his favourite targets, thanks to Burgess, his principal in-house ally. Both men were controlled by Henry.

One of Guy's most spectacular strokes at that time was to arrange an interview with one of his journalist colleagues, Ernst Henri (an NKVD 'illegal'), who proclaimed with absolute assurance that the Red Army was certain of victory at a time when our troops were retreating all along the front. With magnificent impudence he even ventured to pay homage, live on the BBC, to the Soviet secret service – which he qualified as the 'very finest in the world'.

Burgess found another opening for his talents in 1943, when Stalin decided to dissolve the Comintern. The image of the USSR had to be changed, made less aggressive, more human and more in tune with the aims of the Allies, now that the Red Army so badly needed Churchill to open a western front. The suppression of the Comintern, that symbol of world revolution which had hitherto scared everybody to death, was intended to show that a new era had dawned in relations between the USSR and other nations. In his broadcasts Burgess did everything he could to promote this idea.

On Henry's instructions, he broadened his range of contacts by cultivating friendships with civil servants occupying important posts in ministries such as the Foreign Office or the Ministry of Defence. While the war lasted he had full clearance to go in and out of the main ministerial buildings whenever he chose. The sentries and janitors all knew him and he circulated freely on premises where even MPs were unable to go.

During this period Guy became friends with another personality who interested us, Dennis Proctor, the private secretary of former Prime Minister Stanley Baldwin. Proctor, like Burgess, was a Cambridge man, and had been a member of the Apostles in the years before Burgess's arrival at the university. Proctor unwittingly supplied Guy with revelation after revelation about political relations between Great Britain and the United States. In all innocence he revealed details of the secret talks between Roosevelt and Churchill during the January 1943 Casablanca conference, supplying one priceless nugget of information in the news that the Allies were definitely planning a landing in Sicily in June of that year, but had postponed any major invasion of France until 1944.

In August 1943, the Germans had suffered a heavy defeat at

Kursk, when Proctor mentioned 'Quadrant', a secret meeting between Churchill and Roosevelt that had recently taken place in Quebec. In the course of this meeting the two leaders decided to make Operation Overlord (amphibious landings on the French coast) their main priority for the next phase of the war. They also gave their approval to Eisenhower's plans for the Mediterranean, which involved an invasion of the Italian peninsula. These excellent news items came directly to Stalin through Burgess, well before either of his two allies saw fit to inform him.

By virtue of his job, Proctor knew not only the contents of confidential documents, but also a number of secrets that the British, out of elementary prudence, made a point of not setting down in writing. Everything written down leaves its mark. The mere act of scribbling a few words is in many respects tantamount to leaking information. Documents have a life of their own; they also have futures that nobody can control. In certain highly sensitive areas, to write at all is to take a colossal risk; and the only way to eliminate that risk is by transmitting information verbally. This technique is used in every country in the world. Politicians and functionaries meet, deliberate and decide, but no notes are taken and no minutes are drawn up. Dennis Proctor had access to this 'oral material', as it is called in secret service parlance, and he unknowingly passed it on to us, through Guy Burgess. When people say that the only agents of any value are those that can lay their hands on crucial documents, they are wrong, as Guy Burgess proved again and again.

Burgess was particularly brilliant at establishing unusual contacts with people in every walk of life. As the years passed, his principal value for the KGB shifted from his ability to recruit first-class agents, to his knack of gathering information without making his source aware that he was being interrogated. Burgess was friendly with cleaning ladies, taxi drivers, ministry orderlies, janitors, aristocrats, academics, civil servants and politicians, but not one of them was in any sense an agent of Guy Burgess. It wasn't remotely necessary that they should be.

The vindictive attempts of former officers of British intelligence (specifically Peter Wright and Arthur Martin) to unearth these so-called agents recruited by the arch-fiend Burgess make me laugh. I hate to think that the organizations against which I strove all my working life were run by people whose thought processes never went beyond the most simplistic notions of true or false, good or bad, necessary or desirable; but Wright and Martin are certainly people of that ilk.

Like Burgess, Anthony Blunt had an active war. Shortly after his return from the front he was introduced by Victor Rothschild to Guy Liddell, the deputy director of the British counter-espionage services. Any earlier doubts about Blunt must have been dispelled, because Liddell found him a place at MI5. With this development, part of his mission, as defined by Henry (Anatoli Gorsky of the NKVD), was accomplished.

Blunt quickly won the favour of his superiors, above all of Guy Liddell, who became a close friend. Liddell was a major figure in the British intelligence community; he loved his job and went about it with cunning and finesse. He was also very fond of Blunt, so fond that he was ready to tell him things that under normal circumstances one would be reluctant to tell one's own wife. Yan (our code name for Blunt) was also on excellent terms with Dick White, the future head of SIS. They saw each other frequently, ate together at the canteen and talked about a wide variety of subjects. Blunt seized every chance he was given to speak to White. They shared a passion for art; White was a cultivated man and he was intrigued by all the same subjects as Blunt, notably architecture, literature and above all painting, which he never tired of discussing. Their meetings were a welcome relief from the stress of wartime intelligence work, and White welcomed the occasional chance to relax and talk about the things he loved with his junior. Like Liddell, White spontaneously and naturally confided his innermost thoughts.

Later on, when he learned that Blunt was a Soviet agent, Dick White was deeply upset and saddened by what he called Blunt's 'betrayal' of their friendship; and indeed he had placed enormous confidence in him, revealing items of information that taken separately might seem innocuous, but proved vitally important when pieced together.

During these heart-to-heart conversations with Anthony Blunt, Guy Liddell and Dick White were so indiscreet that at one point I seriously suspected, from the documents that came my way, that the British were deliberately feeding us with false information. Blunt learned so many things that a junior SIS officer should never have been party to that I found it increasingly hard to believe we weren't being duped. Nevertheless the facts soon proved me wrong.

Through Blunt, the Soviet Embassy in London was always informed well in advance of any actions against us contemplated by British counter-espionage. We knew exactly which aides at the embassy interested SIS, and when and how they would be approached by our opposite numbers. We had the names of all those who the British believed could be persuaded to defect.

We were also fully aware of every detail of the work being done by British counter-espionage against the British Communist Party. We knew the whereabouts of their bugs, the identities of their *agents provocateurs*, who their agents were and what information they were providing. At one point we even received detailed information about operations being mounted by the British against the Danish Communist Party. And all of this vital intelligence came from Blunt. It may not have concerned state secrets or global strategy, but all the same it ensured that our position in London was rock solid.

In hindsight, I can claim with absolute certainty that for most of the war we were able to work under ideal conditions in the British capital, simply because our risks were negligible. We operated with the extraordinary advantage of knowing in advance exactly how far we could go. Very few secret services in the world have been able to work under such fabulous conditions. Blunt was now a confirmed asset of great value – and so he remained, because he knew how to stay in touch with the leaders of his country's intelligence services. Nor did they stop confiding in him.

The first specific mission the British gave Blunt was to examine the way their services went about watching and following people, and thereafter to come up with suggestions as to how their methods could be improved. It should be pointed out that every intelligence service maintains specialist sections whose sole function is to follow individuals, be they politicians, diplomats, journalists or agents of foreign powers operating on their territory.

Blunt carried out this work to perfection, observing British agents closely in the field over a period of months. He made a careful study of their methods of camouflage and orientation, how the various surveillance teams went about relieving one another and how they broke contact when danger threatened.

Then he sat down and wrote a report in which he pinpointed the weaknesses of the counter-espionage surveillance teams and proposed a series of measures to make them more effective. In the process he perfected a number of new procedures, along with ingenious ways of keeping an eye on the subject under surveillance, in a variety of situations. The watchers might be on foot, in cars, in a cordon sealing off a whole area, operating alone or in groups. The rules Blunt devised were approved, codified and taught to agents – and naturally the KGB reaped its own benefit from them, because Yan passed a copy of his work on to Henry.

I read his report with considerable interest, and found it full of tips that proved easy to apply in the field. For example, when you are tailing someone, where should you be to avoid being noticed? Behind him, on the same side of the street? On the pavement opposite? Not necessarily: it may even be best to move well ahead of your target if the conditions are right, because people alert to the possibility of a tail usually look behind them only. Another trick, this time to get rid of a follower, is to suddenly turn on your heel and retrace your steps. This way you catch him by surprise; you walk past him at close quarters and make it impossible for him to carry on after you unrecognized.

Anthony Blunt's report enabled us to adapt our methods to those of our adversary. Above all we perfected the *parcours de sécurité* system which every agent had to follow before establishing a contact. These procedures were richly instructive to us; for example, from then on we were quickly able to establish which of our Soviet diplomats were being watched, when, how and by whom. Thereafter it was a simple matter to hoodwink the British without their suspecting anything. They never dreamed that a mole inside their surveillance services had taught us every detail of their methods.

Guy Liddell was delighted with Blunt's work and soon enough had him working on a fresh project. This involved analysing the information extracted from captured German spies. Liddell's people were highly successful at intercepting Germans operating on British territory, or abroad in the African and Middle Eastern theatres. Sent back to London, these agents were closely interrogated; their remarks were recorded on tape and subsequently analysed by specialists who cross-referenced the different sources, compared the information and finally compiled reports which more often than not ended up on the desk of the Minister of Defence. Blunt quickly showed himself to be a born analyst: his artistic intuition, coupled with his mathematician's rigour, was extraordinarily effective.

After this second success, Dick White and Guy Liddell devised an even more important task for Blunt, this time involving a degree of risk. They wanted to examine the correspondence of the various governments in exile in London, along with that of the embassies of the countries at war and of those neutral countries (Switzerland and Sweden) that interested the German and Italian espionage services.

At that time there was only one method of sending diplomatic correspondence. The documents were transported in a valise sealed with a State seal; nobody had the right to open, even less take possession of, a diplomatic bag. Governments in exile, however, tended to lack the means to use the usual procedures, so they merely sealed their bags of diplomatic correspondence as best they could and sent them by ordinary post.

Naturally, Blunt's agents intercepted these bags. They were immediately taken to specialists who opened them without leaving any trace. The material was taken out, photographed, put back, resealed and sent on its legitimate way. Very often the harvest of intelligence was extremely rich: the bags contained not only interesting diplomatic gossip, but also accounts of the positions of various personalities in exile *vis-à-vis* British policy, of the support they were receiving from British leaders, of the opposition evinced by others. There was also information about the organization of resistance movements in the field, about internal divisions within those movements, and masses of other information that could be hugely useful to the KGB at the end of the war, when these countries were ready to free themselves from German occupation. In this way we found out, well before February 1944, that the Polish government in exile would refuse to accept the 1919 Curzon Line as the future frontier between Poland and the USSR.

Thus Yan became an expert at spiriting away diplomatic bags, sifting out documents that might interest one or other of his two masters and recording them on film. The contents of the diplomatic bags of Switzerland, Sweden, Belgium, Poland and Czechoslovakia all passed under his eyes before proceeding on their way. It goes without saying that a copy of anything that might conceivably interest us was routinely passed on to Henry. Frequently Blunt seasoned the documents he sent with personal comments revealing the other side of the coin – in other words, the opinion of the British Government concerning the various governments in exile, and the friendships and resentments subsisting between the heads of the British intelligence services and certain prominent Polish, Czech, Belgian and Danish personalities then in England.

At one point Blunt was even in charge of recruiting agents for SIS among the members of the exiled governments; in this he was highly successful, and in time was able to pass on their names to us.

During the second and third years of the war, the information provided by Yan made him one of our most prized agents in Great Britain – though even now I find it hard to say which one of the ring rendered us the greatest service. Blunt was working in a different register to Maclean, for example. On the other hand he produced a brand of intelligence similar to Philby's, which allowed us to cross-reference their sources, to our immense advantage.

Anthony Blunt spent nights on end working for his two employers – SIS and ourselves. This double life seems to have perturbed him not at all; he remained his usual charming self, courteous with his colleagues yet somehow keeping his distance from nearly all of them. In his KGB dossier there is a curious document dating from this time. The Centre – why I don't know, because it never did this for anyone else – wanted at all costs to make Blunt accept money for his work, perhaps as a ploy to compromise him. For years he steadfastly refused Henry's repeated offers, until one day, rather mysteriously, he accepted the small sum of two hundred pounds. The receipt for this, signed by him, features prominently in his Moscow file – though for what reason is anybody's guess. A single receipt could hardly prove that we had bought Blunt and were actively paying for his services.

Blunt was several times congratulated by the KGB, via Henry, for the brilliance of his work: notably when he sent us a detailed operating chart of the British counter-espionage services and a full list of its agents abroad. Everything he could glean in the way of information from his day-to-day activities within the service, and from his friends and colleagues, was written up with admirable clarity and precision and passed straight to our London resident.

Not the least of Blunt's talents was his uncanny ability to win the confidence of all his colleagues, from the highest-placed to the lowest, to such effect that everyone entrusted their thoughts to him without the slightest misgiving. For example, he was able on several occasions to provide us with data on the strategy of the Wehrmacht – the German armed forces – and its operations in Russia. To obtain this, he used the services of his friend Leo Long, the fellow student at Cambridge whom he had recruited in 1935. Long, who worked at the War Office, had access to the deciphering work of the GC and CS at Bletchley Park, and could read at leisure the messages decoded by the Bletchley experts. The information filtering through from Long via Anthony Blunt frequently complemented the facts provided by Philby. In the world of espionage, the greater the proliferation of source material defining the same subject, the greater its credibility.

At no time did the KGB have any direct contact with Leo Long. We knew him to be one of Blunt's most vital informants, but personally I am in no position to say exactly which items of intelligence originated with him, because everything was attributed to Blunt as a matter of course. In the KGB's archives the name of Leo Long does not feature in the chronological file of the information given to us by our English agents.

Blunt was doubly valuable to us because he was able to consult the files of SIS about anything concerning Soviet diplomats posted in London. Nor did he hesitate to do so. As far as I know, these files did not contain any documents of really capital importance, but when the British wanted to carry out operations against Soviet citizens, such as recruiting them or even arresting them, Blunt could be relied upon to let us know immediately.

The fourth file to which I had unlimited access was that of Donald Maclean, at various times code-named Stuart, Wise, Lyric and Homer. Of our Cambridge agents, Maclean was the one I was least familiar with: indeed, I met him for the first time in Moscow, after his operative career was over. On the other hand, I processed the lion's share of the documents he relayed to the Centre, so I knew very well who he was, how he operated, and what information he provided to us.

Donald Maclean was the son of Sir Donald Maclean, a Presbyterian barrister who entered politics early on in his career. Sir Donald was a liberal; he was Minister of Education in Stanley Baldwin's government, and proved a somewhat neglectful father. In effect, Donald Maclean junior grew up a sensitive, uncommunicative, somewhat withdrawn child.

He was sent very young to Gresham's School, at Holt in Norfolk. His academic results were good, but he formed no bonds with his schoolmates (with the exception of James Klugman) and was never really accepted by them. This early solitude was to set an indelible mark on his later life.

On leaving Gresham's School he won a scholarship to Trinity, Cambridge, and went up as an undergraduate in 1931 to study foreign languages and literature. At Cambridge he met the unavoidable Guy Burgess, with whom he talked politics and Marxist theory late into the night. Inevitably he conceived a profound loathing for the United States in particular and capitalism in general, as he fell more and more deeply under Burgess's spell.

Donald Maclean's haughty manner and air of disdain won him a reputation for snobbery, but in reality this was a cloak for emotions that ran very deep. As with many Oxbridge students of the time, his main interests were sport and politics. His idealistic indignation over the wretched plight of the workers in the 1930s clearly aligned him with the Communists. In contrast to Blunt, who shrank from openly discussing his political convictions, and in contrast to Burgess, who argued at the top of his voice but ultimately avoided giving anything like a personal opinion, Maclean took part in demonstrations and saw himself as a thoroughgoing political militant.

I once saw a photograph of Donald Maclean in the British press. The image showed him marching with an air of determination in the vanguard of a crowd of workers. He looked like a young man ready to sacrifice everything for the sake of a cause. This was the real Maclean – the expression on his face told it all.

Maclean remained loyal to his Communist convictions until the day he died. He believed completely in the truth of Marxism–Leninism. Even at Cambridge, he was often heard to say that his highest ambition was to teach English to Russian children. Why English? 'Because,' he said, 'world revolution will be accomplished in English. The Russians must know the English language.'

All his life, he nourished a secret yearning to become a teacher, to instruct and enlighten young people. He was never meant to live in the murky, constrained atmosphere of secret work. It depressed him beyond measure.

Unlike many of his friends, Maclean did not openly adhere to the Communist Party. Instead he joined a clandestine cell, as if he had guessed even at that early stage how his life would turn out. His first experience of leading a double life was when he had to conceal his new-found atheism and Socialism from his father, who had just joined Ramsay MacDonald's government as Education Minister. As it turned out, Sir Donald did not occupy this post for long; he died suddenly in 1932.

Donald kept up his clandestine work until 1934, when he was finally recruited into the Cambridge ring. There are three versions of how this came about. The first has it that James Klugman, his classmate from Gresham's and fellow Trinity undergraduate, brought him in; other sources claim that he was recruited by Burgess, with whom he had a brief homosexual fling. And finally there is a theory that it was Philby himself who convinced Maclean to work for the Soviet Union against Fascism.

I have no idea which of these theories is the true one; I never found any reference to the recruitment of Maclean in the files, though it was a subject that interested me greatly. It must be admitted that the work of the NKVD residents at that time was far from brilliant: they habitually sent back ill-constructed, incomplete, slapdash reports, and in the course of things the important question of Maclean's recruitment was overlooked.

In June 1934, Donald Maclean completed his course at Cambridge, taking first-class honours. Thereafter our contact with him was maintained through Philby. Some experts claim that Theodor Maly and Arnold Deutsch met Maclean at this juncture in his career, and that Deutsch was the instigator of Maclean's breaking his links with the Party. They are mistaken: Deutsch came to London only in May 1934, and was introduced to Maclean much later in the year, while Maly did not arrive in the British capital till early 1936.

As in the case of Burgess, as soon as Maclean came down from Cambridge the Centre enjoined him to apply for the civil service, preferably the Foreign Office. Donald agreed to do so, but was manifestly uncomfortable with the idea.

During the summer of 1934, he broke the news to his mother that he no longer wished to teach English in Russia and planned instead to aim for a diplomatic career. Mary Maclean, who had always known about her son's political convictions, was amazed and delighted by this volte-face.

Donald set about preparing for the Foreign Office entrance exam, which he took in August 1935. His university report was a catalogue of brilliance, but a shadow lay over it in the form of his membership of the Communist Party. About a hundred people – far too many – knew for certain that Donald had been a member of a clandestine Communist Party cell. Naturally, the men on the panel considering his application had been informed.

At his final oral, after he had passed all the other tests with flying colours, he was confronted head on: 'Mr Maclean, it is rumoured that you have Communist beliefs, and these, as you know, would make it impossible for you to work in the Foreign Office.'

Donald was prepared for this question.

'Yes, at one time I did share the ideals of Communism; nor was I the only one. I would add that I haven't entirely shed those ideals, but I'm working on it.'

This answer was calculated to please the set of old gentlemen sitting in judgement; and sure enough Donald Maclean's application was formally accepted by the Foreign Office in October 1935. He was the first of the four to penetrate Britain's corridors of power. His first job was that of secretary to the Western Department, meaning the Western Section of the Foreign Office, with responsibility for the Low Countries, Switzerland, Spain and Portugal.

Theodor Maly, who arrived in London in early 1936, now took Donald Maclean in hand. He taught him basic knowledge of spy work: how to turn up information, how to get it to us and how to shake off surveillance. He also urged the young man to train himself in patience. As a first assignment, and to test his ability, he asked Maclean (along with the other members of the ring) to keep an eye on pro-Fascist individuals within the British governing classes. Maclean carried out this task satisfactorily enough; in addition, he managed to produce a few minor items of intelligence about the war in Spain (though the Moscow files give no record of exactly what these were).

The NKVD, Arnold Deutsch and Theodor Maly were unconcerned at that time about the quality of the information supplied by Maclean. Their long-term plan was to establish him as a 'sleeping' agent, who could be activated when the right moment came: in other words, when he had risen to an important position within the Foreign Office. Maly and Deutsch, who were soon to meet such tragic ends, proved themselves masters of their profession when they selected Donald Maclean. So brilliant was he at his work that by 1938 the Foreign Office was offering him a post as secretary at the British Embassy in Paris. Maclean was overjoyed about his promotion. In a letter to the ambassador which accompanied his nomination, his superior in London wrote that 'Donald Maclean has done remarkably well in the two years he has worked here . . . he is charming, intelligent and refined.' His colleagues at the Foreign Office were, it must be said, somewhat less enthusiastic about his personality.

He adored Paris, quickly gravitating to the artistic, Bohemian milieux of the French capital. He met painters, writers, wealthy Americans, students. The information he passed on to us about the Spanish war, now in its final stages, was more valuable now: it concerned refugees and prisoners of war, and the attitude of the French Government to the emerging Franco regime. Anything he thought might be of interest he sent to the NKVD residence in Paris without the slightest difficulty. Here again, there is no trace of Maclean's reports in the KGB archives: in my opinion the relevant documents must have been destroyed during the evacuation of Moscow, when the Germans were advancing on the city.

In his new job, Maclean worked hard and effectively, making his way with ease through the lower echelons of the diplomatic corps. In the spring of 1940, he was made third secretary; already his friends and colleagues had begun to see him as a future Foreign Office permanent secretary, the highest office in the British diplomatic service.

At this time Maclean met his future wife, Melinda Marling, a wealthy, intelligent American brunette living in Paris. He fell head over heels in love; but to begin with, Melinda was cool to him. Then, just as her defences were beginning to crumble, the phoney war came to an abrupt end. The Germans crossed the French border in overwhelming force. Nazi troops were already at the gates of Paris when the couple were married at the *mairie* of the 7th *arrondissement*, on Rue de Grenelle.

A few days before the ceremony, Donald revealed to his future wife that he was an agent of the NKVD. Apparently, she took this in her stride, promising to stand by him come what might. She kept this promise to the letter. I think she must have sincerely loved him to accept such a giant, lifetime burden. To this day she has always maintained that she knew nothing of her husband's activities on behalf of the NKVD prior to his sudden flight from England in 1951.

In lieu of a honeymoon, the Macleans were forced to run for their lives. At the British Embassy there were scenes of panic: neither the ambassador nor the staff were in any way equal to the situation, their only thought being to get back to England as soon as they could. Young Maclean was among the few who kept their heads. He helped formulate an orderly plan of evacuation, assembled the embassy's documents, destroyed some of them and removed the most important files. His steadiness, flexibility and sang-froid were later noted and acknowledged by his Foreign Office superiors.

Maclean and his wife were the last to leave the British Embassy. They left nothing behind them for the Germans. Travelling by car, they reached the coast in time to be taken off by a motor torpedo boat, one of the last vessels to embark for England.

Immediately on his arrival, Maclean was attached to the Foreign Office general department, with the rank of second secretary. This post, which was not particularly prestigious, nonetheless gave him access to a wide variety of documents, notably those pertaining to the Foreign Office's liaisons with the Admiralty, as well as with the Supply and War ministries.

Six months after setting up house in London, Melinda was on her way home to the United States to stay with her family. She badly needed rest: in December 1940, she had given birth to a stillborn child. Donald, who remained behind on his own, underwent a period of deep depression which affected his work; nevertheless, he continued to provide his new handler, Gorsky (alias Henry) with a steady flow of intelligence. At that time he had full access to diplomatic correspondence, notably the dispatches that went to and fro between the British and the Americans. At the same time he relayed any rumours he heard within the Foreign Office.

After the Nazi invasion of the USSR, Maclean's spirits revived. His job now gave him access to much more important information, including telegrams and documents proceeding from the War Cabinet's military bureau. This new institution co-ordinated the handling of all questions to do with the day-to-day running of the war.

The cabinet ministers whose job it was to determine British military policy towards Germany took part in its meetings.

Donald Maclean also received an avalanche of documents from general military headquarters, in addition to the correspondence between the Foreign Office and its representatives abroad. The correspondence with Washington was of huge interest to us, as were the various communications between Maclean's ministry and the Allied forces stationed in England. Stalin, though he was officially the ally of General Wladislaw Sikorski, the head of the Polish Government in exile, was deeply mistrustful of him. As a result he was enchanted one morning when detailed minutes of Sikorski's negotiations with the British, as well as Sikorski's rude remarks about Stalin himself, arrived on his Kremlin desk. All of this material was filched by Maclean.

It was also Donald Maclean who in April 1943 got the news through to the Centre that Sikorski didn't believe a word of the Russian version of the massacre of Katyn, according to which the thousands of Polish officers liquidated in that unhappy place were murdered by the Germans. Stalin, of course, didn't give a hoot what Sikorski thought – only a scandal of global proportions could have shaken him. All the same, when the Polish Government in London demanded an inquest by the International Red Cross, Stalin immediately broke off relations with it, in the knowledge that nothing was to be gained by further co-operation. Later he was again to take close interest in Poland, but only after he had decided to seize that country.

It has been claimed by various newspapers, and by the authors of books on the Cambridge ring, that Stalin used to await Maclean's dispatches with impatience. This is nonsense. I doubt that Stalin even knew his agent's name. He wasn't interested in names – only the intelligence counted, whether its source was Maclean or any other agent.

On the other hand, since his compulsive mistrust of others made him suspicious of all the information that was brought to him, Stalin seemed reassured by the fact that this particular intelligence came directly from our idealistic British agents, and gave it his undivided attention.

The information Maclean supplied was limited to items that directly concerned the USSR. He had access to much more, but we could hardly have expected him to take it all. For instance, in 1943

Henry asked him to concentrate on Franco–British relations, given that disagreements appeared to be surfacing between the two Allies about the fate of the French colonies and the countries of the Middle East after the war. The USSR, which had been commendably prompt to recognize the French Committee of National Liberation in Algiers and de Gaulle, wanted badly to know whether France would regain her empire when the conflict was over. For their part the British were more or less openly expressing the wish that some of the French colonies should be given their independence. Maclean was able to give us precise information on this question as it developed.

In March 1944, at a moment that almost exactly coincided with my own promotion to officer in charge of the Cambridge ring, Donald Maclean was given the post of first secretary at the British Embassy in Washington, DC. For the KGB this was in the nature of a dream come true; for Maclean himself it was a personal triumph, not least because he had successfully concealed his visceral aversion to the Americans to get the job. Oddly enough, when the Macleans were going through US immigration formalities, Melinda quite naturally gave her future address as the British Embassy, Washington; but Donald stated that he would be lodging in New York with his father-in-law Mr Dunbar, Melinda's mother's second husband.

The Centre took Maclean's work so seriously and had such high hopes of his new posting that it gave in to his demand that he should continue to work only with Henry, his London handler. Henry was accordingly packed off to the United States in October 1944, where he devoted himself exclusively to Maclean, rebaptized Homer by the Centre. This compulsion to work always with the same people was one of Maclean's particular foibles. He had always paid the most meticulous attention to security: obsessively vigilant, even conspiratorial, he systematically refused to have any dealings with anyone from our Washington residence if he didn't already know him well.

The KGB hierarchy could hardly contain its glee. We had no idea what Maclean would come up with in Washington, but in the light of his earlier work we were sure that it would be good. By dint of patience and foresight we had manoeuvred an agent into a vital post, at a decisive moment in the war. The Normandy landings were imminent, and we awaited developments with impatience.

101

When I took over the handling of the Cambridge ring, our section of the KGB (the First Directorate, in charge of foreign intelligence) was riding high. We had two moles – Donald Maclean and Kim Philby – in key posts for the coming Cold War: in the British Embassy in Washington, and in the section of the British Secret Service entrusted with the struggle against Communism.

No other spy organization in the world, before or since, has ever accomplished such a devastating coup.

Chapter 4

MEN OF THE SHADOWS

In 1944, when I had begun processing the documents sent through to us by the Cambridge agents, I never dreamed that one day I might meet them. Apart from my forays into their KGB files, everything I knew about them I had gleaned from the reports of our London residents. I quickly understood that their current handling officer, Anatoli Borisovich Gorsky, code name Henry, held them in pretty low esteem – particularly Burgess, whom he viewed as a rogue, an adventurer, a liar and a drunk. Gorsky himself was a petty functionary in the NKVD, an employee at our embassy since well before the war who had risen in the service as a result of the 1938 purges. He had his points, notably perseverance and a sense of diplomacy, but his judgements of agents and his behaviour towards them left a lot to be desired.

Gorsky's raw energy enabled him to extract the best from a certain type of agent, but he worked on at least one principle which to my mind was deeply offensive. This was 'Demand more, get more'. He was domineering and bossy with his agents, belittling their work even when they produced excellent material – and this our British contingent cordially loathed. They were willing to work for us and to take desperate risks on our behalf, but they had no respect whatever for Gorsky.

To begin with, I took Gorsky's reports for gospel, but when Boris Mikhailovich Krötenschield (alias Krechin, alias Krotov) took over from him, my view of the Cambridge agents altered completely. Krechin was as effective and bright as his predecessor, but there the similarity ended. He was a charming character, with whom our agents enjoyed working; and later on, all of them were to remember him kindly. His attitude was friendly; he gave no orders; he just said, 'Listen, it would be marvellous if you could bring this off,' and left it at that.

In Krechin's opinion, Burgess had evolved a profoundly intelligent vision of life's difficulties. He particularly admired the man's wide culture. When I met Krechin at home in Moscow, he told me with conviction that in his view Burgess had given us his soul. Moreover, he believed that Burgess was so wedded to the cause that he was willing to sacrifice himself physically for its advancement. Certainly he was a drinker and a homosexual, a touchy character with a tendency to be aggressive and violent; yet overall, the picture Krechin painted was positive.

At the close of 1944, the name of John Cairncross, code-named the Carelian, was added to the four agents to whose cases I had been assigned. He was the 'fifth man'. Cairncross had at one time or another been in contact with the others, but he was hardly a member of their group.

Looking through his file, I soon formed the impression that the profile of this agent – born in 1913 in Glasgow – was far from typical. To begin with, his origins were resolutely lower middle-class. His brother Alex – who, I hasten to add, never had any dealing with us – forged a brilliant career as an economist and senior civil servant. The brothers were always on the best of terms.

John Cairncross won a scholarship to Cambridge from Hamilton Academy near his home city, to study modern languages. As soon as he arrived at Cambridge he found himself hampered by his origins, and more particularly by the scorn and hostility of the upper-class students surrounding him; nonetheless, he carried out his studies with such brilliance that his name was put forward for a scholarship to study French literature at the Sorbonne. There were very few such scholarships available at the time, and young Cairncross had to overcome the obstacle of privileged Oxford and Cambridge rivals who had excellent connections and did not hesitate to use them. He resented this injustice, and spoke of it often to me in later years. I think it may have tipped the balance in his decision to become a Communist.

The scholarship was finally awarded to him, against the will of the university administration, which resisted it to the last. Cairncross spent the university year of 1933–34 at the Sorbonne. He loved life in Paris and made a number of friends among his Communist fellow students. At that time the left–right political struggle was out in the open and growing more and more savage by the day. On 6 February, a Fascist demonstration at the Place de la Concorde led to vicious street-fighting with the police in which sixteen people died. On 9 February, a counter-demonstration called by the Communists also ended in a bloodbath, with seven dead. Cairncross followed these events with great interest; the banning of unions in Germany, discriminatory laws like the sterilization decree of 1 January 1934, and the re-arming of the nation by Hitler were steadily bringing Europe closer to war.

John Cairncross's ideas were clearly of a Socialist nature. His Communist acquaintances, however, didn't press him to become involved with the Party or to neglect his studies. He achieved brilliant results and obtained a *licence ès lettres* (a first). His passion for Molière was born then, and he later became an expert on the dramatist, highly respected by the best French academics. He returned to Cambridge, to Trinity College, in the autumn of 1934. He took his degree two years later. According to his file, he was already a Communist.

John Cairncross was *not* recruited by Theodor Maly, one of the NKVD's illegal agents in England, nor by one of our Cambridge agents. Burgess and Co. may have known him by sight as a fellow student, but they weren't remotely interested in him. He belonged to a different social class, and he could never have featured in Cambridge's more fashionable circles.

In 1936, the NKVD residence in London asked the agents we had recruited in Cambridge for their opinion of John Cairncross. They applied themselves to the questionnaire with good grace and each one gave his views, such as they were; but not one of them had a hand in bringing Cairncross in. Certainly they must have known he interested us, and indeed they may have expected us to make overtures to him, but nothing more. In any case, their answers showed that they took a fairly dim view of Cairncross: in the report that arrived at the Centre there was a reference to him as a man who 'hadn't a clue how to behave in company, nor any idea of how to get on with people socially.' Nevertheless, Burgess, Philby, Blunt and Maclean accepted that he was both cultivated and highly intelligent, though he would never be part of their world. And finally, it was James Klugman, the rich Cambridge undergraduate who had been at school with Maclean, who made the decisive advance to Cairncross.

Klugman was a 'high-card Communist', that is, a convinced Marxist whose life was dedicated to the ideal. The founder of a Communist cell at Cambridge, he was on familiar terms with our intelligence services, though he never worked for us outright. From time to time, when he was asked to do something, he would say, 'I will act only on the direct orders of the Party.'

This proviso made our relationship with Klugman somewhat awkward. To get him to act, Harry Pollitt, General Secretary of the British Communist Party, had to be wheeled out. Provided the order came from Pollitt, Klugman would comply.

In this case, he was told straight out by Pollitt that his duty as a Communist was to recruit Cairncross – and he did.

Klugman was an ambiguous character. Though he had been openly Marxist at university, he was able to join British Military Intelligence in 1939. Subsequently he was sent as an operational agent to Bari in Italy, where there was a wireless centre co-ordinating covert actions against the Germans and the Italians in the Balkans. He was even given a mission to establish contact with the Yugoslav resistance movement of Josip Broz Tito.

It may seem odd that an avowed Communist could have entered British Military Intelligence with so little difficulty – and even odder that Klugman was by no means the only one. Many Communists were able to infiltrate both the civil and military services at that time, because SIS simply failed to go into its recruits' backgrounds in sufficient detail. Large numbers of students in the 1930s had sympathized deeply with the Communist cause, and when war came, all they needed to tell the investigators was that this engagement had been a temporary enthusiasm. When the Germans first began bombing London, Wormwood Scrubs prison (from which our agent George Blake escaped in 1966) was gutted by fire. Unfortunately for the British espionage and counter-espionage services, all their archives were stored in the prison. We were lucky enough to get wind of this cardinal fact shortly afterwards, and thereafter we worked in the knowledge that all the lists of active and inactive Communists in Britain had gone up in smoke, along with all the detailed information in their files. Nor were the British ever able to replace this information fully. Anything suspicious in the pasts of James Klugman and several others was annihilated, to the huge delight and benefit of the NKVD. The 1939 routine investigation of him did not even mention that he had led a Communist Party cell at Cambridge.

During Klugman's spell in Bari, the Centre knew perfectly well that he had access to valuable confidential information. He could have passed some of this on, but he didn't.

When he recruited John Cairncross, the Scot was already a convinced Communist but not yet ready for a militant role. Nor was he particularly interested in Party membership. The result was that Cairncross had little difficulty in obeying Klugman's order to make a public break with Marxist theory, afterwards working single-mindedly to attain first-class honours in modern languages in 1936. His tutor for French literature was a certain Anthony Blunt, with whom he had little in common; the rapport with Guy Burgess seems to have been better. But in the main, Cairncross was anti-social and a wretched hand at making friends. This failing was to dog him all his life.

In the wake of his academic triumph at Cambridge, he applied to join the Foreign Office and was accepted immediately. He wasn't even required to take the exam which was otherwise obligatory. For a year he worked in different services, notably at the American desk, without managing to forge any kind of bond with the other staff. His colleagues seem to have found Cairncross boorish, ill-dressed, arrogant, and scornful of either diplomatic or social niceties. He wasn't 'one of us', and they made him feel it in no uncertain manner. To be perfectly frank, I think his collaboration with the NKVD was prompted by the boundless hatred their mockery provoked in him. John Cairncross had a sizeable chip on his shoulder, as the English say.

Why he was given a job at the Foreign Office at all has always baffled me. At that time men like him were routinely turned down. He was highly intelligent, but this was far from the only quality the Foreign Office sought in its recruits. Social background, good manners and good connections counted as much and probably more. Cairncross was the son of an obscure Scottish clerk, and he was hopelessly gauche and prickly. Donald Maclean, who saw a lot of him at this time, wrote to us later that 'Cairncross wasn't a very engaging sort of chap; he never seemed to talk to anyone at the FO'.

Nevertheless, over several months he brought the NKVD a good deal of information regarding Germany. His contacts were Theodor Maly and Arnold Deutsch. In fact, he gave us whatever he could lay his hands on, and his reports were concise and well-written.

Because he was constitutionally incapable of ingratiating himself with his colleagues, he was bumped about from one service to another. Eventually he felt so completely ostracized that it was a relief for him when he was transferred to the Treasury in late 1938. The NKVD was out of contact with him at that time, otherwise we would certainly have urged him to stay in his post at the Foreign Office, which was naturally far more interesting to us than the Treasury.

I don't know what kind of information he provided at this time, or even if he provided any at all. It will be remembered that during this period the NKVD was being devastated by the purges. There were very few people left working at the Lubyanka and the survivors had other things on their minds than looking after our junior agents in the West. Their main preoccupation was saving their skins. All through this period we had no resident whatever in London and nobody to send there.

In the KGB's chronological file on the information furnished by Cairncross, 1938–40 is a complete blank. But after the outbreak of war, his situation changed radically and he became suddenly vital to our intelligence services. The reason for this was his appointment as private secretary to Lord Hankey.

Lord Hankey is one of the more intriguing figures in the twentieth-century political history of England. He began as a Naval Intelligence officer and was a guiding force in the creation of the British Secret Service. In the early 1930s he produced a detailed report on Germany's furious efforts to re-arm and sounded the first alarm that the Nazis were experimenting with biological weapons. In 1938, just after the Anschluss, he was given the crucial task of setting up Britain's Civil Defence Force under the Civil Defence Emergency Scheme.

At the time when Cairncross became Hankey's secretary, Churchill was already in power. Hankey, a former minister without portfolio in the Chamberlain cabinet, had lost some of his influence, but was still the dominant figure within SIS. In a highly intelligent report done for Chamberlain on the state of espionage, counter-espionage and code deciphering in Britain, Hankey had proposed a series of reforms as well as the creation of a brand-new sabotage-and-diversion group, the future SOE.

In tandem with his work for the secret service, Hankey had presided over at least a dozen commissions on defence, security, scientific research, and even the postal services; at one point in his career he had been minister with special responsibility for the Post Office. Whenever there was a problem in the British cabinet, a commission or subcommission would be appointed with the tireless Hankey at its head. He was an indefatigable worker, who liked nothing better than to tackle all the jobs and worries the very thought of which made other ministers feel distinctly languid.

This extraordinary position endowed him with extraordinary privileges. He wasn't a minister per se, but still he had access to all the most important government documents. Sometimes he even saw the telegraphic correspondence of the Foreign Secretary. The most important reports on foreign policy, defence, industry and the orientation of scientific research regularly passed across his desk. John Cairncross, as his private secretary, suddenly became a major asset to us. Any time the name of his boss was omitted from the list of recipients of top-secret papers, he would write personally to complain to the Foreign Office. Result: the documents arrived by the next courier, who delivered them straight into the hands of our agent.

At about this time Cairncross was taken in hand by Gorsky, code name Henry. Fortunately, Cairncross didn't know that the vital and wide-ranging intelligence he was supplying to Moscow was not being used as it should have been. At that time what we needed most was information about the battlefront and, from June 1941 onwards, about the relationships between our allies. We had more pressing priorities than the dissecting of reports on scientific research, about which nobody gave a damn.

That is, until the day Lord Hankey's private secretary became the first agent to inform the NKVD that the Americans and British had been working since late 1940 on the joint manufacture of an atomic bomb.

According to Cairncross, who was by then known to the NKVD as the Carelian, the Allies were capable of producing a nuclear device based on uranium 235. It was a major piece of luck for us when Lord Hankey was appointed as chairman of the British Scientific Consultative Committee; this meant that Cairncross was able to read, copy and borrow thousands of different documents on our behalf. Strangely enough he never took a single photograph; later on I myself tried to teach him the rudiments of photographic technique, but to no avail. He was hopeless at such things.

Reading over his file, I was particularly intrigued by the lists and résumés of documents he forwarded to the Centre. Their sum total was highly impressive. For example, they included most of the forecasts of the war's progress made in late 1940 by Lord Hankey. In this singular document, Hankey, as a former officer of Naval Intelligence, postulated both the failure of any attempt by the Germans to invade Britain, and the stepping up of the submarine war in the Atlantic. He was right on both counts.

Churchill clearly envisaged the possibility of a German onslaught on the south coast of England. He gave orders that the shoreline should be fortified and mined, trenches dug and tank traps set up. This was a very costly exercise to which Hankey was opposed, in the conviction that the Germans would never attempt an invasion. When I arrived in England after the war, I went to see these fortifications for myself, and I was impressed.

As far as the NKVD was concerned, this information on British grand strategy was very useful. The same applied to Hankey's assessments of the differences between the various politicians involved, which could eventually be exploited to our advantage.

Following the invasion of the USSR by the Nazis in June 1941, the Carelian described the detailed functioning of the British side of the Anglo-Soviet commission set up to co-ordinate the sending of war matériel to the USSR. He detailed the commission's reluctance and outright refusal to send weapons that the Red Army particularly needed. Meanwhile, Germany, which had become our common enemy, was advancing all along the front from the north to the south of our country. Cairncross had no difficulty in gathering his information because the president of the commission was none other than the omnipresent Lord Hankey. We also knew that beneath his courteous, co-operative exterior this respectable British politician was a fierce opponent of all assistance to the Soviet Union and never missed an opportunity to remonstrate with Churchill over his indulgence towards us.

In March 1942, Henry asked Cairncross to try a different approach, this time by penetrating the Government Code and Cipher School at Bletchley Park. We were uncomfortably aware that the British were intercepting large numbers of wireless transmissions; it was rumoured that they were transcribing Soviet telegrams as well as German ones. I don't think this was the case at that time. Perhaps they had succeeded in deciphering one or two, but we never had any proof of this.

John Cairncross therefore entered the school with the analysis of intercepted Luftwaffe messages as his principal function. This was another strategically vital post, given that ever since 1940 the British had been deciphering coded messages sent out to the German armies by the Nazi general staff, as well as the answers sent back by units in the field.

The Germans were using a high-quality decoding machine called 'Enigma'. This was a highly practical, fast-operating machine, invented by a brilliant Dutchman just after the First World War. The patent, which was originally designed for civilian use, had been bought by the Germans and adapted for military purposes. Then in the early 1930s a German agent named Hans-Thilo Schmidt, who for ten years supplied the Allies with invaluable intelligence on German re-armament and the intentions of Hitler, managed to furnish the French with a manual for Enigma and a few clues on its encoding procedures. The French, finding themselves unable to penetrate the Enigma system, enlisted the help of the British, who quickly grasped the importance of the work involved. They further decided to bring in the Poles, who at that time had a high reputation as deciphering experts. The three countries made a certain amount of progress, but for every step forward they made, the Germans added another element to perfect their encoding procedure. The Poles appeared to be leading the field when Stewart Menzies, the head of MI6, recruited a brilliant mathematician by the name of Alan Turing. The co-operation between Britain, France and Poland continued until the invasion of Poland and the beginning of the war in September 1939. What was more, during the fighting the Poles managed to capture several Enigma machines, which had been severely damaged. In the meantime the Germans continued to improve their system, but in the summer of 1940 Turing and his team at Bletchley Park, assisted by one of the world's first computers, 'Colossus', cracked the Enigma code once and for all.

This was a success of incalculable importance because it gave the Allies total access to all the messages sent back and forth by Hitler's government and high command. Moreover, all the German regiments in the field were equipped with Enigma.

During the Battle of Stalingrad, Soviet troops captured no fewer than twenty-six Enigma machines, blown to pieces because the German operators naturally had orders to destroy them to prevent their falling into enemy hands. German prisoners revealed the cipher that had been used on these machines, and Soviet technicians were able to decode a few snatches of messages here and there, but they never succeeded in finding the general key to the Enigma system, which the experts at Bletchley Park had laid bare. Among themselves, the British experts called the interception of coded messages 'Ultra' intelligence.

The British Secret Service, which also penetrated the codes of the German Navy and the Luftwaffe, allowed only a few totally trusted people to work on Ultra. The distribution of decoded messages was strictly limited to SIS heads, to the Prime Minister and to certain figures in the government.

Philby, for instance, who at that time was already a high-ranking officer in the secret service, was given no access to these documents. He glimpsed them in the office of his immediate superior, who showed them to him from time to time. The British Government kept exclusive control of the deciphered messages and was careful not to pass on those that concerned its allies, especially those that might interest the Russians.

To conceal the fact that they had cracked the Enigma code, the British habitually attributed the messages they deciphered to the work of their agents in Germany or in the countries conquered by the Nazis. They even went so far as to write on these precious documents 'from X in Austria', or 'from Y in the Ukraine'. Only a handful of men knew the real origin of the information, which was Bletchley Park. Aside from Turing and his team, the only people in on this secret were Churchill, one or two intelligence heads – and the Soviets.

The British refused to share their information with the Soviet

Union – not only for political reasons, but also because they were convinced that German spies had infiltrated the upper echelons of the Red Army. There was something in this; the NKVD had for years suspected as much, and even today the belief persists. During the war two or three members of the Soviet general staff were arrested and shot as German agents; others may have escaped scot-free.

Cairncross, in his new job, was in a position to pass on to us everything that the British Government had hitherto jealously kept for itself. In the winter of 1942–43, for example, he had access to a series of vital texts which saved the lives of tens of thousands of Soviet soldiers during the final Nazi summer offensive, code-named 'Citadel', on the Eastern Front.

At this time, Henry ceased to work with Cairncross and was replaced by Boris Mikhailovich Krötenschield, alias Krechin. The style of this new handler suited the Carelian much better, and he consequently produced twice as much intelligence. Krechin treated his lonely charge with simple warmth and humanity, and the results were spectacular.

Cairncross began to come up with two distinct categories of documents. The first involved technical data about the new German Tiger tank. Built in 1942, this weapon was used *en masse* for the first time during the third and final German offensive on the Kursk salient. Its principal feature was the thickness of its armour, which could not be pierced by our shells. The Germans were convinced at the time that Russian cannons would be powerless to halt this new tank. Thanks to the documents obtained by Cairncross, we were able to analyse the thickness of the armour and assess the quality of the steel – and then to manufacture armour-piercing shells capable of knocking out the Tiger.

The Soviet triumph in the great tank battle at Kurskaia Douga in July 1943, in which two thousand tanks fought each other to a bloody standstill for two days and nights, was thus partly attributable to John Cairncross.

The second category of documents he sent through to Moscow concerned the German offensive itself. In the spring of 1943, the British Government informed the Soviet general staff of the imminence of an attack on the strategic Kursk salient. They also told the Red Army that the Germans knew the exact position of every Soviet unit in the region. This was all. Cairncross, however, went much further; he was able to furnish Krechin with the full texts of the intercepted messages, which contained the identifications of the Soviet units, their proportionate strength and their exact locations. Given this forewarning, the Soviet commander was able to move all his regiments at the last minute and completely outmanoeuvre the enemy. Even more important, Krechin obtained a precise list of all the Luftwaffe squadrons based in the area, which enabled our air force to carry out surprise bombing attacks on no fewer than fifteen aerodromes along a line extending from Smolensk to the Sea of Azov, several weeks in advance of the German offensive at Kursk. This preventive operation, which was followed by several others, was one of the major successes of the Soviet Air Force in the Second World War. Over five hundred Nazi aircraft were destroyed, most of them on the ground. After the victory at Kursk, the counter-thrust delivered by our armies was sufficiently vigorous to drive the invaders out of Soviet territory.

For these two astonishing exploits, John Cairncross was decorated with the Order of the Red Banner. The decoration was solemnly sent to London, where Krechin showed it to Cairncross in its velvet-lined box. He explained to the Carelian that this was one of the highest honours the Soviet Union could bestow. Cairncross held the medal in his hands for a moment: his happiness was obvious. Then Krechin gently took it back, placed it in its box again, carried it home and had it sent on to Moscow.

Shortly after this interview with Krechin, Cairncross told his departmental superior that he wanted to leave Bletchley and take up some other post within SIS. He was accordingly moved to the German bureau, Section V, and thereafter to Section I (political section), where he worked until the end of the war.

When I first took control of him, Cairncross was still sending us everything he could; but at that stage its importance was minimal. The quality of the intelligence he provided was no longer in the same league as that of Philby, who by that time had risen to a very high position within SIS. Cairncross, who worked hard and conscientiously for his country, remained no more than a junior official.

When I finally closed the two beige folders which had enabled me to piece together the biography of John Cairncross, I did so in the belief that for the time being this agent was unlikely to monopolize my time.

The information from London mostly reached Moscow in the form of coded telegrams. At that time our secret service department number one worked hand in glove with the Politburo, which meant Stalin, Molotov and Beria. Our reports seldom reached the lower echelons of the Foreign Affairs Commissariat. The truth was that Molotov was in sole charge of the information we provided, and he did what he liked with it.

Items of military intelligence were forwarded to the GRU (the Russian military intelligence), or else directly to the Red Army high command, but otherwise the heads of the KGB were none too eager to keep the other branches of state security abreast of their business. Their policy was to inform only when absolutely necessary; they preferred to concentrate the efforts of our foreign agents on collecting information for the Kremlin.

Elsewhere in the world, secret services simply try to gather as much intelligence as they can on every possible subject. This information is then filed, assessed and shared out among the various government organizations that may need it. Our work methods were totally different. We almost never went out looking for information at random. Instead, orders to look for certain specific things would come from above. Stalin, for example, badly needed to know exactly what transpired between Churchill and Roosevelt when they met, so our agents abroad were directed to find out at all costs. This highly authoritarian style produced excellent results. The information furnished by our London residence was extraordinarily useful, for example, when the Allies were considering opening a second battlefront. In 1942, Churchill gave his word to Stalin that a western front would be opened the following year. When this possibility was discussed with the Americans it was (of course) decided that the time was not yet ripe, partly because the Western Allies were unprepared and partly because it suited them very well that the Germans should mire themselves for another year in the east. They also wanted the Russians to be brought to their knees, almost bled white, before launching the offensive that would relieve the German pressure on us.

Stalin quickly grasped that no action was to be expected in 1943, despite Churchill's repeated assurances, and thus the value of the secret information brought to him from London was immense in terms of the next phase of the struggle.

The same phenomenon occurred in 1944, when the USSR was begging the Allies for explosives. The end of the war was in sight and the delivery of these supplies was vitally important for our armies advancing in the east; but the British and the Americans concocted delays. Not a single consignment of powder arrived in Murmansk. Stalin was beside himself with rage. He calmed down, however, when he learned via Burgess and Philby that this was a deliberate decision on the part of the Allies. Clearly they were unwilling for the Russians to move forward into Germany too quickly. Yet again, advance intelligence enabled Stalin to make decisions without awaiting the pleasure of our Allies.

We at the KGB were convinced that Stalin and his Kremlin *apparatchiks* placed no trust in Churchill, despite the formal assurances of help to the USSR which he poured forth in his speeches and in his meetings with Russian representatives. We easily guessed why Stalin was so interested in what transpired in the Anglo–American talks, and why he wanted to know what they said to each other about us. Stalin's anxiety increased in 1944 when rumours began to surface of contacts between the Germans, the British and the Americans, in Switzerland and Sweden. Above all he feared a reversal of alliances, now that the outcome of the war appeared certain. If the British, the Germans and the Americans joined forces against the USSR at this point, millions of Russian soldiers would have died for nothing.

When one looks at the situation in this light, it is easy to understand why the foreign policies of the Allies should have been so crucially important to us, and why the main effort of the Soviet secret services should have been concentrated on this single aspect.

In early 1945, more rumours emerged that the Americans were negotiating with the Germans in Switzerland; I myself saw several documents confirming this. I know that there was no question of a separate peace, merely a pact which would allow the Germans to concentrate all their forces in the east, against Russia.

During this critical period at the end of the war, I regularly received telegrams on the secret parleys under way between the British and American general staffs, apropos of a possible war against Russia should the Red Army continue its thrust westwards following the fall of Berlin. From Stalin's point of view, this information was beyond price.

If the head of the Kremlin was haunted by the real or imagined ill turns that the Allies were preparing to deal him, Molotov for his part had placed the Anglo–American discussions on atomic energy very high on his agenda of required information. The word was passed to our networks abroad. Even the smallest item of intelligence on this was given top priority. The telegrams we received did not as a rule contain technical data; they tended rather to detail the minutes of political discussions, the context in which negotiations were conducted, the moral positions adopted by the participants and their ulterior motives. We had known since 1942 through our agents (notably Cairncross) that the British and the Americans were working secretly, with the help of Canada, on a nuclear programme. The goal of the Americans was to attract the foremost scientists to the United States with a view to building an atomic bomb as soon as possible. We also knew that the Americans fully intended to deceive the British every step of the way. In the certainty that they were substantially behind the British in terms of research, their strategy was to use the expertise of their allies – thanks to scientists like Klaus Fuchs, a German physicist and refugee who was later imprisoned for spying for the Soviet Union – and then to jettison them once they had caught up. And this, of course, is exactly what they did.

Without fear of exaggeration, I can confirm that we in the USSR knew absolutely everything about the technical and political aspects of atomic bomb development.

Among our sources, there was one who was very conveniently placed to gather political information on the Anglo–American nuclear programme. This was Homer, alias Donald Maclean. He had taken up his post as first secretary in the British Embassy in Washington in early 1944.

Melinda, his wife, had not followed Maclean to Washington, even though the embassy was the official address she gave. Instead she had gone to New York with her first son, Fergus, and had moved in with her stepfather and her mother, Mrs Dunbar. Moreover, she was pregnant again. It has often been suggested that Maclean was reluctant to live with his wife while he was in the United States. In reality, the only reason why Melinda lodged with her relatives in New York was because Homer's handling officer was also in that city. Donald saw his family as an ideal pretext for visiting Manhattan once or twice a week.

He also went back and forth to London on a regular basis, and there he contacted Guy Burgess and apprised him of the information he had collected.

As soon as he arrived in Washington, Maclean was appointed to an Anglo–American committee entrusted with the drafting of a peace treaty with Italy. The ambassador, Lord Halifax, who had been a close friend of his father's, immediately noticed young Maclean's competence, capacity for work and readiness to help at all times. He was given all the most sensitive files and was allowed to consult ultra-secret documents going in and out of the embassy almost without restriction. In March 1945, after the diversion to Moscow of a London-bound Polish aircraft containing sixteen leaders of the AK (Polish Secret Army), Churchill and Truman exchanged a flurry of telegrams. They agreed to lodge a strong protest with Stalin over this act of air piracy. The fate of Poland was always of deep concern to the British Prime Minister; he frequently raised the subject with Truman, who seemed unaware of the importance of that country in the East–West power balance.

Integral copies or résumés of telegrams exchanged between the two leaders came to the British Embassy in Washington. Homer naturally read them and conscientiously relayed their contents to his handler when he visited New York. The latter encoded them and had them transmitted to the Centre. Two of these telegrams were one day to become famous: numbers 72 and 73, sent on 5 June 1945. I will tell their story later.

In the summer of 1945, Donald Maclean, who was then working on the Combined Policy Committee, was assigned a top-secret mission to co-ordinate the American Manhattan Project to develop the atomic bomb with the British Tube Alloys project. Tube Alloys had been launched in the summer of 1941 by the scientific consultative committee chaired by Lord Hankey, whose secretary at the time was John Cairncross. It is no overstatement to say that the KGB was able to follow the political evolution of the Western atomic programme from its genesis right through to the first test detonation near Alamogordo, New Mexico. I am not speaking of the scientific programme, which was revealed to us by scientists like Klaus Fuchs, Bruno Pontecorvo and Daniel Greenglass.

Since Maclean was no scientist, he never obtained access to

scientific information. On the other hand, everything involving Anglo–American politics in the field of atomic energy sooner or later arrived on his desk at the embassy.

Unfortunately for the British – and, by inference, for us – in 1946 the Americans created the AEC (Atomic Energy Commission) to develop a purely American nuclear programme. The year before, Churchill had been succeeded by Attlee and Roosevelt by Truman; Anglo–American relations were beginning to cool off. This change of direction decided by the White House resulted in the British being cut off from all information about American progress with the bomb. Consequently, the British Government decided to proceed with its own programme. The US decision, perceived by the British as a grave insult, only strengthened Donald Maclean's distaste for the Americans.

For several years the British Government had been sending its leading specialists to the United States without benefiting in real terms from the research carried out there. Now the British scientists were recalled and asked to catch up the ground lost since the end of the war. In effect, restrictions on the sharing of information did not apply either to the research done in common during the Second World War or to strategic raw materials. Thus Maclean was able to continue, though to a somewhat lesser extent, with his intelligence-gathering on behalf of the Centre. As the man responsible for nuclear matters at the British Embassy in Washington, he had clearance to enter the offices of the Atomic Energy Commission. This he exploited to the full for several months, even going there during the night. He visited the AEC on about twenty occasions in all, picking up many valuable items of information, notably records of the quantity of uranium produced or planned for production by the Americans, for the manufacture of atomic bombs.

Donald Maclean did such good work that in February 1947 he was made co-director of the secretariat for co-ordinating British, American and Canadian nuclear policy, from which he continued to provide us with a steady stream of information. Most of it involved dispatches exchanged between the Americans and the British. We were kept completely abreast of every development.

Also during his time in Washington, Maclean obtained information on the attitude of the Allies to the war of nerves mounted by Stalin in his attempt to gain control of the Black Sea and the highly strategic narrows of the Bosphorus and Dardanelles – the sole maritime access to Bulgaria, Romania and the USSR from the Mediterranean. Like the Tsars before him, Stalin dreamed of giving Russia an outlet to the Indian Ocean and to this end cast covetous eyes on Turkey. Great Britain, weakened by the war, was no longer an obstacle as far as he was concerned: only Truman, as Stalin saw it, could prevent his gaining his end. London and Ankara were uncertain whether or not the American President had the stomach to resist the Russians.

The Centre therefore gave Homer the task of finding out exactly how far the West would go to defend this part of the world – and it proved a mission well within his capabilities, because he had direct access to the secret conversations between Ankara, London and Washington. In the event he sent us the full content of the Anglo–American proposals for the control of the Bosphorus by an international commission. A few days after we received this crucial intelligence, *The New York Times* announced on its front page that the British and US Governments had agreed with the Turks on a common position *vis-à-vis* the Russians. Molotov pretended to throw a fit about this double-cross, demanding an explanation. The Allies, unable to find out how *The New York Times* had got wind of the affair, were completely baffled. Tension rose; Stalin dispatched three Red Army divisions from the Czech frontier to Romania and Bulgaria, while Turkey massed its army along the frontiers with Bulgaria and Georgia.

Edwin C. Wilson, the US Ambassador at Ankara, was directed to meet with Ambassador Sergei Alexandrovich Vinogradov and negotiate. He offered a sweeping set of proposals on the situation in the Bosphorus, including one crucial condition allowing warships other than those of the countries directly concerned to be stationed in the Dardanelles area. Of course, this meant allowing the navies of Great Britain and the United States to set up a permanent presence in the region. The American envoy expected a formal meeting in the usual style of the Soviets, with no decisions made by his opposite number prior to consultation with Moscow. But he got nothing of the sort: Vinogradov gave forthright opinions on several of the proposals, and spoke at length about the stationing of foreign warships, which was anathema to the USSR. Wilson was stunned. The Russian had arrived fully briefed, with his answers ready. Little did Wilson know that Homer (Maclean) had sent a transcript of the American proposals.

The Americans were furious and laid the blame for these leaks on the British, openly accusing them of inability to keep a secret. Relations between them hit such a low point that the former Allies refused to adopt a common stance on the Dardanelles. The Turks and the British would no longer hear of the American proposal for an international commission.

Shortly afterwards Homer got word to us that Truman, who was then formulating his doctrine of containment, aiming to stop the spread of Communism around the world, was firmly opposed to Stalin's policies of hegemony and that he would never abandon Turkey. Result: Stalin back-pedalled. In this case the information provided by Homer may well have prevented the outbreak of war.

Every day brought its fresh harvest of intelligence to the Lubyanka, and it was all intelligence that we had ordered, like a suit made to measure. We were directed to find the facts that our leaders needed, by whatever means were at our disposal.

I shared a cramped office with two colleagues; I sat at a desk wedged between an English dictionary and mountains of files; I had to be available to translate or rewrite syntheses day and night when necessary. At the same time I had the most exhausting job of all, because it was I who received the microfilms. To obviate any risk of a leak, even though everyone at the KGB headquarters was painstakingly screened, I often developed the films myself in the laboratory. Sometimes, to gain time, I read and noted the interesting portions while they were still wet with developing solution.

When things weren't quite so urgent, the microfilms would be transferred to photographic paper and I would take my time reading their contents. I classified the information in order of importance, before sending it to our pool of female translators, who put it into Russian. If I judged the documents to be of great importance, I translated them myself. What a responsibility! First of all, I had to avoid translating errors, which might completely alter a document's significance. Next, I had to be completely abreast of the news of the moment, as well as the historical, diplomatic and even economic circumstances, so as to be able to assess the quality of what I was reading. My real anxiety was not so much the likelihood that I might overestimate the importance of some text (which would have brought me no more than a mild reproof), but that I might overlook something on which the fates of thousands of men might depend. This possibility gave me nightmares.

Once I had completed the synthesis or deciphering of a given document, I went to see Lvovich Koghen, my boss. Koghen was efficient but perpetually overworked and in a hurry, since his job was to co-ordinate several groups of agents just like mine. He always gave the impression that he was drowning in his work. Whenever he had a moment to spare between meetings, he read what I showed him; sometimes he ventured a comment, but as a rule he was in agreement with me. Then he would say, 'Yuri, have these documents sent to the three addresses.' This meant Stalin, Molotov and Beria.

A KGB officer would be detailed to take the package, sealed by us, across to the Kremlin. After each delivery, we half-waited for a reaction, but there never was one. All we knew was that the information provided by our London agents seemed to please the masters of the Soviet Union, and that the work of our section left nothing to be desired.

By now Kim Philby had emerged as an informer of incalculable importance. He was, first of all, the rising star within the British Secret Service. When I took over responsibility for the Cambridge Five, in 1944, he was canvassing for the top post in Section IX, the anti-Communist department; but he was not alone as a candidate. Felix Cowgill, his immediate superior, was also in the running. By exploiting his friendship with Valentine Vivian, Kim Philby managed to outflank his rival and secure the job. Cowgill was so incensed by this that he left the service.

Henry, Kim's handler, was wild with delight: his man had brought off a masterstroke. Stanley (Philby), a Soviet agent, had become head of the section within British intelligence whose sole mission was to do battle with the KGB and thwart the spread of Communism worldwide. During the investigation of his background that preceded his appointment, Kim was once again closely questioned about his private life. He explained to Vivian, in even greater detail than he had the first time around, that it was perfectly correct to say that his wife, Litzi, was a rabid Communist, and that her militant Marxism had been the direct cause of their breakup. He repeated that if the divorce had not yet been made official, it was simply because he had received no news of his wife since the beginning of the war. He then reiterated his determination to marry Aileen Furse as soon as he could contact Litzi again.

Valentine Vivian received these explanations with complete equanimity. He assured Philby that he was free to do as he wished, and that his private life would have no influence on his nomination – and this was exactly what transpired. It was true that Kim had lost all contact with Litzi. He had now been living with Aileen Furse for a long time, and had had three children with her. The couple got on very well together, and Kim was a model partner and father, helping around the house and with the cooking and participating with complete sincerity in the life of his family. He was especially fond of Tommy, his eldest son . . . all in all, nobody has ever been able to fault him in this respect.

He finally tracked down Litzi at the end of the war. They exchanged letters and she agreed to a divorce, which became effective on 17 September 1946. This presented no difficulty for Litzi, who was now living with a Communist activist named Georg Honigmann, who never had any contact whatsoever with the KGB. She was living in East Berlin at the Liberation; later she had a daughter with Honigmann, before again divorcing in 1966. I know that she kept up a correspondence with Kim Philby until his death; she herself is still alive, I believe. A few years back I had news of her: it seems she went across to West Berlin in the 1980s and thereafter went to live with her daughter and grandchildren in Austria or Germany. She is a woman of tremendous conviction, for whom I have the greatest admiration.

As usual, Philby settled into his new job with characteristic zeal and enthusiasm. By this time his reputation within the KGB had reached almost godlike proportions. Some people even thought he might make it to the summit of the entire SIS; he certainly had it in him to do so.

Just then an event occurred that was to have serious repercussions on Philby's career. On 4 September 1945, Konstantin Volkov, a KGB agent working in the consular section of the Soviet Embassy in Ankara, presented himself at the British Consulate in Istanbul. He was nervous and anxious, and he wished to see the consul general, Chantry Page. Page received Volkov in the presence of John Reed, first secretary of the British Embassy in Ankara, who happened to be on the spot and who, as a fluent Russian speaker, was able to serve as interpreter. Volkov had been planning his defection for some time, but what he was about to propose appeared to terrify him.

In exchange for £27,500 sterling and a *laissez-passer* to Cyprus for himself and his wife, he was ready to give the names of three highly placed Soviet agents operating in England: two in the Foreign Office and the third at the head of a counter-espionage section. He was, of course, referring to Burgess, Maclean and Philby. Volkov also said he could indicate several NKVD nests in Moscow, and a full list of the Soviet agents in Turkey.

Reed, a diplomat who preferred to abide by the rules, immediately informed the ambassador, Sir Maurice Peterson. Peterson had a horror of anything to do with espionage; he refused to meet Volkov; he told the SIS resident in Ankara, Cyril Machray, to inform London and thereafter washed his hands of the whole business.

The information Volkov was offering the British derived from documents he had read while he was working at the Lubyanka, at Department 3 in the First Directorate, in charge of the United States and Great Britain. There he had access to ultra-secret material, a fact I can formally confirm.

Reed relayed the ambassador's decision to Volkov, who agreed that his offer might be sent to London on three conditions: first, that Reed should write the message himself and not have it encoded by the embassy staff – according to him, there was a spy among them. Second, he demanded that the message should not be telegraphed to London, but should travel in the diplomatic bag, because he thought the Russians had access to some of the British codes. And third, he requested that the whole operation should take no longer than three weeks. Reed agreed to these demands and Volkov slipped out of the consulate, saying he would re-establish contact later.

Cyril Machray's report reached London in early September. As the head of Section IX, Philby received a letter from the diplomatic bag containing Volkov's proposal. The lamb had come to the slaughter, but still Philby had to proceed with extreme care. There was no question of simply suppressing this official message, which was already in the hands of his superiors. That evening Stanley worked very late on a report of the affair, which he passed to his handler, Boris Mikhailovich Krötenschield, code-named Krechin, who had just replaced Henry. He told Krechin exactly what had happened and asked him to make urgent contact with the Centre.

In Moscow, a rapid review of this development showed how serious the situation was. It was more than likely that Volkov knew that the Soviet agent heading a section of SIS was named Kim Philby, and that the two agents in the Foreign Office were called Guy Burgess and Donald Maclean. The enquiry also revealed that Volkov could betray several others. There was no need to panic, however, because the deadline fixed by Volkov gave the KGB plenty of time to react. Krechin's only advice to Stanley was that he should drag things out and gain time. In the meantime, the Centre would work discreetly to neutralize the potential defector. Officers working abroad are usually highly suspicious individuals, constantly on their guard; and Volkov, who knew exactly what he was doing, would be more than usually alert. He was all too well aware that he was playing a deadly game and that if he failed he would face a firing squad. The Centre decided to take every precaution against his disappearing at the first sign of trouble.

In London, the heads of the British services immediately grasped the importance of the Volkov affair. They understood that having a deadline as long as three weeks could torpedo the operation completely. At a crisis meeting attended by Philby, several officers insisted that things should be handled much more quickly than Volkov had stipulated.

Philby proposed to Stewart Menzies, the head of SIS, that an experienced agent should be dispatched to Istanbul to deal with the matter at first hand. Menzies settled on Brigadier Douglas Roberts, of the Middle East security services, a fluent Russian speaker who had worked for years in Turkey. This didn't suit Philby at all, but his luck held. Roberts declined the mission because he was terrified of flying and would never go abroad in anything but a ship. So Menzies delegated Philby himself to go to Istanbul.

Then began a race against time; only the British Secret Service was unaware that we had the ability to hold back the hands of the clock.

Still Kim's luck held. A violent storm over Malta forced his plane to land in Tunis. When he arrived in Cairo, it was too late to catch the connecting flight to Istanbul. He finally got there on the Friday, only to be told that the ambassador was away on his yacht in the Black Sea. He therefore prepared himself for a pleasant weekend, and late on Monday morning made his way to the consulate. In the middle of the afternoon, with the assistance of John Reed, he attempted to make contact with Volkov, through Chantry Page, who could telephone the Soviet consulate in an official capacity without arousing suspicion, given that he and Volkov exercised parallel diplomatic functions.

Page asked the operator at the switchboard to pass him to Konstantin Volkov. Somebody professing to be Volkov came on the line, but Page realized immediately this was not the man he had interviewed. He called back several times in the course of the day, only to be told that Volkov had just gone out or hadn't yet arrived. On Tuesday morning he was informed that Volkov was in Moscow.

At this time a rumour went round the Istanbul diplomatic corps to the effect that a Soviet diplomat had fallen gravely ill and had had to be carried by ambulance to the airport and placed on the first flight to Moscow.

The exact details of what happened to the wretched Volkov in Moscow are unknown to me; suffice it to say that he was summarily tried and shot. The official line was that he had fallen ill in Turkey. I imagine he was simply given an injection to put him to sleep and then sent home on grounds of ill-health. It was the usual practice.

While waiting in hopes of his appointment to the post of head of SIS, which promised to be the supreme triumph of his double career, Kim Philby was made overall controller of MI6's secret agents in the Soviet Union. He was also in charge of recruiting spies and mounting sabotage operations against Communist parties in the USSR and elsewhere. Naturally, he kept us fully informed of these operations, which were usually carried out by the British, only occasionally by the Americans. We were careful not to use his information to conduct a systematic dismantling of the networks concerned. If the operations were of major importance and could cause great damage, we took appropriate action – but otherwise we tended to do nothing, because Philby had to show results to his superiors. At that time the Soviet Union was seething with spies and saboteurs, most of them natives of the Baltic countries annexed by the USSR after 1940.

Every time, Philby gave us notice in a different way. Sometimes he would tell us the name of the agent, sometimes only when and where he or she would be parachuted in, so that we could set up an ambush. The spies entered the USSR by way of the Baltic regions, the

Ukraine, Belorussia and Turkey. We knew in advance about every operation that took place by air, land or sea, even in mountainous and inaccessible regions.

The British had a penchant for parachuting agents into the Baltic countries, where there was already a strong, well-organized resistance. Philby gave us details of every operation in Lithuania and Estonia; they usually involved arms deliveries or the infiltration of combatants or messengers via Sweden or the Baltic. We knew who was coming, and when, and we neutralized these spies and saboteurs; most were arrested and imprisoned; very few, however, were executed. We were at war. The KGB let some of the agents go free temporarily, to avoid jeopardizing Philby, while others were turned and became our own double agents. These turning operations were carried out with such subtlety that Philby was able to continue his work for the British with a solid veneer of success. Ultimately, what the Centre wanted was for him to reach the top of the tree in his country's intelligence services; hence the orders given to the KGB surveillance teams, whose job it was to intercept the spies sent to the USSR by Philby, were extraordinarily exacting. The men involved had to be carefully selected. Any bungling in their work could ruin everything.

By late 1946, Philby's professional future looked assured. He was awarded the CBE, and Stewart Menzies, the head of SIS, was preparing to retire. Menzies was scarcely brilliant as a secret operative, but he cut quite a figure in London's high society. He liked beautiful women and parties, and was a good friend of the King; all in all, he had enormous influence. Menzies was also very fond of Philby, whose name was frequently mentioned as his possible successor. But Roger Hollis, deputy head of MI5 at the time, felt – correctly, in my opinion – that although Philby was an attractive candidate, he lacked practical experience and was too much of a theoretician. Consequently Kim was passed over and sent to Turkey to run operations against the Soviet Union from there. No doubt the SIS chiefs wanted him to use this time to gain more practical experience of his profession, prior to giving him the top job.

From 1944 to 1947, I was engrossed with the material sent by our Cambridge agents, and with the regular discussions I had to conduct with their handlers when they passed through Moscow. Gradually the

127

sheer detail of my work enabled me to acquire a comprehensive knowledge of these men.

From the start, when I was only an apprentice with the NKVD, I eagerly read and memorized everything I could lay my hands on. I became familiar with the working methods of our secret services, and I understood the various mistakes that had been made.

In the war years and after, the personnel of the KGB were very diverse in origin. They were just as likely to be experienced former diplomats or high officials of the Foreign Affairs Commissariat as old officers of the Cheka – the precursor of the KGB – who had somehow survived the purges. These last were men who had 'worked' during the October Revolution and in the 1920s, fighting 'bandits', as enemies of the people were then called. They may have been highly motivated militants, but they weren't very good at their jobs: they lacked both special training and general culture. Their lack of writing skills was perhaps their most severe handicap. They could show flair on occasion and they were far from stupid, but when it came to putting their conclusions down on paper they were lost. This was unfortunate, because our bosses insisted on written précis at all times.

The KGB archives were always chaotic. When Westerners recently started falling over themselves to get into the Lubyanka in search of explosive documents on the work of the KGB from 1917 to 1950, I couldn't help smiling. There really is very little there of the slightest interest.

It may seem paradoxical to anyone who knows Russia, but bureaucracy did not begin to catch up with the KGB until well after the war, in 1948–50. This coincided with the recruitment of new functionaries, who had completed their graduate studies and now thought exclusively of their own careers. And it was at about this time that the Soviet secret services began to go into decline.

For four years, I lived the life of an ordinary functionary. The ambiance at the Lubyanka was more agreeable than not, and our relations with our chiefs were friendly enough. At noon we all trooped down to the canteen with our ration cards and all ate together without discrimination in rank. Groups formed, and we sat round the same table, talking about the war, sport, girls, the shortages, but never about work.

During our rare weekends off, we organized walks around

Moscow. In summer we had the use of a dacha. We had our own sport and leisure centres. In 1945, I was the skating champion and the runner-up ski champion of the KGB's First Directorate.

Away from the office we led uneventful, ordinary lives, like most Soviet citizens at that time. I had a few friends, mostly people from the office, and we saw the same girls. I remember one man in particular, a top-class scientist who ran the technical service of the Anglo–American section: he irritated me prodigiously because his one goal was to prove how clever he was.

Before the war I had been on holiday several times at Sudak, in the Crimea, where I fell in love with a girl. We wrote to each other often; then the war came and we lost touch. In Moscow in 1944, I decided to look her up again. Her address was easy to find; as it turned out, she was living with her mother, who was a teacher in Moscow. Wearing my KGB uniform, with its sky-blue stripes, I went to see her. She received me coldly; no doubt the uniform had something to do with it. There was no question of our resuming our acquaintance.

The fact was, people were growing more and more suspicious of the KGB. For a while I went openly about the street in my uniform; I felt no need to hide the fact that I belonged to the organization, even from my few civilian friends, but this gradually changed. Contrary to what has often been asserted, officers were never forbidden to have friends outside the KGB.

One such friend, a brilliant young soldier, told me in 1945 that he wanted to leave Moscow. The decision seemed rather strange to me, given that at that time virtually everybody in Russia dreamt of living in the capital. He told me it was because he was a Jew.

'So what?' I said. 'There are plenty of Jews in the KGB; my boss Koghen is one, and he has no problems.'

My friend just shook his head. He eventually went away to live at Dniepropetrovsk. He knew he could never carve out a career for himself in Moscow.

Apart from my immediate family, I was pretty much unconcerned with other people. My work consumed me. At that time Philby and Maclean were the undisputed stars in the eyes of the KGB, and the others seemed less important by comparison: the war had ended, and for the moment they were less productive.

Paul, Mädchen or Hicks – as Guy Burgess was known – had by

then ceased to accomplish much. Henry, before leaving for the United States in October 1944, had asked him to do what he could to gain entrance to the Foreign Office, because since Maclean's departure in March 1944 we had nobody left there. It took Burgess about a year to do this. To begin with, he had a job with the press department. This gave him very little access to useful information and he had trouble 'feeding' Krechin with sufficient material. Krechin was unconcerned: he knew Burgess, and he knew he couldn't bear to be unproductive for long.

Krechin was right. In 1946, Burgess found work as private secretary to Hector McNeil, the number two at the Foreign Office in Clement Attlee's Labour government. This key post placed mountains of information at his disposal. To all intents and purposes he had unlimited access to all diplomatic correspondence at the Foreign Office.

Burgess and Krechin generally met outside London, only occasionally in town. Burgess would bring gigantic files with him: these would be photographed, then quietly taken back to Hector McNeil's office. The most interesting items were telegraphed directly to Moscow.

One day, after a meeting with Burgess, Krechin's valise suddenly burst open, strewing top-secret documents and Foreign Office telegrams all over the floor of a pub. Krechin, swearing like a sailor, picked them up one by one; a young man very courteously helped him. Nobody noticed anything untoward, and Krechin went on his way. I dread to think what a colossal political and diplomatic scandal might have ensued had a Soviet agent been arrested in London with a bagful of documents stolen from the Foreign Office. The Cold War, it should be remembered, was in its first hysterical year.

Minister of State McNeil was a highly intelligent, straightforward man: he gave himself no airs. He and Burgess got on well. McNeil's principal weakness was indolence. He preferred going to restaurants, or films, or plays, to working at his desk. Guy immediately grasped this and took advantage of it, doing McNeil's work for him without complaint. When McNeil was asked to draw up a report or analyse a set of classified documents, the job was passed straight to Guy, who was only too happy to oblige. When everything was typed up and ready, all McNeil had to do was sign it and send it on to his colleagues in the government, or to the Prime Minister. In consequence Burgess was held in deep reverence by his grateful boss, who directed him to keep track of all the reports and telegrams proceeding from the post-war international conferences then under way.

In April 1946, Burgess received all the documents prepared by the Foreign Office concerning the conference of the foreign ministers of the Big Four powers which was about to start in Paris. Molotov (USSR), Ernest Bevin (Great Britain), James Byrnes (USA) and Georges Bidault (France) had to determine the fate of the former allies of Nazi Germany. It was more than evident that the Russian proposal for a four-power mandate to govern the Ruhr, and the transfer of control of Trieste to Yugoslavia, would be ruled out.

The same thing happened in March 1947, at the Moscow conference. Molotov knew exactly what the other participants were saying to one another behind his back, and notably that the Americans, represented by their new Secretary of State George Marshall, would turn down all the Soviet proposals for the future of Germany. They would rather torpedo the conference altogether – which is what eventually happened – than accept Molotov's point of view.

Thus Burgess continued to assist us in the immediate post-war period.

Anthony Blunt took a very different course, stretching his links with the KGB to breaking point. His work with British counter-espionage had been on a temporary basis for as long as the war lasted. During the conflict the secret services needed everybody they could get; their ranks were filled with experts from all walks of civilian life, especially engineers, professors and intellectuals. Another consideration was that the authorities were unwilling to allow the nation's élite to be wasted as cannon fodder.

As soon as the war was won, these men went back to their old jobs, leaving secret work to the professionals. Blunt, like the others, was freed from his duties at MI5 and was given the post of Surveyor of the King's Pictures, which suited him perfectly. Charles I had created the post in 1625 to ensure the maintenance of the royal collections and to advise the monarch on the purchase of pictures. At the time Blunt was only thirty-six years old; this appointment came as the crowning achievement of his research career. He consulted with Krechin, who was soon able to tell him that the KGB had no objection to his resignation from active service with MI5.

I believe Moscow had an ulterior motive in agreeing to Blunt's move. Blunt was known to be friendly with George VI, whom he saw often. The two men spent plenty of time together, visiting galleries and discussing art. The powers in Moscow must have concluded that Blunt, given direct access to Buckingham Palace, would come up with valuable information. They couldn't have been more wrong.

In any event Krechin and Blunt decided that if he came across anything of vital importance he would make contact with us directly, or else send it through Burgess.

The fact that the KGB raised no objection to Blunt's departure from MI5 has been a cause of bafflement to British journalists and intelligence officers alike. Peter Wright in his book *Spycatcher* states that the reason why the KGB allowed Blunt to do this was that we had another mole inside MI5. Wright concluded, rather hastily, that the other agent was Roger Hollis. It is not up to me to prove the contrary, but I sincerely think Wright was wrong about this. In 1987, when Wright's book was published, British intelligence carried out a detailed enquiry which turned up nothing new. Peter Wright had no proof of what he said. It's a bit too easy to cast grave suspicion on a colleague, as Wright did on Hollis, without anything like sufficient evidence.

My own view is that the KGB had another excellent reason for its action, quite apart from the hope that Blunt would derive valuable intelligence from his contact with the King. The fact was that Blunt was no ordinary agent: he was a distinguished art scholar whose work was beginning to be internationally renowned. An individual of his calibre cannot work in a nuts-and-bolts counter-espionage capacity: to do so would have been ridiculous and even suspicious. Had Blunt remained in MI5 in the years after the war, at a time when he seemed set for a brilliant career in his chosen field, it would have looked distinctly odd.

Then, too, the reports from Henry, and subsequently from Krechin, that we received at the Lubyanka in 1945 nearly all made reference to Blunt's extreme state of nervous tension and to the risk that he might crack. Needless to say, this was a very serious threat to everyone involved.

Blunt had done sterling work for us during the war. Without the slightest risk of exaggeration I can affirm that over the years he supplied us with literally thousands of documents. He had helped change the course of the war, and his work unquestionably spared the lives of tens of thousands of Soviet soldiers. Now we knew him to be on the brink of exhaustion.

So the Centre left Anthony Blunt alone. We requested no more services from him and we left him in peace to pursue his studies. In 1947, in addition to his job as Surveyor of the King's Pictures, he became director of the immensely prestigious Courtauld Institute, which specializes in the study of art history; and he conferred some of his own international stature on it.

As for John Cairncross, the Carelian, he, too, was demobilized in 1945 and returned to his former job at the Treasury. He did not break contact with the KGB, though his unsatisfactory relationship with Milovzorov, his new handler following the departure of Krechin, led him to give us less and less material.

In 1947, my superiors had the idea of sending me to London to process the material provided by our British agents on the spot. Over four years I had become the principal expert in our section on the agents referred to admiringly within the KGB as the Cambridge Five. Moreover, I was now thoroughly conversant with the Foreign Office's style of work, and I knew how to translate the hundreds of dispatches that found their way through to us every month.

The KGB had very few intelligence operatives abroad at that time. Many agents had been shot before the war during Stalin's purges, and now we were leery of sending people out of the Soviet Union for fear of defections. Most of our officers worked in Moscow, with the result that the few men posted in foreign countries had a work-load so crushing that many of them cracked under the pressure. They all longed to come home, even though conditions in the Soviet Union were far from blissful. It was a very Russian longing, and our superiors understood it only too well. They were allowed to return; but they also had to be replaced.

When I was asked if I would agree to a London posting, I immediately said yes. Koghen told me that I would not be given a diplomatic job, given that the Foreign Affairs Ministry (MID) would not agree to this. I would be officially employed as a cipher clerk, hardly a prestigious occupation but one which I would have to accept: relations at the time between the KGB and the Foreign Affairs Ministry were not good. If the Central Committee ordered the MID to issue someone a diplomatic passport, they would do so, but with very bad grace. On the other hand, the relationship between the KGB and our ambassador to London, Georgi Mikhailovich Zaroubin, was excellent.

My superiors were able to solve most of the immediate problems connected with my transfer, but a few persisted. The first was that a cipher clerk was not supposed to know the local language; hence I would have to conceal my knowledge of English from the rest of the embassy staff. Second, I was not supposed to go alone because cipher clerks are meant to be sent in groups of two or three, so they can keep an eye on one another. Alone, they are relatively easy marks for the opposition secret services. And last, cipher clerks were forbidden all contact with foreigners, something which would hardly make my work any easier. Nevertheless I was young and I didn't give a damn about these obstacles. I told myself I would take them in my stride as soon as I got to London.

So I left for the British capital on 29 June 1947, by way of Paris. My wife and my small daughter came with me – but I was allowed to travel without any other cipher clerks.

Chapter 5

ENCOUNTERS IN LONDON

My transfer to London was made as easy as possible by my superiors, who contacted our ambassador, Zaroubin, on one of his trips to Moscow. The KGB insisted that the embassy give me a free hand to meet all the foreigners I liked. Zaroubin raised no objection.

In Paris, the negotiations over the Marshall Plan, the US scheme for according aid to post-war Europe, were at their height when my wife, Anna, and I arrived on the plane from Moscow, via Warsaw. As soon as we got off the aircraft at Le Bourget, I realized that we were thoroughly conspicuous. We were so different from Westerners, if only in our dress. The second shock came with the realization that people here seemed to be living very well. We had been brought up on official propaganda; we had been convinced that the French and the British were groaning in misery, that poverty was rife and that Russia, the motherland of Socialism, was the only country on earth where folk could live decently without corrupt American gold. The lights of Paris, the gorgeous shop windows, the traffic jams and the cars in the Champs-Élysées struck us dumb.

Hordes of Marshall Plan negotiators had so saturated the city that we were unable to find a room in any of the more reasonably priced Paris hotels, with the result that our compatriots had to put us up in the embassy, on the Rue de Grenelle. There was a problem, however. In the aeroplane my wife's milk had abruptly dried up, with the result that when we arrived our four-month-old baby was very hungry.

Molotov himself arrived in Paris on the same day as we, to head the Soviet negotiating team. He was lodged in the usual manner at the embassy. The first night my daughter shrieked so furiously and continuously that nobody within earshot could sleep a wink. She was hungry, poor mite. Molotov, whose bedroom was just below ours, complained to the ambassador, who grudgingly rented a suite for us at the Grand Hôtel de la Paix facing the Opéra, one of the best hotels in Paris. He had to lay out a considerable sum so that Molotov could sleep properly and arrive spry at the negotiating table next day.

This incident has since became a stock joke in my family, my daughter being the girl who sabotaged the Soviet Union's negotiations over the Marshall Plan!

We were told to take the train to Calais at the Gare du Nord, and then proceed to London. We had first-class tickets, the significance of which I did not at first grasp; so we queued with the other ordinary passengers, while the first-class ticket holders breezed through customs unmolested. Luckily, our porter took control, bundling us on to the train just as it was moving off. Without him we should undoubtedly have missed it.

In our compartment we found a respectable Italian couple, elderly and obviously very wealthy. At lunchtime we cheerfully jabbed our fingers at the menu, selecting a few dishes at random about which we knew strictly nothing. The steward brought the food, which we wolfed down with deep delight. As I cleared the last mouthful off my plate, smacking my lips, I saw that our neighbours hadn't touched their food. They sat there with frozen faces, speechless, eyes lowered.

When the steward came to remove the plates, I realized what had happened. He had given us the food the Italians had ordered, and vice versa. The interesting thing was that our fellow passengers, seeing that we were Russian, had preferred not to rectify the steward's mistake. I wondered why.

We were beginning to understand that life in Europe was far from simple, and that we had much to learn. Chastened, we arrived at Victoria Station.

This was my second visit to London; the first time I had come at the end of the war as a member of the Soviet delegation, to take part in a youth congress. I could lay no claim to any knowledge of the city.

We were surprised at the long queue for a taxi, and the milling crowds. At the airport in Moscow, foreigners were always given priority – the taxis were for them, and the locals came afterwards, if there were any taxis left. In England, everyone seemed to be treated equally, a fact which stunned us. On the other hand, as soon as the others in the queue saw that we had a baby – they could hardly fail to notice her, since she urgently needed changing and was screaming at the top of her lungs – they had the man in charge bundle us into the first available vehicle.

When I think back on that time, the word that mostly comes to mind is 'disarray'. That's what we felt, as we set about making sense of our new life abroad. My employers had taken a big risk letting us loose as they did: our loyalty to our country may not have been in doubt, but our ability to melt into the crowd certainly was.

At the beginning of our stay in London, I stuck out like a sore thumb. People stared at me. I couldn't possibly have arranged to meet an agent and done so unremarked. When I analyse my English début, I have to admit that both Anna, my wife, and I were hopelessly young and naïve. The difference in living standards between the Soviet Union and the West was so gigantic, that for us, coming to London was like arriving on another planet. To paraphrase an old Russian proverb, it was a while before the London dogs stopped barking at Modin.

Ambassador Zaroubin greeted me warmly, but in the first days he had little time to spare, being wholly engrossed by the meeting of foreign ministers in Paris. It was vital for our side to be informed of the position of each state involved, and to know what was going on behind the various closed doors. Sixteen countries had already accepted the US plan, while several others – notably Poland and Czechoslovakia within the Soviet zone – were tempted to accept the manna from heaven proffered by the Americans. Stalin refused out of hand to contemplate this possibility. The KGB was stretched to the limit, and the demands on our agents in London were heavier than ever because Molotov wanted to know everything in advance. He flew into blind rages when he felt he was not sufficiently informed.

'Why,' he roared, 'why are there no documents?'

'Comrade, because neither London nor Washington has yet received word from Paris. Even they know no more than we do!'

In fact, Molotov had no reason to be dissatisfied with the KGB. On one occasion he received London's and Washington's full instructions to the Allied delegations *before they did*; I shall go into the details of that later.

In mid-July, Molotov walked out of the Paris conference, declaring that the Marshall Plan was a plot to rob the countries concerned of their economic independence. Peace returned to our London embassy. Zaroubin called me in for a long discussion. He knew exactly what I had come to do in England; but for form's sake he confronted me with a former translator of Stalin's, Pavlov by name, who tested my competence in English. Pavlov concluded that I was average, but prescribed daily visits to the cinema for a few weeks, so I could get used to the various expressions in current use. The prospect delighted me – in that period I saw a wide variety of thrillers, war films, spy films and home-grown British comedies. I hunted down my favourite actors and actresses: Olivier, Garbo, Vivien Leigh. I gorged myself on movies and picked up a lot of English in the process.

The ambassador quickly understood that I would be of no use whatever as a cipher clerk. Without asking anyone's opinion on the matter, he quietly appointed me an embassy attaché and moved me to an office close to his own. Then, as a trial run, he had me accompany the Soviet delegation attending the negotiations at Lancaster House on the future of Italy's ex-colonies. The USSR was not directly concerned with the problems of Abyssinia, Somalia and Libya, but still we were instructed to find out as much as we could about what was going on. We were especially interested in the attitudes of the countries involved, namely, Italy, Britain and to a lesser extent the United States and France.

We needed to find out what was being said in camera, what the various bilateral agreements were, who was double-crossing whom among the Allies, so that we could manipulate the situation to our own advantage. By the judicious use of disinformation, and by supporting each of the two parties in turn, Molotov was able to obtain concessions from both sides on completely unrelated matters.

I took part in several conferences, along with Zaroubin himself and his private secretary. All I did was sit back and listen.

Shortly afterwards, I was shifted to the press corps to handle relations with journalists, a key post which allowed me to make any amount of useful contacts. I made no attempt, obviously, to win anybody over to our side, but from time to time I was able to obtain information from journalists before it got into print, and this was useful to the Centre.

In the first months of my London posting, Mikhail Alexandrovich

Chichkin, my immediate superior, introduced me to an American correspondent called Russell.

We quickly made friends; Russell was a charming man who had won himself something of a reputation in newspaper circles, having been in London since the outbreak of the war. He had nothing of the usual American bombast and he viewed the Russians as staunch allies. I always enjoyed talking to him. He asked me questions about Lancaster House, and I asked him questions of my own, some of them naïve in the extreme, about the way the British lived and how their minds worked. We also discussed more serious matters such as the fate of the Central European countries and the territories recovered after the defeat of the Nazis, and relations between the victims now that the war was over. Russell occasionally made fun of me, but he did sincerely try to help me understand the point of view of the British and the Americans. When we talked politics, I'm afraid I behaved like a bureaucrat to the bone. I trotted out the official Moscow line and vigorously defended it. In retrospect I can see what a fool I must have made of myself, and it was all the worse because I viewed this as a kind of trial by fire. I was learning how not to let fall my jack-in-office mask, even under pressure.

Russell, who was paralysed for life in a road accident a few months later, helped me in one crucial way. He introduced me to several of his friends, who included the editor of *The Times*. Quite apart from journalism, Russell possessed a political dimension which interested me greatly; and it was he who first took me to the inner sanctum of the Athenaeum, the exclusive London club, where my knowledge of the British improved by leaps and bounds. He also took me to some excellent restaurants and initiated me into the pleasures of the table, which had hitherto been beyond my reach.

Thanks to these contacts, I learned how to ask questions (a real art), how to stay abreast of political developments and, most important of all, how to give answers without coming unstuck and without revealing anything vital. This is a mechanism of double-talk which has to be learned the hard way. For example, my friend from *The Times* knew I was an assistant member of the Soviet delegation to the conference on the former Italian colonies. He, too, was interested in what was going on there, and not only in the line of his official work, I believe. I had very little to tell him, because I wasn't a party to any secrets, but as far as I was concerned, it was good practice to allow him to think I knew more than I did and to answer his questions blandly.

Later I learned how to contact people on my own initiative, especially journalists, and how to talk to them. I loved the work, and when I was eventually moved to the diplomatic section, I continued to deal with press affairs. It was an official cover that suited me perfectly.

To begin with, my wife and I lived at the embassy, because all cipher clerks were supposed to reside where they could be easily watched. Then the ambassador told me I had better find myself a flat in town.

This was a mark of trust which I appreciated. For the time being we took a very expensive two-room apartment in the centre of London and shortly afterwards set about looking for another one at a more reasonable rent. We wanted to stay within range of the embassy, which would be good for my work, and also because Anna felt she would be safer that way. So she put on her white blouse and navy blue dress and went off looking for lodgings. There was a quiet, sunny street just behind the embassy that particularly attracted her. She was walking down it, looking at the houses one by one, when a man accosted her and asked what she was doing. Quite naturally she replied that she was flat-hunting; that her husband worked at the Soviet Embassy round the corner and that she thought this street would suit her fine.

The man muttered something under his breath and went away. That evening Anna told me about her day and mentioned the encounter. I had her describe the house in question, which was, as I well knew, an MI5 address that our own services were fully aware of. Their surveillance teams used it on a routine basis. Anna had walked straight into the arms of the enemy.

Eventually she found a place in Bassett Road, in North Kensington, just as comfortable as the first but a good deal less expensive, and we moved there directly.

We had scarcely settled in our new quarters when someone knocked on the door one mid-morning while I was out at work. He was wearing a postman's uniform and he held out a letter to Anna, asking her if she knew the name written on it. She said no and closed the door. I realized we had just received our first provocation from the British Secret Service. Had Anna admitted knowing the name, it would have been quite simple for MI5 to compromise the person in question.

My wife was regularly followed throughout our time in London, sometimes so blatantly that on several occasions she was tempted to say good morning to her pursuers. After a while it began to get on her nerves, and she mentioned it to Zaroubin one evening in my presence. She wanted him to make an official protest over such lack of diplomatic courtesy. Zaroubin just laughed.

'Certainly not,' he said. 'I'm very happy they're following you, because while they're doing that they'll probably leave Yuri alone.'

In general, our relations with the British were extremely cordial. Their way of life suited us very well, and I for one find it hard to speak ill of them. They are suspicious and reserved when they don't know you, but as soon as they have accepted you as someone who lives up to their own standards, there are no more loyal friends than the British.

In Bassett Road we had two old ladies, very English, for neighbours. To begin with they were less than forthcoming. But when they saw that we lived perfectly normally, that we bade them good day when we met on the stairs and that we had absolutely no snow on our boots, they became courteous, kindly and helpful – even though they knew quite well that we were from the Soviet Union, then so feared and abused by their country's press. The Cold War had entered its first stage. Mr Churchill had declared in the previous year that an 'iron curtain' had fallen across Europe. The climate of Anglo–Russian friendship was glacial, and my wife often had occasion to notice it in her day-to-day existence, with tradespeople and others. There was a phobia about Soviet spies, every Russian was a potential KGB agent and the newspapers picked up on the slightest rumour. I remember reading pages and pages in the press about some wretched Russian discus champion who was caught red-handed stealing clothes from a C&A store.

Personally I was happy as a lark, though it was hard at first for my wife because I was hardly ever at home. When I came back, often late at night, she was asleep, and I was gone so early in the mornings that she was seldom up before my departure. During the long evenings she spent alone reading her English literature, Anna was constantly on the *qui vive*. I never told her what I was up to, but she knew instinctively that there was danger involved.

141

She liked to go to the big parks with our daughter, especially to Hyde Park. She looked more English than Russian by then, and she blended in easily with the nannies and mothers pushing their prams along the paths. One of her favourite spots was the Round Pond, where she spent hours watching the old people pushing out their exquisite model sailing boats. One day a woman came up to her and asked her if she wasn't one of the Churchill family? seeing as our daughter was 'the spitting image of dear old Winnie'.

By the autumn of 1947, Anna had begun to be seriously bored. She loathed the awful London weather, with its smog and drizzle. Consequently, work was found for her in the embassy's translation section and the baby was given to a nurse to look after.

I was working flat out by then, sometimes till 2 a.m. There were only three of us available to handle the huge volume of information pouring in from the Cambridge Five and from our other agents in England. The task involved long hours of concentration, because we were processing quantities of top-secret intelligence, only now it came in the form of real documents, not photographs. I was working on the very same diplomatic papers that were being exchanged between London and Washington.

There was so much material that we had to tell our agents to concentrate on matters of high importance only.

Then a set of new directives arrived from Moscow, which had the effect of turning the London residence upside down. In effect, the ambassador was given co-responsibility for the KGB in all intelligence matters. From now on both he and the official KGB resident had to answer for what we did, and Zaroubin himself had to deal with the Lubyanka as well as with the Foreign Affairs ministry in Moscow.

The goal of this initiative was to deepen our diplomats' involvement in intelligence. Zaroubin deeply disapproved of his new function, but he had no alternative but to comply. Thereafter he had to stay late in his office to be sure our work was proceeding normally, a responsibility that took a heavy toll on him. He would leave the embassy only when the last officer had returned safely from his mission.

Once Zaroubin had to wait up till 3 a.m. for me, at a time when I knew him to be more than usually anxious. My job that night had been a somewhat risky undertaking. When I slipped quietly into my office he heard me, rushed down the corridor and burst in, white-faced. I reassured him that everything had gone according to plan, and he was so relieved that he burst into tears and clasped me to his bosom. I was a little taken aback, and then had to repress a desperate desire to laugh: I realized that this dapper, meticulous diplomat, whose suits were always impeccable and whose shirts were invariably snowy white, had forgotten to put his false teeth back in his mouth when he came rushing out to see me. He must have dozed off in his office.

Eventually Zaroubin understood that if this went on he would collapse from stress; so he simply ignored the new directives. After a while he ceased to interfere in KGB business, except for questions of real importance. This was a great relief to everyone concerned.

In intelligence terms, it was a time of unbelievable abundance, and if Zaroubin had had the slightest inkling of the risks we were running, he would have died of heart failure. Burgess, operating from his post as Hector McNeil's private secretary, was supplying regular consignments, giving us full access to the documents of a number of parliamentary committees and to the secrets of the Ministry of Defence.

Going over all this required unfailing concentration. I wore gloves to avoid leaving fingerprints on the paper, and translated the texts with all the accuracy I could muster. I typed the transcripts up myself, stamped them and passed them on to the KGB resident for signature. They were then put into cipher and telegrammed to the Centre, while the borrowed document was returned to the safe or desk it had come from. Naturally there were risks inherent in this procedure, but our agents didn't always have the equipment to take photographs, and the Xerox machine – that godsend to spies the world over – was not yet in commercial production.

The KGB's London resident, Nicolai Borisovich Rodin, alias Korovin, taught me a lot. His posting was a temporary one but nevertheless he remained in London until 1952. He was a very able man, though at times a thoroughly disagreeable one. He was also a heavy drinker, but this did not deter him from his professional duty, and he shared his long experience of intelligence with me. For one thing, he knew the British extraordinarily well and could judge how they would behave in every instance. To begin with, we got on well: he was a true professional and I respected that. During the war he had been the head of the liaison residence, an outfit whose function was to co-ordinate the military information accumulated by our agents worldwide. He had already worked in London in an intelligence capacity and was an expert at organizing contacts with our agents. The security rules he devised were tried and true: we never once had a serious problem in this regard. Korovin taught me his methods, which I passed on to others in later years.

Unfortunately, Korovin managed to antagonize most of the embassy staff in very short order. His peremptory army officer's manner irritated people. I already had a working knowledge of the type of man he was, and I knew how to deal with him, but my colleagues, many of whom had been well out of the line of fire during the war, were not so long-suffering.

Later on, I, too, came into conflict with Korovin, because as time went by I began to see him as the very prototype of a blinkered bureaucrat, arrogant and contemptuous of his subordinates. Was the cold mask he wore a deliberate ploy to hide his real thoughts? I was baffled by Korovin, until the day I understood that every agent wore a mask, myself included . . .

Korovin treated our humble translation work with supercilious distaste. He told us he had been sent to Europe to take part in conferences laying the groundwork for a new world order. And he was, if nothing else, a genius at intelligence-gathering, completely at home with the other international experts. He knew how to make the best use of the periods of idleness between sessions, the cocktail parties, the official receptions. He made good contacts and his list of acquaintances included everyone who was anyone in the profession. From time to time he would let me tag along; we went often to Paris, where I found myself confined to my hotel room or to an office on the Rue de Grenelle, churning out translations of documents for Korovin to send back to the Lubyanka. Whenever we had a little spare time, we walked together in the parks and talked.

'Yuri, when the NKVD recruited you, surely you asked to be allowed to complete your studies after the war?'

'Yes, of course. But in 1946, when I reminded them of that, they said it was out of the question for the time being. There was just too much work on hand.'

I confided that I didn't plan to spend the rest of my life in the intelligence world. In a few years, I said hopefully, I meant to go back to Moscow and become a teacher. Korovin roared with laughter. I knew then that my life was entirely wedded to the secret service. I would never, never get out.

While we were in Paris, Korovin told me about the worsening relations between Cairncross and his handler, Milovzorov. Something had to be done. I knew all too well that Cairncross was no longer productive, but I held my tongue about that; at the same time I had noted that Milovzorov was also on the wrong side of Korovin himself. The two men had the same rank, but Korovin had come up through military intelligence, while Milovzorov was a counter-espionage man. In any event, Milovzorov had failed to keep the Carelian operational. He had recruited a number of Americans and Britons in his time, but his working procedures, while acceptable in wartime or with low-level agents, were inappropriate now. Milovzorov had come to London mainly to take care of Cairncross; the other major agents were Korovin's exclusive province. Milovzorov's harsh, offensive way of giving orders was utterly unsuited to our star agents. You couldn't tell Anthony Blunt to do this or that. You couldn't speak sharply to a man like Kim Philby. And you certainly couldn't make a firm rendezvous with Guy Burgess and then, for no good reason, fail to show.

Cairncross heartily disliked Milovzorov and had told Korovin as much. Korovin, like the perfect functionary he was, looked at the matter closely, then produced a devastating report which shot Milovzorov down in flames. He showed it to me. A week later, the decision to recall him to Moscow was made. This took place in October 1947.

Korovin called me into his office and broached the subject of our most precious agents. He touched on their importance to the Centre and to the leaders of the Soviet Union. He also insisted that no country on earth had as effective a network of agents within the opposition's camp as we did, and that one of the main advantages of our British contingent was that they were working for an ideal, not for money. Without the least allusion to Milovzorov, he explained that our methods were not always properly adjusted to the sensitivities of these men, who were exceptional individuals. Korovin believed that they should be handled with far greater subtlety, by someone who knew and understood their way of thinking. I began to see what he was leading up to.

'Yuri Ivanovich,' he concluded pompously, 'I want *you* to take charge of the Carelian.'

I wasn't wild about this idea, being only too well aware that my practical experience of intelligence work in the field was virtually nil. Korovin had anticipated this.

'In any event, it's you or nobody. We have no other officers in London remotely capable of working with him, and I wouldn't want Moscow to pitch in with some unknown. Any more mistakes like that and we'll lose the whole ring, mark my words.'

My impression was that he intended to try me out with Cairncross. If I did well, he would hand over the others, too: and this, in effect, was what happened. The truth was that Korovin no longer wanted to shoulder personal responsibility for the Cambridge Five – the job was no longer good enough for him. He would let me conduct the day-to-day business with them, while he stayed in the background to give the orders.

The next time we met, he favoured me with quantities of useful advice. Before unleashing me, he said, he wanted me to know as much as possible about the Carelian, and he gave me several days to prepare my first meeting with that shadowy figure. For my part, now that the die was cast I was eager to meet the agent whose dispatches I had pored over for three long years in Moscow. Would he be anything like what I imagined? I would soon know.

The second time I met Cairncross – I have already described the first – he was half an hour late. I realized that Korovin's warnings were justified: the man had an appalling memory, a grave handicap to our work together. He would regularly forget the hour, even the place, of our rendezvous. As a precaution I decided to set him up with at least two back-up meetings. For example, if he failed to turn up at Hammersmith Grove on either 15 or 16 November, we would meet exactly a week later in the same place.

Everything had to be carefully arranged to cover all eventualities. As a rule I chose locations in the outer areas of London such as Richmond Park or Wandsworth; we avoided the centre, the docks and the East End. The places I chose were always easy to find and remember, but still Cairncross became muddled: for example, he would go to some point we had settled on for the preceding month. This drove me mad with rage, but I had to put up with it.

Apart from the problems with time and place, my relations with Cairncross were very good. I quickly established a positive rapport between us; I made it clear that my first priority was his safety and that I had complete confidence in him. This was deeply appreciated – Cairncross agonized about getting caught and talked about it whenever we met, though he seemed sublimely unaware of the risks he ran by being so vague.

When he was working with Milovzorov, the most elementary rules of spy work were completely disregarded. It was frankly insane to meet in pubs and pass documents across beer-soaked tables. I have never done that. In a pub anybody can see what you're doing, and there's always the danger of being recognized. It's better to glimpse one another in a pub, go out separately, and meet at a prearranged point some way away.

In the first months of our collaboration, there were a number of slip-ups. Cairncross missed each rendezvous in turn and mixed up all the dates. This made it very difficult for me to get back in touch with him. There was no question of my going to his home or telephoning him: both these options were strictly against the rules and would anyway have been extraordinarily foolhardy. I, therefore, had to exercise superhuman patience and spend days waiting for my agent in the open, hoping to waylay him en route between his office and his home. And even then we ran a considerable risk, because I had to improvise, something we hate doing in our profession. Moreover, it's not always easy to track down a single individual among the crowds of London office workers surging homeward after nightfall on a winter's evening.

As a general rule we met in the evening, when Cairncross would hand over his documents; during the night we photographed them all, and they would be handed back to him very early the next morning. This happened once a month. From time to time we urgently needed more information about specific items, and then the contact would be increased from once a month to once every two weeks. Of course, this new place had to be arranged, and as always when Cairncross was involved, it was no easy matter to change the agreed schedule.

I took care to write out a list of ten to fifteen questions in advance of our meetings. These I learned by heart, and then destroyed. I also spent a lot of time framing my queries as carefully as possible: as Dostoyevsky says, 'What matters most is not what people say but how they say it.' The crucial thing was to formulate my comments in such a way that my agent believed the initiative had come not from me but from himself.

This worked perfectly with Cairncross, because I knew at the outset that he was ready to do his utmost to help.

His job at the Treasury was not particularly interesting to us, and Cairncross knew it. The second time we met he explained that he was no longer in a position to supply information of the same quality as before. I fully understood this, and I took him at his word; even had he been lying, there was nothing I could do about it. There was no point in pressuring him. I adopted a different tack.

'Can you get hold of a list of internal ministry phone numbers?'

'Of course I can.' Cairncross looked at me askance. 'What would be the point of that? There's nothing to be had from telephone numbers.'

'I know. It's only that they usually come side by side with office numbers, and office numbers might be interesting.'

Now he understood.

'I see. You want to know exactly where my office is located. Nothing could be simpler.'

The list duly arrived and I set to work analysing the management structure of the Treasury, who worked in what section and who did what. I also located Cairncross's own office, and found out the names and functions of the people in his immediate vicinity. One in particular interested me, a man working in a mysterious 'Section PPB-21'. I wanted to know more.

Cairncross, as it happened, knew this individual well: they had worked together for years. He was nominally involved in 'training work', but in fact his speciality was atomic energy. When Cairncross told me this, I gave him a long stare. He burst out laughing.

We immediately concentrated on this new line of investigation. When did Cairncross's colleague arrive in his office, what time did he go out to lunch? Cairncross didn't know, but he had noticed that the man had a safe in his office, and that he sometimes left papers lying loose on his desk when he went out.

I directed him to find out all the details he could, and before long we knew that on some days he didn't appear at work at all, and on others he habitually left early. Thus we could operate at leisure.

Cairncross had no difficulty whatever in obtaining the keys to the safe, and in having them copied. The next step was to remove the documents for photographing. To cut the risk to a minimum, I suggested that he take the pictures himself, on the spot. It's much easier, after all, to walk out of an office with a roll of film in one's pocket than to stagger past the reception desk with a case full of files. To this end I obtained a beautiful little American camera and told him to practise at home on newspapers. This was a total failure. Either he photographed the top of the document, or he just got the bottom or one side, and if by some miracle he got the frame right, then the picture was invariably overexposed or out of focus. With the best will in the world, Cairncross was the least mechanically minded man I have ever known. After a series of failures, each more dismal than the last, he humbly gave back the camera.

So we would have to remove the documents after all. I would pick them up in the usual way in the evening, get them photographed during the night, and early next morning Cairncross would put them back in the safe.

At first glance, the kind of information that was obtainable from the Treasury, even when it concerned atomic energy, might seem to be of only minor interest to us. What, after all, was the use of lists of figures and accounts of expenditure? However, I already knew that His Majesty's Treasury had standard accounting procedures rather different from our own in the Soviet Union. Not a shilling was allowed to leave the State coffers without full justification. Every item of expenditure had to be specified down to the last detail. When we obtained the documents on atomic energy, we would find full descriptions of each transaction opposite the relevant figure. Briefly, this meant we would have a complete account of work done, research undertaken and materials purchased within the British atomic energy programme. And this interested us no end.

A date had been set and we were on the point of going into action when Cairncross was transferred without warning to another department. The operation would have to be carried out in a great hurry – and we decided against it. But this disappointment was quickly mitigated when the Carelian told me what his new job was: he had been delegated to a section that dealt with the defence industry and the armed forces budget, as well as with future expenditure on weapons and military research programmes. We had failed by a whisker in our first initiative together, but now I was convinced that luck would favour us. I was right: Cairncross began supplying a steady stream of files on every aspect of the financing of the British Army, the Royal Navy and the RAF, along with specific data on his country's war budget – notably the economic contingencies to be planned should war break out with the Soviet Union.

I was overjoyed by the quality of this information. We now knew exactly how much money had been set aside to build tanks and aeroplanes, and how much was slated for nuclear research. All of this was of capital importance to our own military.

My work with Cairncross had begun auspiciously, and the harvest we had reaped together was more than satisfactory to my superiors. In consequence Korovin decided to assign me a second British agent, Guy Burgess, known then to the KGB as Paul. Again, I had been steeped for years in the facts of Burgess's career, and now I was at last to meet him face to face.

Korovin, in his tiresome way, called me in for another avuncular briefing. Burgess, he said, was a far more difficult character than I imagined. I was to watch him like a hawk. I knew this already, just as I knew that despite his brilliance Burgess could be an unmitigated bastard if he thought he was being treated without the respect he felt was due him. I was quite sure that Gorsky, code-named Henry, would have succeeded even more spectacularly with Burgess had he been a little less self-important and blinkered in his dealings. What I knew about Burgess boiled down to this: he was a rogue, but a phenomenally brilliant one; he was ready to die for the cause; he was reliable in a tight corner; and he was the only member of the group who could bring all the others together in one place.

I racked my brains for the most appropriate way to deal with Burgess. I planned to be fairly meek, not to impose too much on him but to show him all the same that I could be firm when I needed to be.

We had our first meeting in the autumn of 1947. It was eight in the evening, at dusk. The venue was an outlying part of London, the weather was fine and you could see people clearly a long way off. I waited alone at a crossing: exactly on time, I saw Korovin approaching with my new charge. After the briefest of introductions, Korovin turned on his heel and left us together; no doubt he had left his car nearby, a risky thing to do. Burgess and I walked off side by side.

He carried himself well, a handsome man in fine clothes, starched shirt collar, gleaming shoes and well-cut overcoat. He was the image of a smooth British aristocrat, with a free and easy manner and a firm step. In the half darkness, his face was barely visible.

I introduced myself briefly. There was a pause, then I said, 'I'm new to this business; you are much more experienced than I; I very much hope you will help me along.'

Burgess said nothing, but made a quick gesture of acknowledgement with his hand. I asked if it would suit him to meet again the following week, in the little square we happened to be walking through at that moment. He agreed to this and we parted.

He was once again right on time for the second rendezvous. I saw him a long way off, wandering tranquilly among the trees, a folded newspaper under his arm. We got down to work immediately. I told him I thought we should meet regularly, and in conditions of absolute security. He assured me that he was an old hand at this. Our first disagreement arose, however, when he suggested we meet in one of his favourite pubs. This was out of the question and I explained how exposed I felt when going into a pub. He laughed aloud, the frank, ringing laugh I was later to know so well. Then he informed me that he was as allergic to the suburbs as I was to pubs – he positively hated leaving the centre of London.

'Guy,' I said, 'I not only loathe pubs, I also understand that to meet in them is to fly in the face of the most elementary rules of security. If you don't like it, write a letter to my superiors and complain. But I will not meet you in Soho, the way my predecessors did.'

Soho, with its restaurants, nightclubs and teeming streets, has always been heavily policed. It was also where Guy Burgess hung out with his homosexual friends. He insisted as a matter of principle and because he wanted to see whether I was able to counter him without antagonizing him.

'You know better than anyone,' I told him, 'that we Russians are closely watched by the British services at all times. Before the war the Germans were enemy number one: now it's us.'

I carried my point: from now on, we would meet in streets, parks and squares, never at bars. I went on to tackle the delicate question of what to do should we be stopped and questioned by the police or by MI5.

I suggested, a bit lamely, that we should say I was lost and was asking him the way. Obviously nobody would believe this, but it might win us a few precious minutes to gather our wits. When an agent gets caught cold, he is, for a few moments, in serious danger of losing control and falling prey to panic. Many agents, overwhelmed by stress, have betrayed themselves completely in those first instants – especially if interrogated by a skilled professional. Again Burgess laughed his ringing laugh and looked me straight in the eye.

'I've a better idea. You're a good-looking boy, and I'm a fiend known all over London for my insatiable appetite for good-looking boys. All we need say is we're lovers and looking for a bed.'

I was young enough to blush to the roots of my hair. Burgess chuckled with glee.

'But, Guy,' I said, 'I'm a diplomat. It's not done . . . I'm a married man.'

'You'd do anything for the cause, now, wouldn't you? And in the time it'll take them to check up on this, we'll be back in the saddle.'

I changed the subject hastily.

So began a long and fruitful collaboration which was to last a full three years. During all that time Guy Burgess was punctual to a fault, took all the customary precautions and again and again gave proof of his excellent memory. He was a welcome change in this regard, after poor Cairncross.

On the other hand, Burgess was a man who stood out in any crowd, and this was far from a good thing in our profession. His shoes fascinated me: I never saw such unbelievably shiny ones, before or since. His shirt was always as perfectly white as at our first meeting. But as I got to know him better, I noticed that his jacket and trousers tended to be stained and wrinkled, and he never seemed to have them pressed. His clothes were definitely odd; they caught the attention of people in the street and, on occasion, of the police. I never could fathom why he looked like a tramp at close quarters, even though his clothes came from the best tailor in London.

Each time we met, I prepared between twelve and fifteen questions for him to answer. Since it was hard for me to remember them all, I developed a system whereby I noted each one on paper with a symbol of its own.

To my surprise Burgess turned out to be an extremely conscientious worker. He answered my questions as best he could. He took no notes, because his memory was faultless: for example, he could remember word for word something you asked him three months earlier. And from the first he treated me with kindness and consideration. When he passed me documents, he unfailingly told me which should be sent to the Centre without delay, and which could wait till later.

Sometimes, when we had run through our various professional chores, we had time to talk of other things; and this was how I eventually came to know him well.

From the start, Guy Burgess saw himself as a consummate secret agent. He bore no resemblance to the ordinary types who followed people, played the informer and picked up bits of intelligence here and there. His task, he believed, was far finer and nobler. He wasn't working for the Soviet Union as such; he was in the vanguard of world revolution. His reasons for collaborating with us were truly ideological and I thought that most admirable. I always hated agents who took money.

Guy Burgess believed that world revolution was inevitable. Like his Cambridge friends, he saw Russia as the forward base of that revolution. There was no alternative, of course: he might have his reservations about Russia's domestic and foreign politics, and I often heard him berating our leaders, but in the end he saw the Soviet Union as the world's best hope. He and his friends were sure that one day soon our country would provide itself with honest leaders more interested in questions of real importance to the world than in their own perks and privileges.

When I asked him what he thought of the USSR when he went there in 1934, he laughed.

'Well, I told everyone who would listen that I was disgusted by Russia. That was a lie, of course, but all the same I admit what I saw was a far cry from what I had imagined Russia would be like. Still, I was impressed. The sheer energy and enthusiasm I saw still make me believe in the enormous reserve of strength your country possesses.'

I saw Burgess turn and turn about with Blunt, at intervals of about a month. I had read in an internal KGB report at our London residence that Paul didn't care to see a job through to the end, that he was superficial and that he lacked firmness and perseverance. The truth was, his original turn of mind drove him to initiate so many ideas and projects that he couldn't possibly accomplish them all himself. He confided his ideas to other people, to his friends in the Foreign

Office and to us as far as his secret work was concerned. Some of our KGB officers suspected that he was liable to panic under pressure. This was absurd. I never heard of a single instance when Burgess panicked.

He was a naturally gifted analyst. He would say, 'This is a very complex, very important problem; I don't know how we can possibly resolve it.' Then he would discuss all the ramifications, and what might have seemed simple to me at first glance turned out to be far more intricate. He had greater insight than I, he knew how to recognize hidden difficulties and, what was more, he knew how to explain them to me. Though the Centre appreciated Paul's work, it was ambivalent in its attitude towards him, because other reports contained harsh judgements of him. Some officers even wrote that he was a coward, a ridiculous assertion. He was cautious in the extreme; before any important decision, he took plenty of time to think, seeking the advice of his friends and anybody else who was competent to help. When problems were particularly thorny, he called in his friend Philby. Some of my colleagues saw his delays as proof that he was an ineffectual ditherer (probably because they themselves were that way inclined, and stupid into the bargain). They couldn't grasp Burgess's real value. Nonetheless, it wasn't hard to see that he was highly intelligent and energetic, full of initiative and above all ready to help a friend at the drop of a hat. In fact he was prepared to risk his life for his friends.

Sometimes the Centre would try to make me see my agents more often than was necessary. I mentioned this to Korovin.

'Give us useful, properly thought-out missions,' I begged him. 'We can run around seeing our agents every half-hour, but the more we do that, the more dangerous it will be. We should pare down the meetings to a strict minimum – though if you really want me to, I can set up contacts twice a day.'

At various times I did in fact meet Burgess on a daily basis.

We had worked out an ingenious method of receiving his information when developing events required virtually continual contact.

Paul would dial a telephone number. The phone would be manned day and night by an agent, to whom Burgess gave a code number before hanging up. The code meant that within the hour we would meet at a prearranged rendezvous. Korovin or I went to this rendezvous, where Burgess would be waiting to pass on the information he had picked up, either verbally or in the form of documents.

We used this system in November 1947 during the conference in London between representatives of France, Great Britain, the United States and the Benelux countries, like the conference in Paris earlier that year convened to discuss vital post-war matters ranging from the future of Germany to the Marshall Plan. The Soviets, who were not invited, saw this event as a distinctly unfriendly manoeuvre aimed at undermining the Potsdam agreements.

Moscow had fired off several notes of protest and Molotov was ranting in his office. He clamoured for fresh information every day. And we were able to provide it. At one point he became seriously overwrought when he spotted a provision in which the British and the Americans appeared to disagree over the future status of Berlin. He wished to know how they planned to get around this.

The two delegations had adjourned the session until the following day, on some irrelevant pretext. The meeting had hardly broken up before the British and American representatives were on the telephone to their respective governments. Molotov, in his usual way, harassed the KGB for results.

'Do what you like,' he said, 'but I must know what they're saying to their chiefs. And I also need to know what London and Washington are telling them to do next. And I want this information by six o'clock tonight.'

The situation hung fire for a while. The two governments were clearly failing to agree. Molotov's impatience grew by the minute.

Burgess called late that night and gave the agreed code. Korovin met him. I don't know what the substance of the message was, but the fact is that Molotov received the information well before the British delegates, who had to wait until they convened the following day.

On the insistence of the Centre, I gave some money to Guy Burgess so he could buy a car. I vigorously disapproved of this move, but according to our masters a modern secret service was honour bound to use motor cars for its contacts with agents. I had to get used to the idea that if you go to a rendezvous with a car it's easier to get there, and safer for talking in. So I gave the cash to Guy. He passed his driving test with admirable celerity, then went out and purchased the vehicle of his choice. One day he announced, 'Next time I'll bring the car.'

The day came, and I made my painful way to Acton, where I only had to wait a few seconds on the pavement before Burgess made his appearance. He had parked a little farther on, and he hurried me up the street to survey his acquisition.

It was a Rolls-Royce. The money I had produced wasn't enough to buy a new one, he said, so he had picked up a powerful second-hand two-seater model with a folding top, the colour of old gold.

I looked at it with horror, but held my tongue. We decided to take a ride while we talked. The car was in fairly poor shape: the door almost fell off when I yanked it open. The giant engine seemed to occupy most of the available space; the two seats were tightly cramped together.

The two minutes that followed were among the worst in my life. Guy gunned the engine and the Rolls leapt forward, reaching a very high speed within seconds. Guy drove like a maniac, looking neither right nor left. I was pressed to my seat by sheer velocity. My eyes bulged. My body went numb.

After a while, I don't know how long, the engine ceased to roar and Guy Burgess pulled up gently at the kerb.

'Well?'

'Guy, do you always drive like that? Do you always go straight through crossroads without looking to see if other cars are coming?'

'You're quite right, I really don't look at all. And that's one reason I bought this old banger, because even if I write it off I won't get hurt. Rolls-Royces are very *sturdily built*, you know.'

Never again did I get into a car with Guy Burgess. I never heard what happened to the old gold Rolls.

We continued to see each other regularly, but on foot, in the old-fashioned style. Our meetings generally took place near Underground entrances, never in the Underground itself, where there were too many people. I never gave much thought to how Guy got there: I suppose he just parked his Rolls a little farther on.

I placed a very high value on Guy's efficiency, steadiness, strength of conviction and breadth of culture and interests. He could stand up for himself in argument against the most logical and persuasive adversary. I began to understand why he knew so many people, why so many upright, conventional, stylish and typically British individuals enjoyed his company, admired his abilities and succumbed to his charm. I heartily agreed with Anthony Blunt when in 1979 he told an interviewer from *The Sunday Times* that 'so much ill has been said of Burgess that I feel bound to repeat that he was not only one of the most brilliant intellectuals I have ever met, but also a man of enormous charm and energy.'

His charm, to which I, too, was very susceptible, did not (I hope) distract me from carrying out my duties as a secret service officer as scrupulously as I could. While I admired his abilities and qualities, I never forgot the priorities of the KGB and I did what I could to make Burgess as productive a spy as possible. He knew, I think, that I hid very little from him. For his part, he never once deliberately deceived me, but at the same time it always seemed that he was keeping something back.

Plenty of people were intrigued by him: he knew exactly how to operate within English society, wherever it suited him. When he was confronted by opposition or by people who happened not to agree with him, nobody could be a harsher enemy. It was all part of his extremely complex make-up.

The expression on his face was habitually cold, even scornful. His features were slightly coarsened by alcohol, though I never saw him drunk at any time, then or later. He was an inveterate drunkard, who went on very heavy, extended binges, but oddly enough I never noticed this during my association with him.

He radiated strength of purpose, and he was far from a romantic. I often heard him quote, supposedly from the Bible: 'Evil may be overcome only by violence.'

When Burgess talked, his words were clear and simple, but the ideas behind them danced like quicksilver. His thoughts leapt effortlessly from one to the next and if he noticed that you had not understood him, he would go back, start over, add more detail and enlighten you. He had a rich imagination.

As an agent, Burgess produced a steady flow of documents. He knew how to classify them on a scale of importance, and he would frequently write out a précis for us of what he had read, thus sparing us the drudgery of sifting through piles of paper. It is hard to conceive of the sheer volume of information carried in His Majesty's diplomatic bags, and the extent of the correspondence between the Ministry of Defence and the other ministries of the British Government. To this must be added the oral information gleaned by Burgess from his discussions with politicians and secret service officers, which was often much more interesting and important than the paper churned out by the bureaucrats of the civil service.

In the case of the London conference of 20 April to 7 June 1948, between France, Britain, the United States and the three Benelux nations, the goal of the exercise was to work out a common position on Germany. For a month and a half we were abreast of all the negotiations which eventually led to the transformation of West Germany into a Federal State made up of autonomous *Länder* (states). According to Burgess – and I agreed with his analysis – the Soviet Union was heading for a major collision with the West. *Pravda* did not wait for the official confirmation before denouncing, on 8 April, 'this lawless plot to divide Germany'.

As usual, the Centre was very interested by the Anglo–American relationship, and by the various difficulties that might arise between Britain and the United States. The slightest hint of a breach was important, because the Kremlin might find some way to cause trouble between the two partners. Thus Moscow learned one day that the British and the Americans were quarrelling over a business that Guy Burgess had told me was inconsequential.

It involved an obscure problem over the European contribution to the Marshall Plan. We had more or less forgotten about it when the London residence suddenly received a directive from the Lubyanka to supply as much information on the subject as we could.

I asked Burgess.

'Of course I can find the thing,' he said. 'But I have to tell you, you won't understand a word of it. We've tangled it up so badly with the Americans that even we don't understand it any more. And nobody's in any hurry to let in the light. If you insist, I'll bring you the paperwork, but I warn you there's a suitcaseful.'

Like all spies, I was a glutton for information.

'I'll take your suitcase – and we'll find a way to use it. I've orders to find out everything I can. Bring me everything you can find.'

'Righto, but you'll regret it.'

In due course I received a bag full of papers. I leafed through them, understood nothing and like a dutiful agent sent the lot on to Moscow. Two weeks later they wired back: 'We understand nothing. Ask Paul to tell us at least where it begins and where it ends!'

Burgess found this very droll. 'Told you so. If you like, I'll distil it into a page or two.'

And so he did. I typed the pages up and dispatched them by telegram. This time Moscow sent no reply. The whole thing must have been perfectly clear.

In addition to the work he did for us, Burgess at that time was acting as the intermediary between Kim Philby, then posted for a few months to Turkey, and the KGB. Philby's official task was to find spies who could be sent into Soviet territory, some for short-term missions, others for extended periods. His zone of activity extended throughout the countries of the Caucasus, the Donbas and the Ukraine. He located people who had left these areas of the USSR before or during the war, and who still had relatives in Georgia, Azerbaijan and Armenia, in the regions of Stavropol, Krasnodar, Rostov-on-Don, the Ukraine and the Crimea: and when he found them he suggested that they return to their countries in the service of Great Britain. Volunteers weren't hard to find. Some of these spies went into the Soviet Union by train. Others crossed the frontier on foot, not far from Mount Ararat. They say that Philby installed a big telescope on the mountaintop, so he could follow the progress of his agents below as they crossed the frontier under cover. Yet other spies were sent in by boat across the Black Sea; they disembarked at deserted spots in the vicinity of Sukhumi, Sochi or farther north towards the Crimea.

Stanley had no full-time KGB handler following his work, so Burgess had to be the middleman between him and us. From time to time Philby came back to London, but as a general rule what he had to tell us – the times and places scheduled for the passage of the Anglo-American spies, along with their names – was quite simply communicated to Burgess by mail.

Burgess, despite appearances and despite what the Centre may have thought of him, got through mountains of work. It told on his nerves. I often enquired how he was holding up; he was scrupulous to a fault about what he was doing, and always let me know (even though he didn't actually say so) when he could do more. Indeed, he suffered agonies of remorse that he wasn't doing enough – unreasonably, in my view.

We often discussed the tactics to adopt to solve a given problem, and once we had jointly decided to act he never hesitated to carry out the work before the deadline we had fixed, even though the risks were sometimes great. I found discussions with him very tiring. His mind was sharp as a tack, quick to grasp ideas, while I always needed time to mull them over. Like a computer, he could work a theory through to its conclusion in a flash, and often I found him hard to follow. The result was that I was constantly on my guard, afraid I would miss or misunderstand something, afraid to make a blunder. This took immense effort and after every meeting I felt completely spent. Invariably, after Burgess left, I would head for the nearest drinking establishment, where I slowly and very deliberately drank down a glass of beer.

My meetings with Blunt were much less of an ordeal, though they were just as fruitful. I encountered him for the first time in 1948, a few months after I had begun working with Cairncross and Burgess.

I knew about his counter-espionage experience, and I immediately asked him if we could not usefully put into practice for ourselves the security procedures he had developed in his wartime report for MI5. I suggested that if we used his methods we could be sure of our safety.

He smiled, then explained in great detail the system of open-air observation the British now employed. I attended carefully to what he had to say, and I think I can claim to have made good use of it.

Blunt was the only agent I never worried about meeting. We both had a thorough knowledge of British surveillance methods, so we could easily short-circuit them and meet under conditions of complete safety to discuss whatever we needed to discuss. We got so good at it that we always knew if we were being watched.

Following the same rules I had laid down with Cairncross and Burgess, we met only in streets, parks and squares, never in bars or pubs, and I imposed my preference for locations well away from central London.

Blunt was proud, aristocratic and severe in demeanour, but he had one overriding trait which I deeply appreciated: he was reliable. Though he was anything but a convinced Marxist, I knew I could count on him to the last.

Sir Harold Nicolson, in his book *Diplomacy*, describes reliability as the most important characteristic of a diplomat. Reliability implies punctuality, loyalty and modesty. These are all qualities which apply equally well to secret agents; most don't possess them, but Anthony Blunt undoubtedly did – and if I myself learnt to be reliable, it was partly thanks to him.

We met fairly frequently because whenever Burgess had something urgent to tell me and couldn't be there to do it himself, he would send Blunt in his stead. They saw one another all the time and were fully informed of each other's activities. Blunt, in effect, served as Burgess's permanent liaison with me.

I would also seek him out whenever I needed information about MI5, where he still had plenty of friends. Sometimes I even asked him to procure up-to-date data on individual agents in the British counter-espionage service.

I asked him to verify whether or not the British were attempting to recruit one of our fellow citizens or whether they were trying to turn one of our men into a double agent. Any time we had the least suspicion, we asked him to check for us. This service was of vital importance, since it allayed all our fears and suspicions of one another. In terms of morale, it was invaluable.

As always, I was intrigued by the internal rivalries among our opposite numbers, and I often questioned Blunt on the subject. He took a perverse pleasure in telling me every detail of the routine dirty tricks the British espionage and counter-espionage services played on each other. His memory was excellent and he knew exactly who was behind what. Occasionally he would pass on information he had picked up while socializing with his former colleagues in restaurants or at parties.

It didn't take me long to conclude that the best use for Anthony Blunt was as a liaison agent between us and Burgess, given that Burgess was in a position to obtain far more crucial information than his friend. When he left MI5 in 1945, Blunt had agreed with Krechin that he would resume his pre-war role as a talent spotter for the KGB. But now I clearly understood that he was no longer willing to recruit actively on our behalf, and I let it drop.

I was all the more disposed to meet Blunt, given that we saw eye to eye about procedures. In general, agents set up meetings in given places. Our approach was different: we agreed on a broad perimeter within which we could set up visual contact, without settling on a precise spot. For example, Blunt might be on a viaduct with me on the road below, or the two of us might be in different parts of a park or in the vicinity of two or three blocks of houses.

After ten to fifteen minutes around the designated area, we would catch sight of one another. At this point, by crossing the road or some such ploy, I would let him know I had seen him. He would then walk calmly off, in the knowledge that I would follow at a distance; and while I did so I would check that he was not being followed by some third party. After a while, we would reverse the roles: he would follow me, checking that *I* wasn't trailing a tail. This merry-go-round would continue for about half an hour – sometimes even longer, if either of us had the slightest doubt. We would then establish physical contact in a place that was often a good way off from our original point of departure. The method was tried and true: we never lost touch. At the merest suspicion of surveillance, I trusted my instinct and aborted the encounter. In this case I would go into a shop and buy a few trifles, or else go to a cinema and stay inside for three hours or more. The fact that in England they often showed two films one after another was always very useful to me in my job, for one could go in and out whenever one chose. I would simply see the movie through to the end, then get up and go straight home.

Naturally, when this happened poor Blunt had a few unpleasant moments, but they were mercifully infrequent. Most of the time my fears were imagined, and on the rare occasions when there really was surveillance, it was being conducted by complete greenhorns. The British Secret Service ought never to have sent out inexperienced agents to follow a man they suspected of being an old hand, but they nearly always did in my case. Surveillance is a real art and it needs to be learned. From time to time MI5 would send out a trainee to keep tabs on Soviet Embassy employees, and on occasion I noticed one of them on my heels. In such cases I never made any attempt to lose the man – on the contrary, I tended to make things as easy as I could for him so that he could be a little bit pleased with himself. But invariably it meant that my rendezvous would have to be postponed.

In contrast to my relations with Burgess and Cairncross, my dealings with Blunt remained on a strictly professional level. He was suspicious at all times and every word he said to me was carefully thought out in advance. As far as possible he avoided confidences, keeping to the business at hand. This doesn't mean we didn't get on well; only that my relations with him weren't quite as warm as with the others. I was fast friends with Burgess and Cairncross, but with Blunt things worked on a basis of mutual respect only.

Despite his haughty manner, Blunt was a most agreeable companion, a tall, distinguished-looking individual with steel-grey eyes. All this tended to keep one at arm's length, but also inspired a certain confidence. One had only to look at Anthony Blunt to understand that here was a man who matched his deeds to his words. In all the time we worked together he never once broke a promise or forgot a detail. And he had a knack of looking at men in the same way as he looked at pictures; he taught me, by example, that one can learn to understand people by noticing the fleeting expressions on their faces, and by contemplating their work. Aesthete that he was, Blunt could comprehend painters by their paintings, architects by their buildings and novelists by their books. In this regard he was the opposite of Philby, for example. The two men had completely different values and references, even though they liked and admired one another. Anthony Blunt did have one curious defect, however: he hated to be looked directly in the eye. If one ventured to do this, he would look away.

When I arrived in London in July 1947, Donald Maclean (Homer) was still posted in Washington. He came to England often enough, but as a precaution the Centre had decided that none of us should have any direct contact with him. If he had any material to give us, he was to pass it on by way of Burgess, whom he could meet with openly, as a Foreign Office colleague.

This did not stop me from following his career as closely as I could, and he was a frequent subject of conversation at the residence. We knew that in the United States Donald Maclean had lived up to his reputation as a brilliant young diplomat. After three years there he rose another rung within the diplomatic hierarchy, being appointed head of the Chancery at the British Embassy in Cairo. He was only thirty-five. Melinda, his wife, was living in London, but she went regularly to Egypt with their sons, Fergus and Donald.

In Cairo, the relationship between Maclean and the KGB hit a low point because of the stupidity of the handler allotted to him. We in London had warned our colleagues in Egypt that a vitally important agent was on the way, that he should be treated with the greatest care and that everything should be done to maintain excellent relations with him.

The Cairo residence reacted somewhat oddly to this message: perhaps the resident never even read it. The fact was that as soon as Maclean arrived his KGB contact started trying to order him around, which caused intense irritation. This was compounded by the arrangement of rendezvous in the Arab quarter, as if Maclean were some kind of skulking informer: the tall, blond Briton in his immaculate suit and tie was about as inconspicuous in the souk as a swan among geese, particularly since no British diplomat would otherwise dream of going there.

Maclean's reaction was to suggest that all communication between him and the handler should cease, and that two liaison agents should take his place: namely, Melinda Maclean and the wife of the Soviet resident. The two women could meet at the hairdresser's, for example. Melinda was quite prepared to do this, but the Cairo residence categorically rejected the idea.

Donald then tried another tack, proposing that the meetings take place openly, on a diplomatic basis, in restaurants and bars. This, too, was turned down.

It was at this crucial juncture that Donald Maclean wrote a letter to the Centre via the Cairo KGB residence. The letter was short, a kind of SOS: in it he declared that he had always wished to work in Russia and felt that it was the best place for him to carry on his struggle against American and Western imperialism. He asked, in so many words, to be spirited away to Moscow by the KGB. The note duly arrived at the Centre, but I am quite sure that nobody looked at it. Had the Cairo resident had the sense to act immediately to get Donald Maclean and his family to the USSR – Melinda was perfectly prepared to go – much of what happened afterwards might have been avoided. In short, if the KGB hierarchy had listened to its British agent's appeal for help at that critical moment, our Cambridge network might never have been dismantled at all. Only Maclean would have been neutralized.

In fact, it was in Cairo, where he arrived only a week after his departure from Washington, that Donald Maclean's life began to unravel.

At the same time, much the same thing was happening to Burgess. The pressure he had carried so lightly during the war, when his country was fighting against Fascism in alliance with the Soviet Union, became more and more burdensome with the coming of peace – and the Cold War. I saw him weakening psychologically and physically, before my eyes. We at the London residence became aware at an early stage that he had begun to drink seriously. He was frequently drunk in public, unshaven, ill-dressed and incoherent. Rumours about his behaviour eventually reached the Centre, which demanded explanations from us. What could we say, except that his nerve was going, and that he could no longer take the stress of his double life. In the summer of 1948, Moscow saw that Paul's behaviour was affecting his work. He was supplying less and less information.

I was among the first to write in my reports that the huge and successful effort made by the Cambridge Five to satisfy both their masters – the British and ourselves – was taking a terrible toll on them. They had been operating for fifteen years. It was time to call a halt, even if only temporarily, to the activities of Burgess and Maclean, and to go easier on Philby, if we did not wish to lose our network altogether.

What I did not know at the time was that it was already too late.

Chapter 6

RUNNING SCARED

Burgess was now causing serious concern. At the residence, the KGB lived in dread that one evening, dead drunk, he might confess everything to some stranger. Personally I was sure that he was not only fully aware of the risks, but was also professional enough to hold his tongue even if he had consumed a barrel of his favourite wine. His boss, Hector McNeil, grew tired of the constant stream of complaints about Burgess received by the Foreign Office. Nevertheless, McNeil continued to protect his friend, even when Burgess hit another civil servant so hard in the jaw that he had to be hospitalized. McNeil hushed up the scandal; this amazed me, even though I knew that exactly the same thing might have happened in the Soviet Union.

Fortunately the vacuum left by Burgess was filled by John Cairncross. In the autumn of 1948, Cairncross was assigned a new job which suited us very well. Within the Ministry of Defence, he was placed in the section dealing with the finances of NATO, which was officially to come into being the following year. This coup raised his stock in the KGB enormously. The Kremlin, viewing NATO as a Western machination against our country, was eager for more information about this new American-led initiative.

John Cairncross dealt on a daily basis with files on the future armed forces of NATO and the proportionate contributions of each member nation. He knew the types of troops involved and their equipment and weaponry down to the last detail. Better still, he possessed exact charts of the command structures of the land, sea and air forces to be committed. In a word, Cairncross was in a position to tell us everything about NATO; and we were entirely familiar with all its structures before they were even implemented.

My own relationship with Cairncross remained excellent, because I took care to conduct it on a friendly basis of mutual confidence. I reminded him often that I was very young, that he could teach me a lot and that I admired the quality of his work. I told him from the start how grateful I would be if he could help me along.

I said much the same thing to Burgess, on whom it produced an equally positive impression.

In general, Cairncross was a calm individual. He liked my attitude, though he rarely showed it, and indeed he did his best to advise me on matters connected with our work, without ever seeming professorial or pretentious. I am sure that he, at least, was relieved to be rid of my high-handed predecessor.

When intelligence was urgently required on a given topic, I took care to ask for it tactfully, rather than demanding it.

'In your NATO material, have you seen any reference to the future siting of nuclear bases in Germany? This is very important to us. The attitude of Russia will depend on whether or not NATO brings nuclear weapons into West Germany. Would it be possible for you to find out?' A month later, I had in my possession every detail of NATO's plans for nuclear arms in Germany.

In retrospect, I think I liked Cairncross best of all our London agents. He wasn't an easy man to deal with, but he was a profoundly decent one for all that. Burgess, Philby and Blunt may have had more panache and imagination; they were flamboyant and each in his way had star quality. But I felt most at ease with Cairncross, perhaps because our backgrounds were roughly similar.

His career within the civil service proceeded at a snail's pace, despite his great abilities. He seemed to get nowhere, which was a pity. Certainly there were things about him that annoyed me. For example, he was stone deaf in his right ear; sometimes I forgot this when I was walking along beside him, in which case he would move to get me on his good side. His inability to be punctual was also a problem, of course, but I had to resign myself to that. The hardest part was hanging around waiting for him to appear, wandering about vacantly and staring into shop windows in the growing conviction that everyone in the street had their eyes fixed on me.

With Cairncross I tended to select places where I could accost him, rather than vice versa. I would appear from the shadows in a public garden, for example, when I saw him walk through the gate. By night, I would lie in wait in some dark street leading off a well-lit highway, where I could check at my leisure that nobody was following him before showing myself. And I know he did make an effort not to be too late; often he would arrive at a shambling run. He did his best.

The NATO documents were so interesting that the KGB sent me a congratulatory telegram from Moscow. Cairncross was back in favour and the Centre, with a view to reinforcing our security, asked me to pass him some money to buy a car. As I've said, I was always opposed to this: I feel that the best way for agents to meet in the field is on foot, after a leisurely *parcours de sécurité* to rule out any possibility of surveillance. In London, with its rush hour, its buses, its Underground, its parks and gardens, this is easy. If you know the city and its vast suburbs well enough, you cannot fail to mark a pursuer and get rid of him.

In any case, Cairncross was never followed . . . but the Centre was determined to buy him a car, so I had to comply.

Korovin, the resident, thought the plan an excellent one, mainly because it had originated in Moscow.

'Just think of the advantages, Yuri Ivanovich. The Carelian will arrive in his car, you will climb in beside him, and once there you can talk for as long as you like while he drives. Or maybe you can stop somewhere quiet, get out and continue your conversation on foot. You'll have so many more *alternatives* than you did before!' This thought seemed to delight him.

So I gave the cash to Cairncross and explained what the Centre had in mind. He was indifferent, unlike Guy Burgess, who became an automobile enthusiast almost overnight.

A month later, we met at our usual rendezvous. No car: he hadn't got round to buying it, he said. The weeks passed, and still the machine didn't appear. I held my tongue; finally Cairncross announced that the thing was done.

'Well, how do you like driving?'

Silence.

'Well?'

'Peter, the thing is, I keep failing my driving test.'

'What, you haven't got your licence?'

'No, and every time I try, I make a hash of it because I keep mixing

169

up all the knobs and pedals. I always seem to do the opposite of what I should be doing.'

Many months elapsed before John Cairncross met me in his new car. It was a Vauxhall, I seem to recall. I was pleased. I got in beside him, as planned. I wasn't too scared; I told myself that if he'd managed to pass his test, he must have made some progress and everything was bound to be fine.

We trundled along for a while, and eventually turned into a broad street where there was plenty of traffic. Ominously, Cairncross seemed far from comfortable behind the wheel. We were in a residential part of West London when suddenly, slap in the middle of a busy intersection, the car stopped dead. Cairncross pressed the starter again and again to no avail. A policeman at the corner of the street watched the performance with keen interest, as Cairncross began to lose his head and the engine turned over ever more slowly. Finally the bobby ambled over to us, motioned to Cairncross to get out and walked round the car, examining it as only a policeman can. Cairncross, managing to keep his composure, brought out his papers and thrust them at his tormentor, who, ignoring him, got into the driver's seat beside me.

As I sat petrified with horror, he examined the various knobs on the dashboard. I knew that if I were forced to speak my Russian accent would betray me. Finally he reached across my knees and pushed the knob farthest to the left – which was the choke, forgotten by Cairncross. The engine was flooded. The policeman waited for a moment or two, then tried the ignition, and after a few tries the car started, belching a thick cloud of black smoke from its exhaust. I thought my anguish was about to end, but not a bit of it. Instead of relinquishing his place to Cairncross, the constable shut the door, put the car into first gear and drove to the far side of the intersection.

Although this took only a few seconds it felt like an eternity. I dreaded that he would turn and say something to me, but he didn't. He parked the car as the breathless Cairncross rushed towards it.

'Now, sir,' said the bobby, measuring his words, 'you really ought to know the choke should be pushed in once the car's started up, otherwise she floods. Good day to you, sir.'

Cairncross was too shaken to say anything. It was all he could do to resume his place at the wheel and drive away.

I arrived in London with my wife, Anna, and our daughter in June 1947. We were both twenty-five and our immediate impression of western life was of 'having landed on a different planet'. Here, we are enjoying one of our frequent weekend picnics.

Although originally sent to England as a decoder, I had to change my job very quickly as Soviet chancellery regulations forbade contact between decoders and foreigners. I was appointed embassy attache by Zarubin, the ambassador, who later made me his press agent. My wife and I were soon drawn into London society.

In the early 1950s, Stalin – shown above with his daughter Svetlana sitting on Beria's lap – Beria and Molotov had devised a new way of gathering intelligence. KGB officers and their agents abroad were instructed not to collect information at random but were given orders by the Kremlin to obtain precise intelligence details, a method which proved very productive. (*Novosti*)

PHILBY

On 8 November 1955, four years after Burgess and Maclean's hurried departure for Moscow, Kim Philby was accused in the House of Commons of involvement in the Burgess/Maclean network. He subsequently gave a press conference at his mother's flat in London strongly rejecting the accusations. Harold Macmillan, then Foreign Secretary, publicly cleared Philby. (*UPI/Bettman*)

Below: Summer 1964. Kim Philby enjoying a holiday under the Crimean sun, two years after settling in Moscow.

The British agents on holiday. Kim Philby and his wife, Rufina, entertain George and Ida Blake at their dacha near Moscow. George Blake, himself a Soviet agent, had arrived in Moscow in 1966 after an incredible escape from Wormwood Scrubs prison in England. (*Archive Photos*)

May 1968. Although Kim Philby had become a Soviet citizen and a KGB colonel, he remained very British. I paid him a few friendly visits, talking of the good old days and of departed friends. (*Archive Photos*)

BURGESS

Guy Burgess in Moscow, April 1957. He had been in the Soviet Union for six years but was still finding it difficult to adapt to Soviet life and missed the London pubs. Although in this picture he is wearing an astrakhan coat and *chapka* like a Muscovite, his suit was made in London and he is sporting an Eton College tie.

Below: In the summer of 1962, Guy Burgess took a holiday by the Black Sea. Undermined by despair, he took to drinking more and more Georgian white wine, and to insulting people on the beach. He missed Britain greatly and became very self-destructive: at fifty-three, he had only one year to live. (*Archive Photos*)

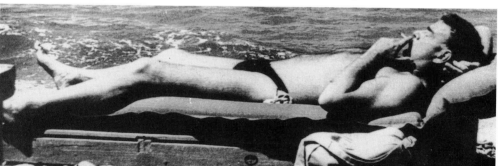

Khruschev had officially recognized Burgess and Maclean's presence in the USSR and granted them Soviet citizenship. Burgess no longer had to keep his identity secret and met many foreigners, including journalists. He is seen here with Terence Lancaster of the *Daily Express* in Moscow, November 1957. He admitted to readers that he missed London. I met him frequently during this period. (*Archive Photos*)

MACLEAN

Donald Maclean, who joined the Foreign Office in 1935 under Soviet intelligence service instructions, became a successful diplomat with postings in Paris, Washington and Cairo. During this time he had a number of KGB code names: Stuart, Wise, Lyric and Homer. (*Archive Photos*)

On 25 May 1951 Burgess and Maclean, about to be found out, fled from England. Melinda stayed behind with their two sons and newborn daughter, Melinda. Press harassment forced her to leave the country with her family in 1952 and settle at her mother's home in Switzerland where she is seen here arriving. A year later she secretly left with her children for Moscow. I was directly involved in the Maclean family's departure from England. (*Keystone*)

Donald Maclean's family – his wife, Melinda, and their two sons, Donald junior and Fergus – accompanied him on his various postings. Melinda had known that her husband worked for Soviet intelligence since their wedding in Paris in 1940. (*Keystone*)

BLUNT

Anthony Blunt, the fourth Cambridge agent, had connections with the Royal Family and was a friend of King George VI. He acted as an intermediary between Burgess, Philby and the KGB, especially after the War. I met him in London as often as I met Burgess. (*UPI/Bettman*)

Suspected in 1951, Anthony Blunt, a world-renowned specialist in eighteenth-century paintings and adviser to the Queen, resisted the questioning of MI6 until 1962. He refused to flee to the USSR, and when I suggested it he replied, 'Can you guarantee me access to Versailles or the Louvre if I come to Moscow? No, then I prefer to stay here.' Blunt's involvement in the Cambridge network was finally revealed in 1979 by Prime Minister Margaret Thatcher. (*Archive Photos*)

CAIRNCROSS

John Cairncross was the first agent I dealt with in London in 1947. He had studied in Cambridge for a year but was not really involved in the Burgess, Philby, Maclean and Blunt group. However, his role was as important as that of the others, especially during the War. The fight against Fascism was Cairncross's main motivation when he joined the Foreign Office in 1937. He is still alive and living in France. (*Jacques Munch/France-Soir*)

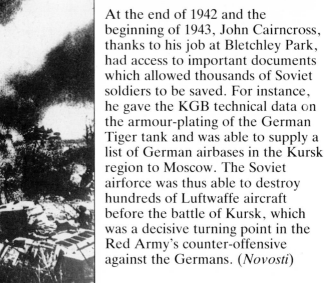

At the end of 1942 and the beginning of 1943, John Cairncross, thanks to his job at Bletchley Park, had access to important documents which allowed thousands of Soviet soldiers to be saved. For instance, he gave the KGB technical data on the armour-plating of the German Tiger tank and was able to supply a list of German airbases in the Kursk region to Moscow. The Soviet airforce was thus able to destroy hundreds of Luftwaffe aircraft before the battle of Kursk, which was a decisive turning point in the Red Army's counter-offensive against the Germans. (*Novosti*)

Dzerjinsky Square in Moscow. Opposite the statue of the founder of the Cheka (forerunner of the KGB) is the Soviet intelligence service building, better known as Lubyanka. This is where the information provided by the British agents was sent and where I also worked. (*TASS*)

A picture of me at Box Hill in 1950 – a rare photograph of a Soviet intelligence officer at work.

In 1960 I was back in Moscow, here seen at the KGB headquarters with my colleagues from foreign intelligence.

I could obviously not return to London after Blunt had revealed my name to MI6 in 1963. However, I was able to carry out other assignments in 1967 and 1968, particularly in India.

I was delighted that my work for Soviet intelligence earned me a chair at the KGB training school, a position I retained until I retired to live quietly in Moscow.

Unless otherwise specified, these photographs were provided from the author's collection.

Dzerjinsky Square in Moscow. Opposite the statue of the founder of the Cheka (forerunner of the KGB) is the Soviet intelligence service building, better known as Lubyanka. This is where the information provided by the British agents was sent and where I also worked. (*TASS*)

A picture of me at Box Hill in 1950 – a rare photograph of a Soviet intelligence officer at work.

In 1960 I was back in Moscow, here seen at the KGB headquarters with my colleagues from foreign intelligence.

I could obviously not return to London after Blunt had revealed my name to MI6 in 1963. However, I was able to carry out other assignments in 1967 and 1968, particularly in India.

I was delighted that my work for Soviet intelligence earned me a chair at the KGB training school, a position I retained until I retired to live quietly in Moscow.

Unless otherwise specified, these photographs were provided from the author's collection.

I'll never forget that incident, during which I experienced the first real cold sweat of my career as a secret agent. In those few minutes anything could have happened. The policeman might have demanded our papers. He would have wondered, no doubt, what a press attaché from the Soviet Embassy was doing in a car with a civil servant from His Majesty's Treasury. A cursory investigation, a quick call from the police station to MI5, and we'd have been cooked. Furthermore, Cairncross had a number of highly classified documents with him, marked top secret. Had we been caught, the situation would have been delicate in the extreme – though not quite as delicate for me as for Cairncross, because I wasn't yet in possession of the papers he had planned to give me. It is a cast-iron rule of procedure when dealing with agents never to receive compromising documents until the very last second of an interview with one's contact.

After this we changed our tactics. When there were documents to deliver, we met for no longer than the time it took to pass them from hand to hand, saying nothing. We saved the talking for the next rendezvous, when no papers were involved. After one or two adjustments of this kind, I felt that Cairncross and I were working in relative safety. True enough, I had difficulty adjusting to his chronic lateness and vagueness, but in the end I managed to do so. Meanwhile, he produced a steady stream of valuable intelligence.

NATO was established in April 1949 and the North Atlantic Council, which is composed of representatives of its member states and which co-ordinates NATO's military forces, began functioning the following August. From the start, we knew what the American bases in Turkey, Norway, Iceland and Italy had cost to set up, the value of Britain's contribution of equipment, how many civilians were employed and how much they earned, who provided the food and who maintained the bases at what price. We also knew the nature of the weapons involved, how much they were worth and which country had supplied them. Likewise, we were later fully informed of the costs of the army units stationed in West Germany.

We worked in this manner until 1951, to the great satisfaction of the Centre, which several times sent messages of congratulation to Cairncross and me through Korovin.

Far less satisfactory was the progress of Homer, alias Donald

Maclean, who began to cause major concern a few months after his arrival in Cairo.

Maclean was utterly exhausted, and his problems with the KGB in Egypt didn't help at all. One day we got wind that he had begun drinking heavily, just like Burgess before him. This didn't stop Maclean working with his usual professionalism, but his binges nevertheless began to cause ripples of outrage in the Cairo diplomatic corps. The KGB Cairo residence reported back to the Centre that its British agent was making an ass of himself. In London, week after week, the tales of Maclean's increasingly unpleasant behaviour filtered through.

The first major incident occurred on a Nile cruise. Maclean got so drunk on this occasion that he exchanged punches in public with one of his colleagues.

This was followed by a series of similar exploits, culminating with a night out with the journalist Philip Toynbee (son of the economic historian Arnold Toynbee), in the course of which the two men, blind drunk, decided to pay a visit to the secretary of the US ambassador. The girl was rash enough to let them in, upon which they began to trash her apartment. They smashed the furniture and the bathtub, then began ripping up the girl's clothes and flushing them down the toilet. After this they set to work drinking every drop of alcohol they could find. Finally the girl managed to get out and call the police, who came and arrested the two men. The resultant scandal was the talk of Cairo for weeks afterwards.

Meantime, Guy Burgess had quieted down somewhat. Hector McNeil had left his post as Minister of State and consequently Burgess was out of a job. He put out feelers for another post which would give him access to classified information, and with his usual skill contrived in October 1948 to penetrate the Asia section of the Foreign Office. After the series of drunken incidents he had caused, his staying in the diplomatic service at all was a tribute to his resourcefulness.

Although now a grade 4 employee (i.e. one grade beneath his previous level), he somehow obtained access to the analyses of the committee that co-ordinated intelligence at the Foreign Office. He also obtained information emanating from the Ministry of Defence:

and the result was that Guy Burgess was once again able to 'feed' me as he had in the old days. His field of action was highly varied, ranging from Asia to NATO by way of the calendar of international conferences, and he passed on all the information coming his way which he thought might have some interest for us.

Thus he was able to send on details of future British policy towards Mao Tse-tung, whose consolidation of power in China was now virtually complete. At the close of 1948, Asian problems were beginning to play a major role in the foreign policies of all nations. Anything that concerned this area of the world was of interest to us, and once again Burgess was in the right place at the right time. The Far East was hardly his speciality, but during his stint as private secretary to McNeil he had gained a certain familiarity with the region – and Burgess, as always, was a fast learner.

By 1949, with his army poised for victory, our then ally Mao declared the nationalization of all foreign assets in China. He did just what the Bolsheviks had done in Russia in 1917, when the property, factories, businesses and financial assets of the British, Germans, Belgians and French were seized. The Americans in particular were outraged by this move and adopted a hard-line position, declaring themselves ready to go to war to defend their interests.

The attitude of the British was more subtle, probably because they knew the Chinese a good deal better. Their experts counselled patience, in the belief that after their revolutionary orgy the Chinese Communists would see sense and find ways to make amends. In their discussions with the Americans, the British assured them repeatedly that within a few years the Chinese and the Russians would have a serious falling out; in view of this, they felt that Truman should not act too hastily and aggressively.

Burgess was informed day by day about the substance of the Anglo–American secret negotiations. One day he arrived at a routine rendezvous with me and offered a suggestion. 'At the moment,' he said, 'I'm producing documents galore, but I think we can go one better. I might be able to launch an active operation, if you agree to it. We could try to exploit the contradictions in the British and American positions. We could poison things to such a degree that a real conflict could break out between them. I can't exactly guarantee it, but we could try to drive some kind of wedge between Britain and the United States *vis-à-vis* China.'

173

This was an important enough suggestion to warrant a report to Moscow before taking any further measures. Nevertheless, I let discipline go by the board, given that we had little time to act and also given that I feared the Centre might torpedo the initiative.

So Burgess and I set about discussing ways of putting his plan into action, and when we had reviewed them I gave my consent. He feigned amazement.

'Well, I'm damned! You've developed a mind of your own! Whatever happened to consultation with Moscow?'

I made no reply. The fact was, we both knew I often gave the 'need to consult Moscow' as a pretext for giving myself time to think.

Burgess began his campaign the very next day, and highly effective it was. He moved around the Foreign Office sowing doubt and resentment among his colleagues and superiors about American intentions in China. He went about it so cleverly that certain high-ranking civil servants were incensed enough to write letters of protest to their minister about the 'American attitude'. I have no doubt at all that Burgess's one-man campaign had something to do with the transformation of Anglo–American differences on the question into outright opposition, and eventually real conflict. The diplomatic face-off between the allies went so far that the two sides began to exchange irate letters of protest.

It is worthy of note, I think, that this radical disagreement over China persisted until long after Burgess's death, indeed until the 1970s.

In June 1949 our attention shifted from Asia to Paris, where the foreign ministers of the Big Four – the USSR, France, the United States and Great Britain – were once again conferring on the status of Germany and Austria. The negotiators were Ernest Bevin, Robert Schuman, Dean Acheson and Andrei Vyshinsky, who had replaced Molotov earlier in the year, with Andrei Gromyko as his second-in-command.

The talks proved extraordinarily tense. The USSR had just swallowed a major humiliation over the Berlin airlift, and there was no question of our making any further concessions. We knew we would give away nothing on the German question save a few vague promises of economic exchange between the Eastern and Western zones. Instead our aim was to make gains in Austria. In the course of the conference, our three partners consulted closely with one another and usually presented us with a solid front. Luckily for us, however, their delegations were in the habit of telegraphing accounts of the negotiations back to their respective governments every evening, along with the conclusions they had reached in secret among themselves. Clement Attlee communicated his instructions back from London, and copies of these instructions circulated to one or two ministers in his cabinet. The three Western states might appear to present us with a concerted front; but since we knew about their secret consultations, we were able to exploit their differences. I cannot say for certain that Vyshinsky's success in the Austrian negotiations was entirely due to the information he had from our British agents, but it had a major hand in the business. In return for signing a peace treaty, the USSR obtained an overall indemnity of 150 million dollars payable over six years, all the assets of the Danube Steamship Company, and sixty per cent of the oil revenues within the zone occupied by us.

At this time I was seeing either Burgess or Blunt on a weekly basis. They brought me so many documents that it was impossible to carry them loose in folders, so we fell into the habit of exchanging a small suitcase each time we met. Back at the embassy, I had the documents photographed before returning the case the following day.

On one occasion Burgess and I were walking side by side in an empty square, engrossed in discussion; Burgess was carrying the suitcase as usual, since I adhered to my rule of not taking possession of it until the last possible moment. Suddenly two policemen appeared in our path and detained us.

I was stunned. We didn't look remotely suspicious: more like a couple of friends on their way home, or heading for their club. Burgess was completely calm. In a split second he analysed the situation and held up the suitcase.

'Is this what concerns you, Officer?'

The policeman nodded. Burgess stepped up to him boldly, opened the case and showed him its contents. The man slipped his hand into it, felt under the documents, looked at one or two of them and motioned to Burgess that all was well.

'Sorry, sir. Everything's quite in order.'

The two bobbies saluted and turned away. I was completely mystified and very shaken indeed, rooted to the spot: I have always found that in situations like this my head takes over and the rest of me becomes virtually dysfunctional.

Burgess explained why we had been stopped. Apparently burglars in London used suitcases similar to ours for carrying the tools of their trade, such as jemmies, skeleton keys and various types of pliers. There was room enough in the case for a whole range of specialist equipment, hence the policemen's concern.

In that moment we had been as close to catastrophe as it was possible to be, but Burgess had kept his head. He had given me a proof of his reliability and strength of mind, which I found deeply reassuring. Yet in the ordinary course of his life, his behaviour grew more and more dangerous for him, for his British superiors and for us, too. His irascibility and aggressiveness increased by the day.

I was powerless to do anything, apart from keeping the Centre informed of the situation. I hoped for a while that Guy's new job in the Asia section of the Foreign Office might calm him down, especially since I myself was making virtually no demands on him. But things only got worse.

His regular – and rising – consumption of alcohol did not help at all. By the autumn of 1949, he had become a real problem to work with, and I preferred whenever possible to deal with Anthony Blunt when delivering or returning documents.

Despite the danger, I did not feel the moment had yet come to break with these two agents, who were still producing useful and important information.

I always felt safer when it was Blunt's turn to come to the rendezvous. I particularly appreciated his way of keeping a certain distance while remaining perfectly straightforward and accessible. He never showed me the slightest discourtesy. Even when he disagreed violently with what I had to say, he heard me out calmly before giving his own opinion. I especially remember one incident that took place towards the end of the year, when relations between the USSR and the West were rapidly deteriorating. The eleven-month blockade of Berlin, the creation of NATO, the appearance of the Communist-inspired peace movement throughout Europe, the birth of the Federal Republic of Germany and the witch-hunt for Marxists in the United States had brought East–West tension to the boil. Some of our own intelligence chiefs believed that the Soviet policy of blockading Berlin had affected the commitment of our

British agents, and might cause them to abandon us. I, too, felt this was a real possibility, and I was glad when I was directed to raise the issue with Anthony Blunt.

It was no easy matter to explain the obstructionist, even hostile Soviet policy towards the West, and to justify Molotov's post-war refusal to agree to even the most harmless proposals, which earned him the sobriquet of 'Mr Niet' in the free press.

I did what I could to make Blunt understand our foreign policy as I saw it, though I suspected he was just as aware of the real Soviet motivations as I was. At the time my own view was that the Western attitude was just as bad; indeed I felt that the West had seized on every opportunity to raise questions about the frontiers of the Soviet Union without the slightest regard for the consequences.

To back up my reasoning (which was heavily tainted, I admit, by the propaganda of the time) I told Blunt that the Western position had not changed substantially since Anthony Eden, Britain's Foreign Secretary, visited Moscow in October 1943. At that time the Soviet Union was insisting that Britain should recognize the frontiers established at the beginning of the war. Eden wouldn't hear of this: Britain, he said, would never accept a Soviet annexation of the Baltic nations. As far as he was concerned, the same applied to eastern Poland and Bessarabia, which had been ceded to the Soviet Union by the terms of the Molotov–Ribbentrop pact.

The leaders of the Soviet Union viewed the British stance as an attempt to divide our country. As an illustration of Western bad faith, I reminded Blunt of the British and American reluctance to deliver munitions to us in 1942, a time when the situation on the Eastern Front was really desperate. We had been forced to abandon vast areas to the Germans, along with major munitions factories, and consequently we suffered a chronic shortage of explosives, which had been repeatedly promised to us by the Allies. Yet virtually nothing came, and what deliveries there were proved so irregular that they were useless to our forces, which remained on the defensive on all fronts. I tried to make Blunt understand that we were only too aware that the Western nations had done, and would do, anything in their power to prevent the Soviet Union from becoming a great power in the post-war era, and that our foreign policy had to be viewed in this light. A continuing confrontation between the two great power blocs appeared inevitable in the short term, and at that point we felt that the West, backed by NATO's military force, was intolerably aggressive.

I also told Blunt that our agents were keeping us fully informed of attempts to subvert the Balkans and the Ukraine then being made by the Western allies and their agents. The attitude of the British in Yugoslavia was a proof of their outright hostility, if ever there was one: they were overtly attempting to detach the Communist leader Tito from the Soviet Union. As for Poland, Churchill had clearly expressed his intention that the Poles should spearhead the struggle against Bolshevism. At one point he had also contemplated placing the west of Ukraine and Belorussia under the control of the United Nations. Blunt knew about some of these projects, both those that were talked about openly and those that were established in secret. He himself, through Burgess, had revealed some of them to us.

At the same time, since the defeat of Germany, the allied governments had been afraid that the Soviet Union would attack them. As far as we were concerned, there was no ground for this fear. I explained to Blunt that we had lost too much strength and too many human lives in the last conflict to dream of advancing westwards. We had taken Berlin and we had obliterated the military power of Germany. It was enough for us that the Nazi danger was neutralized for many years to come.

I suppose I tried to express my view that the nature of Soviet foreign policy was defensive. Blunt listened calmly throughout, never once interrupting me. I even thought I might have convinced him. But when I had finished, I saw a slow smile spreading across his face.

'Is that all you have to tell me?'

Then he pointed out that I had just spent half an hour without a break talking about a subject which had nothing whatever to do with our work together. This was quite true: as a rule we spoke only of business. He went on to say that he was well aware of everything I had told him. None of it would change by one iota his firm view of Russian policy, which he considered to be frankly imperialist.

He gave the example of Turkey, which Stalin had coveted in 1947 as a way of attaining access to the Bosphorus, the Dardanelles and the Mediterranean, something the Tsars had always dreamed of. He made it clear that I was wasting my time trying to persuade him otherwise. He found our present policies ill-conceived, damaging to Communism, and every bit as imperialist as those of our predecessors in Russia. He, Blunt, collaborated with us not because he agreed with Soviet policy but because, like his friends from Cambridge, he believed in one overriding truth, that the happiness of humanity could be accomplished only in the wake of a world-wide revolution. Burgess, Philby and Maclean were the most active in this cause; they were struggling hard for the triumph of the revolution. Blunt himself was not a driving force within the group, but he shared its ideals. He believed that the foundations of the revolution were set in the USSR, but that its dynamics lay in the West.

When he told me this, I realized what a completely honest man he was. He could quite easily have agreed with me, thereby making his own life easier. It would have cost him nothing: yet he preferred to tell me openly that his views were diametrically opposed to those of our country's rulers. The most important thing to us was that Blunt was loyal and honest with us. Moreover, he made it clear that our relationship would in no way be affected by this, and indeed it was not.

The next time I saw Blunt, he handed over a sheaf of documents from Burgess on the newly formed North Atlantic Council. On this occasion he did not merely play the role of messenger. He knew the contents of the dossiers he was giving to me, and he did not hesitate to comment on them. The siting of NATO bases in Europe was a nightmare to us and we were going full out to discover what the West was planning. The deliveries of arms and munitions from America to the various signatories of the treaty, at that time twelve countries in all, including some that were at our very gates, like Norway, terrified the Soviet Government. Maclean, Burgess, Cairncross and sometimes even Philby were concentrating hard on this topic – and their efforts paid off, because before long we were able to know with precision exactly how NATO worked at every level: political, economic, financial and military. On this last point, the characteristics of the most insignificant military weapon supplied to the Norwegians, the Danes, the Belgians and others were known to us.

Before my meetings with Blunt, I would often prepare a series of questions about the documents at hand. We needed clarification on certain points, notably when we learned in November 1950 that West Germany was being considered as a possible participant in the West's defensive system. We wished to know what the terms of German collaboration would be. The rearmament of that country so soon after the end of the war frightened everyone in the USSR. Blunt relayed my questions back to Burgess, who replied to them in less than forty-eight hours. This system allowed me to work quickly, without waiting for further meetings and without taking risks.

From time to time, Anthony Blunt rendered us services outside the field of intelligence. For example, on several occasions he travelled to Germany in his capacity as Surveyor of the King's Pictures. He went there to review the works of art looted by the Germans and recovered by the Allies after the destruction of the Nazi regime. In this connection he met with Leo Long, who had been assigned to the British commission in Germany following his departure from SIS in 1945. I have no idea what information Long may have given Blunt at that time, and despite everything that has been said about this, I myself never had any contact with Long.

I was to continue seeing Blunt on a regular basis until 1951. I felt more and more that his work for us was irksome to him, but I think he went on doing it for the sake of the past, in memory of the war and, above all, to render a service to Burgess, to whom he was still utterly devoted. This loyalty of his was soon to show itself in spectacular fashion, when Burgess ran into really serious trouble. Anthony Blunt was there, ready to take the direst risks to help his friend; and long afterwards he remained the only man who was ready to stand up and defend him. In this he never wavered until the day he died.

As the months passed, Guy Burgess's self-destructive behaviour grew progressively worse. While on holiday in Ireland, driving recklessly, he ran over a man and killed him. He successfully pulled strings to hush up the affair and avoid legal complications, but this time some of his colleagues in the Foreign Office began to suggest openly that he should go. This incident was hardly calculated to calm Burgess down. A few months later he beat up yet another of his colleagues for 'liking Americans'.

On holiday in Tangier, he went completely off the rails. He was permanently drunk in the city's bars, pointed out British Secret Service agents in public and walked out of restaurants and hotels leaving unpaid bills. In the street, he made open advances to young men. When he met an old friend, the local secret service head, he again got into a violent fight over American influence in Europe, then went on and did exactly the same thing with the representative of

British counter-espionage in Gibraltar. Both men wrote irate letters of complaint to London, but again Burgess's network of friends protected him. He contrived to persuade his superiors that he had been the aggrieved party in both cases, and was forgiven with the warning that this was the last time. His days in the Asia section were numbered.

During one of our meetings, I raised the subject of what might happen if the worst came to pass and he was forced to leave England for ever. I vividly remember his face when he told me: 'Peter, I couldn't live in Russia.'

Burgess's nerves were giving way, but still he continued to provide us with vital information. In April 1950, two months before the outbreak of war in Korea, he sent me a long hand-written account taken from a report by British military intelligence detailing the extent of Soviet aid to the Chinese armed forces. It should not be forgotten that since 14 February, China and the USSR had been bound by a treaty of friendship and mutual assistance. In this way, a few weeks before the first hostilities broke out, we knew exactly what the West had managed to find out about our co-operation with the Chinese.

I sent this document back to Moscow as quickly as possible, but I have no idea if it was subsequently passed on to the North Koreans.

In June 1950, Burgess began working in partnership with Maclean, who was by then back in London, having been repatriated by the British ambassador to Egypt. Melinda had been furious about the behaviour of her husband in Cairo, but she had nonetheless defended him to the Foreign Office hierarchy. She forcefully gave her opinion that his condition was entirely due to overwork: Donald had not had a single break since the beginning of the war. She won her case, and Maclean was given several months' leave, during which Melinda had him closely supervised by doctors – and by a psychiatrist, who reported acute depression and marriage problems.

After six months' rest, in June Donald went back to work as head of the American section of the Foreign Office. The Cairo incident seemed to have been forgotten; in any case, there was no longer any question of drinking orgies and debauchery. The conscientious diplomat in Donald Maclean had regained the upper hand, more professional than ever. For its part, the KGB had decided to leave him alone, and it was for this reason that I myself never met him in

London. We asked for nothing; he sent us information on his own initiative, via Burgess.

With the outbreak of the Korean War, the main question for the Soviet Union was how far the Americans were prepared to venture down the road to world-wide conflict.

On 25 June, the day the North invaded the South, Burgess and his friend Maclean were more active than ever. Burgess gave me what he could: usually he annotated the documents in his own hand with comments about the attitude of the British Government and the possibility of an escalation of the war.

Maclean, too, supplied his own comments: he was far from optimistic about the American position, which he judged 'dangerous and wrong-headed' after MacArthur's appointment as commander-in-chief. I believe this was the first time he revealed his anti-Americanism openly.

Two months later, in August, when East–West tensions were at crisis point, Burgess was appointed first secretary at the British Embassy in Washington. This post was obviously his last chance to succeed as a diplomat, and he failed to take advantage of the opportunity. No doubt his superiors thought the job might shake him into behaving sensibly; not a bad idea on the face of it, but why on earth choose the United States when Guy Burgess was publicly renowned as a Yankee-hater and a violent critic of American policies? I can only explain it in terms of a somewhat warped British sense of humour, of the same kind that allowed Donald Maclean to be named head of the American section at the Foreign Office.

It would have been better had Guy Burgess been posted to some more congenial country, where he could have stopped drinking. His problem was now much worse. He had become a real alcoholic, never quite drunk but always between one glass and the next, and it became all too obvious. We at the KGB felt that Washington was at the least an ill-considered choice, but all the same any job that would get him out of London was better than nothing. We weren't too concerned from an intelligence point of view, because at that crucial juncture we knew we could still count on Maclean.

Burgess might come back when everything had blown over; the Centre was resigned to putting him on the back burner. Personally, I knew the man well enough to understand that he would never accept this. He would merely work that much harder.

At one of our last meetings before he left for the United States, I asked him how he planned to solve his problems.

'Problems? I have no problems. I'm not alone. I have my friends, and they'll help me when I need help.' He was bitterly resentful of some of his colleagues. I tried to convince him it was pointless to get into fights about nothing.

He wouldn't listen; Guy Burgess was a real fighter; he never apologized, just carried on blindly. In my reports to Moscow I stated explicitly that the move to Washington would do his nerves no good whatever. What he needed was serious medical treatment, after so many years of hard work under constant, debilitating pressure. During the war he had achieved much in the struggle against the common enemy, and when the war was over he had maintained the same level of effort. He was suffering from long-term fatigue. Only Philby and Blunt, whose nerves were of steel, were immune to this affliction.

Once Burgess was gone, Blunt took over his duty as middleman between Maclean and ourselves. A new world war threatened: at the close of 1950, President Truman shocked the Soviets by stating that the utilization of a weapon is implicit in its possession, a reference to the atom bomb.

Clement Attlee, the British Prime Minister, who was already seriously concerned about the rising tide of American militarism, was also shocked. He arranged to visit Washington immediately to obtain an explanation from the President. Maclean passed us all the prepared texts for this visit, and on Attlee's return he obtained a full account of what had been said. According to this material, Attlee had come back reassured.

Nonetheless, Stalin was sure that a Third World War was imminent, and I believe he was not far wrong. MacArthur had clearly stated his view that the atom bomb should be used against North Korea. The tension reached an intolerable level as the American forces neared the Chinese border. The West was convinced that the attack on South Korea by the North was part of a broad Soviet plan to conquer Asia; they couldn't believe that the conflict's only goal was to satisfy the expansionist ambitions of Kim Il Sung, the North Korean President. Each camp attributed to the other much more warlike intentions than they really had.

Homer's information strengthened Stalin's certainty. In March

1951, Maclean sent us the minutes of a meeting that had taken place in the Foreign Office, along with an account of his own alarmist view of the situation. The British Government's experts were apparently convinced that American aggressiveness was 'pushing the world into a pointless war'.

It is correct, also, to say that it may well have been on account of a piece of news brought to us by Homer that East–West tension finally began to relax. As soon as the decision had been made, he informed us that Washington had forbidden General MacArthur to invade Manchuria and set up a blockade of the Chinese coast. Shortly afterwards the crisis was further defused when Truman relieved MacArthur of his command; the general had been a strong advocate of extending the conflict at a time when both the United States and the Soviet Union were already in possession of the ultimate weapon.

Burgess, who had arrived in Washington on 4 August 1950, was not entirely isolated from his friends. He found Kim Philby, who had arrived the previous October, awaiting him.

The post of representative of the British Secret Service attached to the recently created CIA had fallen vacant, and SIS heads had deemed it important that the man slated to be its future director, Kim Philby, should cultivate his relations with the American cousins. Philby had requested our views on this idea, and the Centre had warmly approved.

In August 1949, Philby had left Ankara for London, where I myself had been working for over a year. I did not meet him. Moscow insisted that all our contacts be conducted through either Burgess or Blunt. After going through the formalities for himself, Aileen and their four children, and after a few weeks of briefing, Kim Philby moved with his family to Washington.

The night before he boarded the plane, he sent Burgess to me with news that was to have fearsome consequences for us all. A colleague at SIS had told him that an American cipher expert from the Army Security Agency (later the National Security Agency), William Weisband, had just informed SIS that a brilliant analyst in his service named Meredith Gardner was attempting to decode telegraphic messages sent to the Lubyanka during the war by various KGB posts around the world.

This caused a ripple of alarm at the Centre. We had no idea what the Americans might uncover, and this investigation hung over us like the sword of Damocles.

When he took the plane, Philby was already aware of the sudden grave danger to the Cambridge Five, among others. He told a worried Burgess that he would do everything in his power to parry this new thrust.

In thoroughly professional style, Stanley set about building excellent working relations with the CIA from the moment he arrived in the American capital. In this he was assisted by another SIS agent, James McCargar.

The CIA had been created in 1947 out of the old Office of Strategic Services (OSS). To begin with, it had serious organizational difficulties. The Americans knew only too well that if the CIA was to become a secret service to be reckoned with, it had to work in a fundamentally different manner from the OSS, an organization specifically geared to wartime. A completely fresh structure was badly needed. Philby, who had an excellent knowledge of covert operations against both Fascism and Communism, was just the man for this job. He shared his experience with the Americans, who were glad of it and suitably grateful for his advice. In a sense, he was one of the true founders of the CIA. He had, for instance, remarkably good working relationships with the CIA heads, particularly with James Jesus Angleton (the future head of American counter-espionage), who became a close friend. Philby helped Angleton with a wide range of issues. After Kim's defection to the USSR, Angleton predictably said that in his heart of hearts he had always suspected his friend was a KGB agent.

Contacts like these permitted Stanley to obtain virtually all the information he required. All he had to do was ask. His relations with the interception services were just as good. The only problem was the FBI.

Philby never succeeded in gaining the confidence of the FBI's director, J. Edgar Hoover, who objected to him from the start. In fact, he was not so much against Philby personally; it was just that he didn't want any Brits in his hair in Washington. It was as simple as that. He believed that Philby had been sent by SIS to penetrate the CIA with a view to gathering confidential information about the American services. As far as Hoover was concerned, this SIS–CIA

185

co-ordination business was no more than a cover for a British cell-building operation. When he was asked what he had against Philby, he said his intuition told him that the man was a 'British spy'.

Hoover stated openly that he was formally opposed to any collaboration with Philby, and forbade anyone in his service to furnish him with the least item of information.

J. Edgar Hoover was a hard man to fathom, for both Americans and British alike. One may only imagine how delighted he was when he heard the news that Philby was suspected of spying for the Soviet Union. He proclaimed from the rooftops that he had foreseen it all, that he had always known what was going on and even that he had personally warned the CIA. This was all nonsense.

As it happened, Philby himself paid little attention to the FBI, having focused his activities on the CIA, within which he could move about more or less as he liked. Thus it came about that he participated in the preparations for the Anglo–American effort to subvert Albania.

In December 1949, SIS and the CIA organized a first landing of special forces in Albania. Their goal was to carry out subversive actions against the regime of Enver Hoxha, a hard-line Stalinist and a fierce adversary of Tito's Yugoslavia. Albania had been devastated economically by the war. Its people lacked even the most basic necessities, to such a point that when Hoxha visited Moscow he told Stalin he would welcome a consignment of bootlaces, if Stalin could spare nothing else.

Albania was on the brink of famine, hence an ideal target for an anti-Communist attempt at subversion. The idea was simple: to infiltrate groups of Albanian refugees, who had left the country at the time of the Nazi defeat because they had collaborated with the Germans or with Mussolini's Italians. A first commando group was organized, armed and trained to land on the Adriatic coast, then advance to the interior of the country, calling on the people to take up arms against Hoxha's regime.

Philby, from his eyrie in Washington, took part in the planning of the coup and in due course sent us all the necessary details in a letter to Burgess. He gave us vital information about the number of men involved, the day and the time of the landing, the weapons they were bringing and their precise programme of action.

Here I should point out that during the eighteen months he spent in

Washington our agent Stanley never had the least contact with any KGB agent based in the United States. The Centre felt that this would be altogether too hazardous, and went out of its way to expose Philby as little as possible; for in spite of the deciphering operations then being undertaken by the Americans, we hoped that Philby might yet become head of the British Secret Service. If he needed to make contact, he did so through Burgess; but this was rare, for the very act of sending a letter or a telegram was liable to put the network at risk.

The Soviet authorities duly passed on Philby's information to the Albanians, who set up ambushes on their coast. The commando force was surrounded. A number of its members were killed and some captured, while a few escaped in the life-rafts they had used for the landing.

This first operation was followed by another in the spring of 1950, this time involving a parachute force. Again the Albanians were fully apprised in advance and the invasion was a complete disaster.

In August 1950, when Burgess took up his post as first secretary at the British Embassy in Washington, Philby committed a rare error. He lodged Burgess at his own home. This was extremely unwise, and had I known about it at the time I would have strongly advised against it. Perhaps Kim felt that he would be able to keep an eye on his friend if he had him to stay: at the time, Burgess was playing an important role because, since he was less exposed than Philby, he was the one who sent Philby's messages on to me. I would see him from time to time when he came to England on leave, or for reasons connected with his work.

As I had dreaded, there was no improvement in Burgess's pattern of behaviour in his new job: rather the contrary. The distance from London and the change of scene did nothing for him. He quarrelled repeatedly not only with his colleagues, but also with the ambassador himself.

For example, he parked his car wherever he pleased when he arrived for work at the embassy. The police immediately complained; Sir Oliver Franks, the envoy, summoned Burgess several times to remonstrate with him. But he took not the slightest notice.

Again, in any embassy it is customary to respect a certain set of procedures when consulting confidential archives. Such papers cannot simply be taken out of a filing cabinet at will and replaced when they are finished with. Burgess utterly ignored the procedures;

he didn't give a damn for secrets (hardly surprising, since he had spent his entire career divulging them to the KGB) and often left classified documents lying around on his desk. Nor did he return them to the files, where a staff member was supposed to set a new seal on them. At the end of each working day, the surveillance agents discovered Burgess's carelessness and regularly reported it to Franks, who, despite reprimand after reprimand, completely failed to make his subordinate see reason.

In the United States, Guy Burgess had no friends to protect him, and he had lost no time in making powerful enemies within the embassy. This did not improve his state of mind, any more than the activities of Senator Joseph R. McCarthy's witch-hunt against Communists, which coincided with his arrival.

In the autumn of 1950, SIS and the CIA launched a third commando assault on Albania, this time overland. The Anglo–American agents crossed Yugoslavia from Italy. Inevitably, this operation also failed dismally, again because of Philby. Thereafter the British and American ardour for the fight against Enver Hoxha was somewhat dampened.

In October 1950, a court in Tirana condemned twelve of the infiltrators to life imprisonment and two others to death. The CIA and SIS were unable to figure out why they had failed so repeatedly. The Americans in particular suspected a leak, but Philby still remained beyond suspicion: after all, many other agents had worked on the project apart from him.

Thereafter, Philby continued to attend the various Anglo–American conferences on intelligence co-ordination – notably that of February 1951 on the Baltic states. Harry Carr, who had been the SIS Stockholm resident during the war and who was head of the Northern Europe section of the British Secret Service, was present on this occasion. Philby sent us a complete breakdown of the meetings which reassured us mightily, given the many misunderstandings between SIS and the CIA. It was clear that they stood little chance, in their present state, of destabilizing the Baltic countries. However, the KGB was worried by the ongoing British and American operations within the Ukraine.

Their aim in the Ukraine was to parachute in or infiltrate groups of agents which would then disperse around the country. During his tour of duty in Istanbul, Philby had already helped us to wreck several attempts to send in agents. He did the same thing from Washington.

The CIA and SIS had no trouble recruiting spies among the large number of Ukrainian émigrés in the United States and Canada. They took advantage of the fact that many displaced individuals still had family in their country of origin and could be sent back under the pretext of rejoining their relatives.

In March 1951, Philby gave Burgess, who was heading home to London, the names and arrival points of three groups of six men who were to be parachuted into the Ukraine. This information eventually reached me through Anthony Blunt and I made good use of it. Burgess also mentioned the American deciphering operation, still under way; the project was code-named Venona and it was now known for certain that the analyst Meredith Gardner had discovered a blunder in a telegram sent from New York to Moscow.

At the Lubyanka, our own deciphering specialists were immediately put to work to discover what this blunder might be. They went through all the telegrams received from New York with great care, eventually unearthing two messages in particular. They noticed that the encoding clerk at our Washington embassy had committed a serious error in 1942, which was then compounded by his superior. Having exhausted his stock of 'one-time' pads for encoding telegrams to the Centre, he used the same pad twice. This breach of the rules was attributed to a delay in the transportation of diplomatic mail between Moscow and the United States, which at that time was still going by sea. The captain of the ship bringing the diplomatic bag, which contained the new pads from Moscow, had decided to stay longer in port in Britain, on account of intense submarine activity in the North Atlantic.

The heads of the KGB then asked their experts how long it would take for the Americans to decipher the whole text of these telegrams, given the means at their disposal. Several years was the prognosis: and it proved wildly optimistic. The authors of the original error were severely punished, but apart from this there was nothing the Centre could do.

We were at a loss to know how to handle this development. We could have closed down our networks, of course, but that was well-nigh impossible, given the sheer size of the spider's web we had woven since the war.

Once again Philby came to the rescue. Burgess told us that Philby had made the acquaintance of Meredith Gardner, the brain behind the deciphering operation who each day was burrowing a little further into our secrets. The two men were on such good terms that Philby was able to enter Gardner's office while he worked and was consequently in a position to follow the progress of the deciphering operation on a day-to-day basis.

We knew now that Venona would blow our network apart at any moment and unmask some or all of the Cambridge agents. In the meantime, however, Philby's relationship with Gardner gave us the advantage of prior warning. We could expect to remain in control of the situation right up to the last minute, thereby avoiding unpleasant surprises and springing our agents while there was still time to do so.

In general, this worked well, once the inexorable process that was to culminate in the exposure of the Cambridge Five had begun. I knew instinctively that the game would soon be up, and I prepared myself psychologically to save what I could from the ruins. To me at least, the idea that our Cambridge agents might spend the rest of their lives in a British prison was deeply disquieting.

Chapter 7

THE END GAME

As late as 1950, we in the KGB were serenely unaware that for ten years a base in the Australian outback had been intercepting virtually every radio message – whether civil, diplomatic or military – between the Soviet Union and a number of other countries, notably the United States.

By 1945, a priceless trove of intelligence had accumulated in the archives of the Allies, but how priceless nobody could know. The information still lay beyond the grasp of our enemies, securely locked into codes that they could not decipher.

It happened that our agent Homer (Donald Maclean), first secretary at the British Embassy in Washington, contrived to pilfer a highly interesting document. This turned out to be a report on two telegrams sent by Churchill to President Harry S. Truman on 5 June 1945, officially numbered 72 and 73. In these two messages the British Prime Minister answered a query from President Truman, who had been keeping him abreast of progress in the negotiations between Stalin and the US special envoy Harry Hopkins, who had been President Roosevelt's closest and most trusted adviser. The war was won; and Hopkins, despite the fatal illness which was to kill him the following winter, had gone back to Moscow one last time to negotiate with his 'dear old friend' Stalin, for whom he appeared to harbour a sincere respect.

The Stalin–Hopkins talks mainly concerned the fate of Poland and – more precisely – of the sixteen members of the AK (Polish Secret Army), whose Warsaw–London flight had been diverted to Moscow and there held indefinitely by the Soviet authorities. After a week of negotiation in relaxed surroundings, Hopkins, and by implication the American President, appeared satisfied with the stance adopted by Stalin, who blandly declared in regard to Poland that he would accept 'any government which proved both acceptable to the Polish people and friendly to the Soviet administration.'

This ambiguous statement, though apparently good enough for Truman and Hopkins, was far from satisfactory to Churchill. In his 5 June telegrams to Truman, the British leader argued forcefully that whatever the result of Poland's forthcoming elections, Stalin had not the remotest intention of freeing the AK captives; also that, whatever happened, the Allies should throw their full weight behind the Poles and keep it there. The way Churchill saw it, Truman would commit a very serious tactical error, *vis-à-vis* world opinion in general and the Russians in particular, if he gave the impression that the Polish question had been settled.

The possession of a précis of these telegrams was of crucial importance to us. Because of it we had clear advance warning that the British would refuse the Hopkins–Stalin compromise on Poland at the conference in Potsdam, which was due to take place the following month.

By virtue of his job at the British Embassy, Homer had access to the contents of telegrams sent by his Prime Minister to the White House, and had personally passed on a copy of this particular communication to his KGB contact, Henry, at the latter's New York apartment. Maclean had an excellent pretext for going frequently to New York from Washington; his wife, Melinda, was living in Manhattan at the home of his mother-in-law, Mrs Dunbar. Moreover, Melinda Maclean was pregnant.

But at this point our hitherto smooth-running system abruptly and disastrously failed us. When the cipher clerk posted in New York set about encoding Homer's résumé and Henry's comments for dispatch to the Centre, he made an appalling blunder. Out of stupidity or negligence or both, he included in his own telegram the internal British Foreign Office code of the original brought in by Maclean. Armed with this code, the most naïve Western investigator into whose hands our telegram might fall could find out in a matter of hours exactly where it had originated: to wit, the British Embassy in Washington. A time bomb had been planted which was to blow our network sky-high four years later.

Four years; yet only eight days after Henry's text had been dispatched to Moscow, the FBI's agents might have unmasked Maclean practically overnight.

On 15 June 1945, Drew Pearson, a well-known American journalist, published a seven-page magazine article revealing the full substance of the Stalin–Hopkins talks at the Kremlin, as well as that of Churchill's telegrams to Truman. His piece contained so much exact detail that the FBI's suspicions were thoroughly aroused. There was another reason: Pearson seemed to have gone out of his way to paint Stalin as tolerant, genial, open-minded and respectful of democracy, whereas in fact there was no question whatever that Uncle Joe planned to offer the West the smallest possible concession over Poland.

The FBI immediately (and correctly) suspected some kind of Soviet propaganda coup. After analysing the contents of the article in depth, American agents deduced that a serious leak had occurred somewhere along the way. They soon discounted any possibility that the White House, which possessed complete transcripts of the Churchill–Truman telegrams, could be the source: had this been the case, the article would certainly have included other details which did not feature in the résumé. Thus the culprit could only be someone within the other two organizations through which the résumé had passed – the State Department, or the British Embassy.

Since J. Edgar Hoover, the director of the FBI, despised all diplomats, and most especially British diplomats, he gleefully focused the investigation on His Majesty's Embassy. Initially the press attaché, John Russell, was suspected of being Pearson's informant, but this scent went cold when Russell returned to London.

The FBI then shifted to a fresh line of investigation. Its people had noticed that some of the factual information in the article seemed fanciful in the extreme: for example, direct telephone conversations between Hopkins and Churchill were mentioned. The FBI checked this with the communications control room at the White House, and received the answer that no trace existed of any such contact between the two men. Purely on the strength of this, the FBI deduced that the journalist had been drawing on his imagination rather than on some sinister contact.

It was a close call for Maclean. Had the FBI delved one inch deeper, they would have discovered that the White House was mistaken; that, in the event, Churchill and Hopkins had had five telephone conversations in three days, but had not deemed it necessary to send transcripts of their conversations either to Truman or to the White House communications control room. And from this the Bureau could have deduced with absolute certainty that there was only one other place in Washington where a third party might be in a position to know the substance of the conversations: and that place was the British Embassy.

What really happened? The American journalist was an unwitting tool of Moscow. His article was orchestrated by the Soviet secret services without his knowing it. Naturally, his information was lifted straight from the document that had been purloined by Maclean and transmitted by Henry to the Centre.

On the other side of the world, the same crucial message from New York to Moscow had been recorded by the Australian eavesdropping facility. There, for a while, it slumbered – until 1948, when Meredith Gardner, the American analyst working for the Army Security Agency (ASA), set about the complex task of working out the key to the Soviet codes. Gardner's job was to work through the hundreds of messages intercepted during the war by the British, the Americans and the Australians. This was the project that was given the code name Venona.

The Gardner team was helped in this mind-numbing drudgery by fragments of a badly scorched book of Soviet ciphers captured by Finnish forces in June 1941. After the USSR entered the war, the Finns successfully launched offensives in Carelia and north of the Gulf of Finland to recover the town of Petsamo (renamed Pechenga), which had been annexed by the USSR after the 1940 conflict between the two countries. It was the duty of the Red Army's cipher clerks to destroy their code books before they themselves were taken prisoner, but in Petsamo one of them was actually taken in the act of burning his manual: the Finns were just in time to snatch the book out of the fire before it was completely consumed. Certain names figured in it, along with their corresponding codes in cipher.

The Finns clung to this intelligence nugget throughout the war years. Then, in 1944, hoping to please the Americans and having no use for it themselves, they handed the Russian manual over to the US Army. Thereafter the Americans found themselves in possession of an important tool for breaking the codes of Soviet telegrams, even though it was not sufficient to reveal all their contents. The US cipher experts took several months of hard labour to transcribe only a few fragments of text; but then the research took a giant step forward when Gardner and his ASA specialists noticed that the Soviet Embassy in Washington had used the same pads for coded messages on two separate occasions in 1942.

To break any code, you need at least one of its basic elements – such as the Finns' manual or a repeated use of the same pad. This can lead first to the identification of complete words, and thereafter, with luck, to identification of the special terminology used in the military, diplomatic and scientific spheres. With patience, cunning, imagination and intuition, you can then hope to translate one or two coded phrases, and by following the same Ariadne's thread enlarge the research to cover whole sentences and finally whole messages.

It happened that in the summer of 1948, Gardner became interested in a text which eventually turned out to be the résumé of telegrams 72 and 73, sent by Churchill to President Truman in 1945.

The translation of one or two odds and ends of sentences took about a year, but it was the deciphering of the signature which was to create a breakthrough for the investigators tracking our mole. From here on, MI5 and the FBI were in a position to launch a full-scale enquiry on the spot.

In the autumn of 1949, our agent Kim Philby, alias Stanley, sent a message from Washington to our services in London containing information of crucial importance. Gardner, with whom he had carefully nurtured a friendship, had shown Philby some passages from a newly deciphered telegram. The text concerned messages that had passed between Churchill and Truman, along with fragments of comments inserted by the KGB handling officer. The name of the mole at its source appeared in black and white for the first time: Homer. Philby had no idea who lurked behind this pseudonym, but he was fairly sure it was one of our agents. A few months later the unsuspecting Gardner tipped him off that there was now no question that the mole was lodged somewhere in the entrails of the Foreign Office.

Our cipher clerk's catastrophic error had finally come home to roost.

The ASA researcher had now worked out that the figures at the head of the message represented an internal Foreign Office code number. Hard on the heels of his first warning, Philby sent another message through to us in London which, after decoding, read: 'I think it's Maclean'. Of course, we knew this already, but we decided to keep Philby in the dark for the time being. In his next dispatch he was less urgent, reassuring us that the clues and allusions to Homer were still very vague. Homer could be any one of hundreds of people; it was enough for a man to have had access, either in London or Washington, to the secret transatlantic communications of 1945 to be a potential suspect.

To begin with, MI5 in Britain was clearly disconcerted by the sheer scale of the investigation which would have to be carried out within the Foreign Office. As for the FBI, Hoover's men focused at the outset on the domestic staff of the British Embassy in Washington, so Maclean, a senior diplomat, could sleep fairly soundly for the time being. Nonetheless, the Venona decoding operation remained, in Philby's words, 'a serious source of concern'.

Korovin and I transmitted all Philby's reports back to the Centre, trying to be objective in assessing the danger. Moscow's answer came back in short order: 'Maclean must be kept in place for as long as possible.'

The trap began to close inexorably in the final months of 1950. The investigators had narrowed their field of suspects to thirty-five individuals. By January 1951, that number had been further reduced to four, all of them diplomats: Paul Gore-Booth, Roger Makins, Michael Wright and Donald Maclean.

In Russian, the name 'Homer' is pronounced 'Gomer'. By a strikingly odd piece of reasoning, MI5 speculated that this fact might establish a link between the names 'Gomer' and 'Gore-Booth'.

Paul Gore-Booth was all the more deeply suspected by the British because they remembered the confessions of Walter Krivitsky. This celebrated spy, the head of GRU (Soviet military intelligence) for Western Europe, was based in Paris. He realized the game was up for him when a friend, Ignaz Reiss, another GRU agent and a covert opponent of Stalin's regime, was found brutally murdered. When Moscow sent Krivitsky a ticket and a false passport to return to the USSR, he smelt a rat and decided to run for it. After a series of hair-raising adventures, he turned up in New York in November 1937 and told everything he knew to the FBI. The following year Krivitsky wrote a book entitled *I Was One of Stalin's Agents*; a few months after its publication, he was found dead in a Washington hotel room, shot in the head.

During his debriefing by the American services, Krivitsky had mentioned a Soviet agent inside the Foreign Office, an old Etonian and an Oxford graduate. The description fitted Gore-Booth. The suspicions hung fire for a while, then abruptly faded. MI5 had turned up some fact – what it was, I never found out – which completely absolved him.

Kim Philby had nothing to do with laying this false scent. Some writers covering the Cambridge ring have claimed he deliberately pointed MI5 in Gore-Booth's direction. This is nonsense. There was no reason for him to intervene, so he confined himself to monitoring the progress of the enquiry: with what fascinated interest, we may well imagine.

The short list of potential moles had now been reduced to three names and it was clear that Maclean might be exposed at any moment. Philby therefore consulted with Burgess, who was still living at his house. The two men decided that the KGB and, above all, Maclean himself should be warned.

Since for reasons of security neither Philby nor Burgess maintained any direct contacts with KGB agents in Washington, the residence in London remained their only link with us. A telegram would be too risky, because the FBI knew quite well that Philby had been informed of the names of the main suspects. Finally Burgess suggested that he himself should go back to England to sound the alert. But how could he get out of the United States without arousing suspicion?

Guy Burgess, who worked at the embassy, could hardly leave his post from one day to the next, and he could hardly tell Sir Oliver Franks that his aged mother had been rushed to hospital in London. Under the circumstances, the rawest MI5 recruit would have put two and two together. So Burgess, who was never at a loss for ideas, suggested he play on his reputation for out-of-control behaviour to get himself sent home. All he needed was a way to set the process in motion.

Burgess's freakish behaviour had long since discredited him in the eyes of his ambassador, who not only hated him personally, but also had a healthy dread of his sharp tongue. This dread was the only real reason why he had not yet fired Burgess from his staff. All Guy needed to do was go altogether too far, and the ambassador would pack him off to England. Guy Burgess therefore seized the first opportunity for scandal that presented itself.

On 28 February 1951, he was invited to Charleston, South Carolina, to represent Great Britain at a conference on international relations to be held by the cadets at the Citadel private military academy. Early in the morning he climbed into his Lincoln to drive the 560 miles from Washington to Charleston. Along the way, he picked up a hitchhiker in US Air Force uniform named James Turck. Barely twenty miles from Washington, near Woodbridge, Virginia, Burgess was pulled in for speeding by a motorcycle cop. He showed his diplomatic pass and the officer let him carry on, but not before he had informed his superiors of the incident. Burgess repeated the same exploit at Ashland, Virginia, where he sped past a military convoy at over 90 mph, with similar results. The officer released him, having checked his papers. South of Richmond, Burgess told his passenger to take the wheel. On Highway 301 near Petersburg, the Lincoln grossly exceeded the speed limit for the third time and was pursued by a police car. Turck showed his driver's licence, but Burgess intervened, drunkenly flourishing his own diplomatic pass and bellowing that the American was his 'chauffeur'. This time the officer was less inclined to be lenient and ran the pair in to the local police station. A call to the highway communications centre confirmed that Burgess had already broken the traffic laws twice that day. He was fined fifty dollars on the spot, and the district judge remitted the case to the governor of Virginia.

At Charleston, Burgess parted company with Turck and checked into a hotel. Next day he calmly attended his conference and drove quietly back to Washington on Monday 5 March.

Ten days later an irate letter from the office of the governor of Virginia reached the State Department head of protocol, complaining of Burgess's repeated and flagrant violations of the Highway Code, which could have caused a serious accident, and accusing the British diplomat of gross arrogance and abusive behaviour towards officers of the law.

In due course the governor's letter reached the British Embassy, along with a copy of the declarations made by the police officers, which of course were deeply uncomplimentary about Burgess. Ambassador Franks consulted his Foreign Office superiors on 7 April. Nine days later, on his return from the weekend, Burgess was summoned by the ambassador and given notice that he was to be sent back to England in disgrace. Burgess simulated a furious tantrum and stormed out of the room. On 18 April the British Embassy informed the US State Department that Burgess would be recalled by the Foreign Office and would leave Washington at the earliest opportunity.

At the beginning of 1993, I met with agents of the FBI who had worked on the Burgess affair in 1951. They were still convinced that Burgess's departure from Washington was involuntary, that his scandalous behaviour with the highway patrol had nothing to do with any deep-laid plan. They couldn't have been more wrong. Philby and Burgess concocted the whole simple stratagem to get Guy home to England.

The two friends dined together the night before Burgess was to leave, and for the first time Kim explained the full gravity of the situation. Another piece of the telegram had been decoded by Gardner and his team, and it revealed a new detail of Homer's identity. The KGB duty officer, in a sentence accompanying the main text, had referred to his *Washington* agent, and this despite the fact that the telegrams had been cabled from New York, where he himself had to be based. According to Gardner, it was very much on the cards that whoever was the embassy mole had made the journey from one city to the other in the days immediately following 5 June 1945, with the purpose of delivering the substance of telegrams 72 and 73 to his Soviet contact. Philby instantly realized that this must mean Maclean, that Maclean was Homer. He remembered only too well that Melinda Maclean had been living in New York with her mother in 1945, and that Donald frequently travelled to and from Washington to see her.

Still over dinner, the two men worked out a plan in two stages, the first being to warn Maclean in London, and the second to arrange his now inevitable defection. There was not a moment to lose: MI5 might arrest their man at any moment. At the end of the evening, Philby made Burgess swear that he would sit tight in London after Maclean's departure for the Soviet Union. He explained to him in the strongest terms that if he broke now and scrambled off to Russia with Donald, MI5's logical next step would be to arrest Kim Philby. Guy Burgess gave his word he would do no such thing, and on this note the two men parted. They knew they were caught in a race against time – and they also knew the *Queen Mary* would take at least five days to carry Burgess across the Atlantic.

Meanwhile I was waiting anxiously in London. Anthony Blunt had heard nothing from Maclean since their last contact in April, at which time he had seemed feverish and wretched; close to breaking point, Blunt claimed. Of course, Maclean was intensely aware of the deep suspicion surrounding him at work. His colleagues avoided him, and secret documents no longer seemed to come his way.

On the *Queen Mary*, Burgess, true to form, struck up an amorous acquaintance with a young American student named Miller. The two men got on well, and Guy invited his new friend to stay at his flat in London. As soon as he disembarked, Burgess made contact with Blunt, who habitually served as the intermediary between him and our branch of the KGB. He alerted Blunt to the seriousness of the situation and relayed his own and Philby's views about what should be done. Briefly, they felt that Donald Maclean should slip out of England and cross over to the Soviet Union as quickly as he could. Blunt immediately agreed to warn our side, since he was due to meet Peter (my code name) very shortly.

'Shortly' turned out to be the very next day. Anthony Blunt arrived at our assignation his usual calm, controlled self, but I knew something was desperately wrong. Behind the mask he was deeply worried. Under normal circumstances I was the first to speak: this time, he was.

'Peter, there's serious trouble. Guy Burgess has just arrived back in London. Homer's about to be arrested. MI5 has focused on three men, and now it seems they have a lead which points straight to Maclean. It's only a question of days now, maybe hours.'

He went on to explain that according to Burgess, Philby and himself, Maclean's imminent interrogation would wipe out our entire network; and that we must move immediately but with extreme caution, because no doubt Maclean was already under heavy surveillance.

I listened impassively. I had expected this moment to come sooner or later, ever since I heard that the Americans were making progress in their efforts to decode our telegrams.

'Donald's now in such a state that I'm convinced he'll break down the moment they question him,' added Blunt with finality.

I knew I couldn't take any decision on my own at this stage – my superiors back in Moscow would have to be consulted. We scheduled a meeting for two days later, but this time I told Blunt I would rather Burgess himself came to see me. I felt Burgess might have some fresh information for us, and, given the urgency of the situation, I would rather do away with the intermediary and meet the agent face to face.

To impress on Blunt that we were taking the matter very seriously, I told him I would bring the KGB's London resident along with me. Naturally enough, Korovin was determined to play his part in this affair (it was his duty anyway to do so), but I was far from happy about it because latterly he had begun disregarding the tight security rules he himself had laid down for the rest of us. Korovin considered himself above such things. He had been known to go to clandestine meetings in one of the embassy cars, and sometimes was foolhardy enough to place direct calls to agents in their offices. Carelessness like this could easily prove fatal under the present sensitive circumstances; but there was nothing I could do about it. It was hardly my place to denounce my superior in the service. Moreover, I knew Korovin had contracted a heart disease, which might well be affecting his behaviour. So I confined myself to an account of the gravity of the situation, making it seem even worse than it was in the hope that it might scare him into behaving with greater caution: and the ploy seemed to work, because thereafter he scarcely put a foot wrong.

We had about forty-eight hours to contact Moscow, receive our orders and plan our moves. The Centre reacted very quickly. Its message was clear and unambiguous: 'We agree to your organizing Maclean's defection. We will receive him here and provide him with whatever he needs, if he wishes to go through with it.'

At the meeting with Korovin, Burgess confirmed Blunt's remarks in every detail. We ordered him to contact Donald as soon as possible, to put him in the picture and convince him there was no alternative to defection.

On his arrival in London, Burgess had asked the Foreign Office personnel department for a few days off to settle some private business. Thereafter he was our only link with Maclean, because Blunt could no longer contact him in safety.

In the most official manner possible, Guy paid a call on his friend

Donald in his room at the Foreign Office. The two chatted for a few minutes about one thing and another, like a couple of civil servants, good friends meeting on their return from different missions. As they did so, Burgess discreetly scribbled a note suggesting an urgent meeting at the Reform Club. His precautions were wise enough – it was clear that Donald was already under close watch, probably with his phones tapped and his office bugged.

They met later at the Reform. Guy explained what he knew at some length; Maclean showed no surprise. 'They've been watching me for some while now,' he said. 'I see no more confidential telegrams or documents. I told Blunt all about it. I'm expecting a summons from my superiors, or from MI5, any day now.'

Burgess then set out his reading of the case, which was shared by Philby, Blunt and the Centre: Maclean's best course now was to run. Donald sagged visibly.

After a long silence, he confessed that he hadn't the strength to face the coming confrontation. He was aware of his own weakness. He knew he would never be able to soldier on for months, maybe years, stolidly denying everything. He knew he would end up confessing; but still he couldn't make up his mind to leave. And there was his family to think of. Melinda was due to have her baby in three weeks' time: he couldn't bear to abandon her.

Throughout this period of emergency Korovin and I took turns meeting with Blunt and Burgess. It was to Korovin that Burgess reported in the evening on his discussion with Maclean that very day. Within the hour, the news was relayed to the Centre, which immediately responded: 'Homer *must* agree to defect.'

Korovin went back to Burgess and told him to insist. Burgess duly did, and this time Donald came up with a new, alarmingly specious objection. He announced that if his way to Russia led through Paris, he would never reach Soviet territory. Burgess didn't understand what he meant.

'You *have* to understand,' said Maclean. 'I've got friends in Paris from way back, and if I see them I'll hit the bottle again and never find the strength to leave.'

Burgess swept this extraordinary argument aside with the assurance that we could find somebody to go with him if he wished. And this, in fact, was exactly what Maclean wanted – he wasn't strong enough to do the thing alone.

The problem of Melinda, heavily pregnant with her third child, was much thornier. I advised Burgess to authorize Maclean to raise the issue of his defection with her, to see how she felt about it. The Centre had agreed to this because, contrary to what the experts have written since the event, Melinda was very much in the know. Before they were married, Donald had so far disobeyed the rules of the profession as to tell her every detail of his intelligence work for the Soviet Union. He felt it his duty to inform her of this before she became his wife. Astonishing though this may seem, it was the exact truth. Melinda, who even then could not have been described as passionately in love with Maclean, had nevertheless accepted this state of affairs. Moreover, in 1943, when we decided to change our system of liaison with Maclean, he had himself suggested that Melinda act as the go-between for all our contacts. This idea was rejected, but all the same the fact remains that Melinda Maclean was fully abreast of her husband's activities as a Soviet spy.

When Donald spoke to her of his conversation with Burgess, revealing that we all thought he should run, she concurred immediately. 'They're quite right,' she said briskly. 'Go as soon as you can, don't waste a single moment.'

It was quite clear to Melinda that should the blow fall, her husband would fold very rapidly under interrogation. Therefore she did her utmost to help us get him out quickly and efficiently.

So now we had to find someone to go with him. Again the Centre was consulted. It radioed back: 'Burgess will leave with Maclean, but only as his travelling companion.'

In retrospect, I believe that these few short, ambiguous words ultimately sealed the fate of our Cambridge network. If Maclean had been willing to leave alone, the network might never have been exposed and Guy Burgess might have lived out his days happily in England: and he might perhaps be still alive today.

At the next meeting, Korovin and I asked Burgess if he would go along with Maclean to keep him out of trouble along the way. He was stunned.

'If I do that, I'll never be able to come back. I could *never* live anywhere but London, you all know that.'

Korovin didn't think this was much of an objection. Then Burgess tried a different line, which to him appeared conclusive.

'It's out of the question. I gave my word to Kim that I wouldn't run.

Before I left him in Washington, he said: "Warn Maclean by all means, but don't go with him when he goes. If you do, that'll be the end of me. Swear that you won't," he said, and I swore.'

He was talking nineteen to the dozen, close to hysteria.

'Very well,' said Korovin, 'I take your point; I understand your concern over protecting Philby. All I want you to do now is accompany Maclean. You should behave in such a way that should you be investigated, it will be obvious you hadn't the least intention of defecting. You'll be able to tell anyone who asks that all you meant to do was help a friend who asked you to drive him abroad in a hurry.'

I've no idea whether Burgess actually swallowed this baloney, but in any event he agreed. It's my view that he was paralysed by the rapidity with which everything was unravelling; for one thing, Korovin conspicuously omitted to tell him exactly where he and Maclean should part company on the road to exile. Nor did Korovin instruct Burgess on whether or not he should go beyond the Iron Curtain – and Burgess certainly didn't ask.

How on earth could Burgess be expected to convince the British counter-intelligence services that he had helped Maclean escape for motives of pure friendship, and, having done so, that he had strictly nothing to do with the latter's espionage? Why he agreed to go without any guarantee of return is beyond my understanding. I should add, however, that the Centre was no longer greatly concerned about what happened to Burgess. As long as he agreed to go with Maclean, the rest mattered precious little. Cynically enough, the Centre had also concluded that we had not one but two burnt-out agents on our hands. Burgess had lost most of his former value to us, even if he retained his job, an eventuality that seemed remote enough, given his recent antics. He could never again feed intelligence to the KGB as he had done before. He was finished.

In retrospect, I think we could have acted otherwise. Instead of bringing both men out, it would have been possible for one of our own people, or even for me, to tail Maclean through France at a discreet distance. As we say in Russia, the best ideas all too often occur to you after the event.

Next day I saw Blunt again. He had more bad news. Philby had taken the huge risk of contacting Burgess from the United States.

Ostensibly the message was about what should be done about Burgess's Lincoln, which he'd left in the embassy car park. This innocuous message ended with a deeply ominous sentence: 'It's getting very hot over here.'

Behind Philby's warning was a chain of events about which we as yet knew nothing: Geoffrey Patterson, the MI5 officer in charge of the Homer investigation, had told Kim that his final report would reach London on 22 or 23 May. Hence we had barely a week to spirit our man out of England before the British would be ready to act – but, as I say, of this we were unaware.

Blunt also told me that Burgess was dangerously overwrought and might even become uncontrollable. Both Donald and he had to be extracted double quick – but how?

Pacing along side by side through Regent's Park, we reviewed the various alternatives. Trains and planes were out of the question. Burgess might be able to cross frontiers unsuspected, but there would be police watching for Maclean at every border. Given that he was already under investigation by MI5, the immigration services must surely have been informed.

False papers were another possibility, but there was no way these could be produced in England in the short time at our disposal. There was also that classic spy-novel device, a submarine appearing at a discreet rendezvous somewhere along the coast – believe it or not, this was always a serious option for us where England was concerned – but again time was far too short.

Then Blunt suggested one of the ships that sailed from the southern English ports and cruised along the French coast. These vessels left England on Friday evenings, put in at two or three Continental ports over the weekend, and returned the following Sunday night or Monday morning. Above all – and this was the main interest for us – immigration controls on these excursions were virtually non-existent. I was astonished by this, but Blunt explained that such cruises were particularly favoured by businessmen and senior civil servants, people who might want to spend a few days in isolation with a secretary or a mistress. For this reason, the immigration services showed unique restraint.

I thought the idea a sound one. We agreed on a further meeting with Burgess and parted. The next step was to arrange the practical side of the journey.

With Korovin's approval, I collected a pile of brochures, compared schedules and embarkation procedures and selected what I thought was the most suitable ship. This was the *Falaise*, due to leave Southampton at midnight the following Friday, cruise along the French coast for forty-eight hours, and return to England on Sunday evening. Two or three short stopovers were scheduled, notably one at St-Malo. After checking carefully with the tour organizers and giving out that I planned to travel incognito accompanied by a young woman, I discovered that Blunt was right: passengers' papers were not checked, since it was felt that in theory the ship constituted British territory. I reported my findings to Korovin, who accepted the plan immediately.

Korovin then met with Burgess, explained the plan we had devised and told him to book two berths on the *Falaise* for the weekend of 25–27 May. He also recommended that Burgess set up some kind of false trail to confuse the opposition.

Burgess, who seemed to Korovin considerably less nervous than before, pointed out some of the drawbacks. At the Reform Club, Maclean had told him MI5 was watching his every move; he had had to work hard to get to their rendezvous without being followed. On the other hand, according to Maclean it was very possible that the tail left him at Victoria Station when he took the train home to Tatsfield in Kent. He'd also noticed that somebody was waiting for him every morning at Victoria when he got off the train and made his way to the Foreign Office. In short, all his comings and goings were closely watched by MI5 – but only in London.

This seemed quite plausible to me, because I knew by experience how hard it was to arrange a tail outside town. In the urban milieu, it's a simple matter for a watcher to keep out of sight, but in the country, in a village for example, it's another story. To follow Maclean to his home in Tatsfield would be awkward for MI5. On the train, too, Donald would know the other passengers by sight, all of them being people who had taken the same trains for years, to and from their offices. A follower would stick out like a sore thumb at the little station at Tatsfield, especially since Donald always went home from the station by car, never on foot. MI5 might manage the thing successfully once or twice, but certainly not on a daily basis. Thus we were sure there were serious shortcomings in the surveillance of Maclean, because even though the English intelligence services clearly expected the worst, they had not yet deployed in force around our agent.

We mounted a counter-surveillance operation at short notice which confirmed that Maclean was correct on all points. At Victoria, MI5's men saw the train out of the station, then headed home like good little functionaries. There was no one at Tatsfield to take up the chase. We concluded that Donald could leave his home without the slightest fear of pursuit.

Burgess rose to the occasion splendidly. On 24 May, he bought two tickets for the weekend cruise and set up a serviceable false scent. He told his new boyfriend, Miller, that they were off on a trip together, then dropped in at the Reform several times and fumbled ostentatiously with unwieldy road-maps of the north of England. He even discussed the merits of various routes with one of the club servants, before renting a car and letting it be known he was 'going to Scotland'.

On Friday 25 May, the big day, Burgess called Miller and suggested they embark on a friend's yacht that evening. He went to a shop, where he bought a suitcase and one or two other travelling articles, and chattered on about his forthcoming holiday in the north. All this, he thought, might help him if he was interrogated by counter-intelligence on his return.

And then for once in his life Burgess followed his orders to the letter. In the early evening he drove down to Tatsfield in his rented car. It happened to be Donald's thirty-eighth birthday. Melinda was busy preparing a special dinner in the kitchen when Burgess appeared at the door and introduced himself as 'Roger Styles', a fellow employee of Donald's at the Foreign Office. Melinda, who knew Burgess perfectly well, called her husband; the two men spoke in private for a few minutes, then everybody settled down to dinner. At around 9 p.m. Maclean went upstairs to kiss his sons good night, while Burgess waited in the hall. Donald then took his leave of Melinda, and the two men vanished into the night.

Officially, they had gone off to finish the evening at a local pub – at least, this was what Melinda told the MI5 agents who came to see her the following Monday morning.

Melinda heard Burgess's car start smoothly, and then nothing. Guy and Donald had very little time to get to Southampton. They took turns at the wheel, driving as fast as they dared.

They couldn't know that the decision to interrogate Maclean had been taken that very morning, at a meeting between the heads of MI5 and the Foreign Office. I learned later that once again we had been unbelievably lucky because MI5 was caught in something of a bind by this decision. The British Secret Service had resolved never to produce an official confirmation of the results of the Venona decoding programme, and of course Venona was the only concrete proof they had against Homer (Maclean). Hence the investigators would be obliged to extract a confession from their suspect if they meant to bring him to justice – and as they knew all too well, there is nothing so awkward to obtain as a true confession.

This partly explains MI5's indecisiveness and delay; the fact was they couldn't settle on which method was most likely to be successful in breaking Maclean.

The Deputy Under-Secretary of State at the Foreign Office, Roger Makins, was present at the fateful Friday morning meeting when the mandarins finally settled on a course of action. The same afternoon Herbert Morrison, who had succeeded the late Ernest Bevin as Foreign Secretary, gave the green light for an interrogation as soon as Maclean arrived for work the following Monday.

After the event, the press not surprisingly seized on the fact that Maclean vanished on the Friday evening, when his interrogation had just been appointed for Monday. To many journalists this seemed to be a highly suspicious coincidence. Some said straight out that the diabolical Soviets must have installed a mole at the highest level of government or the intelligence services, a mole who had tipped off Maclean and Burgess to the coming interrogation. This assertion was completely false. Our side knew only too well that sooner or later Maclean would be put to the question, but we had no idea at all when this would happen. Our timing of his disappearance was pure luck and nothing more.

Two minutes before midnight on 25 May 1951, the car containing Burgess and Maclean screeched to a halt on Southampton dock. The two agents leapt out and sprinted for the *Falaise*, whose crew was already in the act of pulling up the gangway and casting off. They left the car just as it was, skewed across the middle of the road.

Later, journalists speculated that Burgess's abandonment of his car at the dockside was some kind of signal for his accomplices. Far from it; the two men simply reached the ship with seconds to spare and they had no time to park properly.

On the morning of 26 May, Maclean and Burgess disembarked at St-Malo. Along with their fellow passengers they entered French territory without passing through any border checkpoint, leaving all their luggage aboard. Under a steady drizzle, they made as if to explore the town, then quietly hailed a taxi and had the driver take them to Rennes, over forty miles away. Questioned later, the driver said he had dropped them at the railway station, but had no idea what train they might have taken thereafter. In fact they went straight to Paris, crossed the city from the Gare Montparnasse to the Gare d'Austerlitz, and travelled on without a break to Geneva and Berne.

On their arrival at the Swiss capital, Burgess made his way to the Soviet Embassy, where he was given two false British passports with photographs slightly altered and different surnames. He and Maclean had been outside British territory for twenty-four hours and still no one had raised the alarm. Carrying their new documents, the fugitives pressed on to Zurich, where they caught a plane to Stockholm via Prague. In the airport of the Czech capital they walked out of the international zone and were immediately taken in hand by KGB agents. By Sunday night, Burgess and Maclean were safely within Soviet territory.

On Monday morning I received word that the operation had been a total success. Our mission had been accomplished in every detail: not only had we spirited Maclean out of England, but we had also done so in such a way that nobody could prove that his final destination was the Soviet Union. Of course, you didn't have to be a genius to guess that he had gone to Russia, but we didn't mind that. The important thing for us was to keep the whole affair shrouded in mystery for as long as possible.

But still I wondered why Burgess hadn't turned back at Prague. I think now he may have been subjected to certain pressures; he may even have been offered some kind of guarantee that he would be taken back to England fairly rapidly. Knowing the man's character, I believe he may have imagined he'd be given a few days to enjoy himself in Moscow, and then would drift back to London as if nothing had happened. Little did he know what really awaited him.

* * *

On Monday, Melinda Maclean made two calls to the Foreign Office. The first was to the American desk to ask if her husband was there, or if he had left any message for her. The second was to Carey Foster, the ministry's security chief. She told Foster her husband had gone out on Friday night with a Foreign Office colleague and she hadn't heard from him since.

It wasn't until 30 May, five days after Donald's disappearance, that Melinda was finally interviewed by MI5. She was at the Kensington home of her mother-in-law, Lady Maclean, when a couple of inspectors rang the doorbell. She stated that her husband had gone away on the previous Friday evening with a Foreign Office colleague named Styles. She described Styles's appearance and made a show of deep anxiety. The officers asked both women to say nothing to anyone about the matter till further notice, and went back to their headquarters. It didn't take them long to establish that there was no such person as Roger Styles.

Around 7 June, Lady Maclean received a reassuring telegram signed 'Teento', the nickname she had given her son when he was a child. Shortly afterwards Melinda, too, received a message, this time signed Donald. In a few short sentences, he begged his wife to forgive him for his sudden departure, assured her that he was in good health and sent her his love.

The defection of Burgess and Maclean wreaked havoc among the British authorities. A blanket check of the political opinions of literally hundreds of civil servants was set in motion, the emphasis being laid on those men and women who occupied, or had occupied, sensitive positions in the intelligence services. Naturally, the press set up a corresponding hue and cry. Any top official who might have flirted with leftist elements at Oxford or Cambridge in the thirties was specifically targeted.

This was not all. Everyone who at some time or another had known Burgess or Maclean or both was called in for questioning by MI5. Their university friends, including Blunt, and hundreds of other former Marxists were interrogated. Some got off the hook by stating that they were by no means the only students at great British universities to have been Communists or Communist fellow-travellers in their youth. But for others it proved not so easy.

Alan Maclean, Donald's brother, was like him a top civil servant, and a member of the British delegation to the United Nations. He was forced to resign. The husband of Donald's sister Nancy also lost his job. These men, who had nothing whatever to do with espionage, saw their careers shattered by the paranoia which had set in among the various arms of the British Secret Service.

From 1951 onwards, the MI5 officers Peter Wright and Arthur Martin orchestrated a witch-hunt for agents supposedly recruited by Burgess. As time went by, their determination to smoke out traitors in the British Secret Service became an obsession. They were convinced, for example, that Burgess had constructed an extensive network of agents under his own direction, which over the years had spread to every level of the intelligence community. They could not have been more mistaken. Burgess had no tame informers, just friends and acquaintances from whom he extracted information without their noticing. Nevertheless, the thrashings and posturings of Wright and Martin cast suspicion on the entire secret establishment of their country. Indeed, the witch-hunt created so deeply unpleasant an atmosphere within the British intelligence community that many of the most valuable officers simply resigned from MI5 and MI6.

Peter Wright was extraordinarily proud of his methods of investigation. Later he boasted that to obtain good results in the enquiry into the activities of Russian spies in Britain, MI5 had spread a remarkably fine-meshed net which was guaranteed to bring in the maximum number of suspects. In fact, the procedure was criminally stupid, because its only concrete result was to humiliate a number of innocent people. Dozens of agents were sacked, disgraced and insulted; some confessed to errors they never committed; and a few were harassed into suicide. In my own view, Peter Wright loathed not only Soviet agents, justifiably enough, but also all intellectuals and professors into the bargain, particularly if they came from Cambridge. To be precise, he despised the British Establishment.

The atmosphere of paranoia was short-lived. To their credit, those at the head of the secret services soon understood that the enquiry had taken a disastrous turn. A halt was called within SIS; but not before a great deal of harm had been done by Peter Wright. For several years his obstinate insistence on seeing Burgess's henchmen behind every tree distracted the attention of the British intelligence service from its real job, which was to win the struggle with the KGB. The blunder was all the more damaging because our own services were going through a crisis at that time. We had to cope with a wave of defections all over the world, and most of the networks we had set up during the war were either destroyed or destabilized. So we reacted to the furore within the British intelligence community with profound relief, coming as it did at a juncture when they were in a position to do us irreparable harm.

It is my considered opinion that SIS was, and remains, a highly effective organization, perhaps even more so than the KGB. When I worked with our British agents, I had plenty of time to evaluate MI5, and the qualities and defects of the people working for it. It was my general impression that their agents were thoroughly competent – and honest.

On 30 May 1951, Geoffrey Patterson, Philby's MI5 colleague in Washington, told him that Maclean had gone over. Philby feigned astonishment, but when Patterson added that Burgess had also defected, his horror was real. He instantly realized that he, too, was now heavily compromised within the service, but he kept his head. Characteristically, he reviewed in his mind the various items in his possession which might convict him. He had no trouble disposing of the documents, which he burned in his fireplace. A few days after the news of the defections broke, he slipped away to Virginia to 'relax' for a couple of days. There he disencumbered himself of the cameras he had used to photograph CIA and MI5 internal documents in the United States.

Less than a week after his return to Washington, he heard that the director of the CIA had demanded his immediate recall to England.

It must be said that the normally efficient SIS made a complete hash of this particular affair from start to finish. To begin with, they took an astonishingly long time to work out how we had got our agents out of England. We had, of course, spoiled the scent fairly comprehensively by sending reassuring notes to the families of Burgess and Maclean from Paris, Beirut and Cairo. It was not until mid-June, however, that the press got hold of the story, with the *Daily Express*'s sensational announcement that two British diplomats had disappeared.

The affair was instantly launched on to the front pages of newspapers throughout the world. Reports of sightings flooded in:

the fugitives had been seen in Montmartre, Montparnasse, Bayonne, Cannes, Andorra, Brussels and Prague. Prague perhaps – but we were certain that nobody had been able to identify them during their brief stopover.

Now that Burgess and Maclean were safely out of the way, I had only to eradicate any clues they might have left behind which could compromise the remaining members of their network. In this Blunt proved very useful to me, because he still retained the confidence of our adversaries.

At the beginning of June, MI5 had been in no hurry to break the scandal and reveal its own negligence by having Burgess's flat and Maclean's house thoroughly searched. So they asked Blunt, who was widely known to have been a close friend of Burgess, to get hold of the key to his home. Apparently, the investigators were hoping to accumulate as much proof as possible against the two traitors, but they wanted to do so discreetly. Blunt, of course, agreed to perform this small service for his chums at MI5. Jack Hewit, another former lover of Burgess, gave him the key to the flat. This breathtaking, almost comical stroke of luck gave us several hours to tidy up after Burgess and destroy anything there that might possibly compromise us or one of our agents. Knowing Burgess as well as I did, I was sure he hadn't taken even the most elementary precautions. One or two clues to his secret work were bound to have been left in plain view. Furthermore, he had left in such a hurry and in such a high state of excitement that I was convinced he hadn't bothered to do any more than the most basic 'housework', as we call it.

So Anthony Blunt paid a quiet visit to Burgess's lair. From the chaos of newspapers, files and books scattered about he retrieved what he could of anything damning. Best of all, he found Philby's last telegram, with the fatal last line, 'It's getting very hot over here'. This he burned, along with a sheaf of other papers. When I told Burgess about this episode in Moscow, he denied everything, swearing up and down that he had gone through the flat as carefully as possible before leaving.

When Blunt finally turned over the key to MI5, they rushed into the flat and searched it thoroughly. Later they said they had come across one or two hand-written notes referring to a confidential meeting in Whitehall in 1939. According to them, John Colville, one of the participants, recognized the handwriting of John Cairncross. I think this story was pure invention and bluff: there was no link whatever between Paul (Burgess) and the Carelian (Cairncross), particularly at that time.

Nonetheless Cairncross, like so many other civil servants working in the Foreign Office, was under MI5 scrutiny. This was brought home to me in June, exactly a month after the departure of Burgess and Maclean.

It was a glorious summer evening; I had an appointment with Cairncross at Ealing Common tube station, at our customary hour of 8 p.m. Cairncross was due to hand over a bundle of documents. The sky was cloudless and I felt relaxed and sure of myself, despite the threat hanging over the remains of my network. The Carelian's latest delivery of documents about NATO had earned me the congratulations of our bureau chief.

I was on a street that ran straight into the thoroughfare where the tube station was, walking slowly along with a newspaper under my arm, window-shopping. The sinking sun cast a deep shadow over the pavement fronting the shops, so it was hard for people to see me in the half-shade but easy enough for me to observe exactly what was going on in the broad, sunlit road beyond.

Cairncross and I had agreed that he would emerge from the Underground, cross the street and enter the public lavatories set slightly back from the pavement on the far side. About a hundred yards away from me was a bus stop; I noted the figures of two people waiting there. Nothing out of the ordinary. As I walked along I checked my wristwatch. In three minutes my agent should appear, cross the street and enter the lavatories, and I would follow. There, from one stall to another, he would pass me the envelope full of documents.

I was only fifty yards off when I spotted Cairncross. He was a trifle early, unusually for him. I stepped up my pace.

Turning into the main road, I glanced at the figures at the bus stop – an old woman and a young man. Something wasn't quite right about the man. He wasn't standing slightly back from the kerb, as Londoners normally do, but right on the edge, in a posture that had nothing remotely to do with waiting for a bus. I don't know why I thought this; I just did. Glancing to the left, I saw a second man, slightly older, seated on a bench a few yards back from the toilets.

I had been an operative for nearly seven years at that time, and by now I knew I could rely on my intuition. I sensed danger. This impression grew when I spotted the young man at the bus stop glancing furtively at the bench, as if to indicate that all was well. I thought the seated man threw him an answering look. Were they watching Cairncross, who had reached his destination? At the point of crossing to join him, I hesitated. I had a split second to decide. Should I carry this thing through? No. I veered off to the right along an alley, where I knew there was a second-hand jewellery shop. I examined a display of necklaces in the window and considered what I should do next. Perhaps I was imagining things; perhaps this was paranoia. I didn't always meet the Carelian in deserted places, after all, and this wasn't the first time other people had been around at one of our contacts. Finally I decided it was best to abort the meeting. I turned away from the window, walked off and made my way straight home.

Korovin was less than understanding. He didn't bother with basic security precautions any more and even took his embassy cars to secret meetings. Of course, I couldn't say anything and had to listen to his contemptuous reprimands. 'What's happened, Yuri Ivanovich? Scared of something, were you? Impossible. The Carelian's never been tailed, you told me so yourself.'

I told him in detail what had passed – I even made a detailed sketch of the rendezvous, explaining exactly why my suspicions had been aroused. But Korovin was sure I had lost my nerve. 'When a man has the wind up,' he sneered, 'he always uses intuition as an excuse.' He went off and wrote a negative report to Moscow, asserting that a vitally important contact had been called off entirely by my fault. The Centre responded with a severe reprimand, barely stopping short of an open accusation of cowardice.

I got out of this situation by explaining very clearly to my superiors that all was not lost, that the contact with the Carelian wasn't broken off entirely, because Cairncross and I had made three provisional rendezvous in the event of just such an incident as this one. In eight days we were to meet at the same place and the same time. Should this plan also abort, there was a second fall-back: and if even this did not work, we would apply the procedure of long-term contacts.

This calmed everybody down for a while, but unfortunately

Cairncross didn't show up at any of our fall-back assignations. My conviction was strengthened that I had been right to abort the first Ealing Common contact, but Korovin wasn't happy at all. Thereafter it was open war between us. I had to find a means of reaching Cairncross. It took me several weeks, because he very seldom went out, and when he did he was never alone. I spent hours on end waiting to intercept him between his office and his home. Finally I managed it, in a spot where I was certain we were safe. I walked a few yards behind him and spoke straight at his back, naming an hour and a place where we could meet. He nodded his head once and went on.

This time, he showed up. The rendezvous was outside town, and as soon as I saw him I knew something had happened. I explained my reasons for backing off at Ealing Common and asked him if he had noticed anything out of the ordinary. No, he had seen nothing. As to the other prearranged meetings, he hadn't appeared because he'd been frankly terrified.

'Immediately after the first meeting, I was interrogated by counter-espionage. They were courteous enough, but then the tone got more and more disagreeable. They held over my head the fact that I'd been a Communist at Cambridge. I repeated over and over again that I had never hidden the fact, that my Communism was just youthful folly and my opinions had changed long since. That's why I didn't turn up to meet you, Peter.'

I considered. It was obvious that Cairncross was under huge pressure, but I sensed his breaking point was still some way off. I reassured him as far as I could, pointing out that he had come through several hours of interrogation and there was no reason why the same procedure should be repeated. After all, we had left no trace of our activities for the investigators to follow up. But then he told me the worst part, which was that for the time being MI5 had barred his access to confidential Treasury information, on account of the general climate of suspicion within the civil service. Cairncross had accepted this with a show of complete understanding, agreeing without a murmur to work in a different department.

I realized at once that my association with the Carelian was about to terminate, but before any decision was made I felt I should consult with the Centre. Cairncross understood this and we settled on yet another meeting. As I watched him leave the square, slowly, his shoulders slightly bowed, I thought to myself, 'There goes a brave man.' He certainly appeared less concerned about his own fate than I was.

As soon as I got back to the embassy I dispatched a report to Moscow, expressing my personal view that the British Secret Service would continue to hound Cairncross in the foreseeable future. The answer came back promptly. I was to cease working with him altogether.

Before our final meeting, Korovin gave me a large sum of money – exactly how much I forget – to hand over to Cairncross. The Carelian had never asked us for anything in return for his services, but in this instance our people had decided a gift of money was the best way of showing our gratitude. As a rule I was strongly against paying agents; the element of money made for ambiguous relationships and the craving for it could lead to deception. But in the case of Cairncross, with whom we were about to break relations entirely, I felt that a cash offering was a good idea. The man had recently married a young woman named Gabriella and a little money would come in very useful for fixing up the couple's flat. At the least it would allow him to live comfortably for a year or two.

At our final interview, I noticed no change at all in Cairncross's manner. He listened calmly as I told him the news.

'The Centre now feels that it would be best for all concerned if we parted company for good. You've done plenty of useful work for us and we have no right to endanger you any further at this point. If we stop now, the opposition will never have any grounds for accusing you. In any case, as things stand at present they have no actual proof against you, and we would rather it stayed that way.'

Cairncross grinned. 'I really don't think I've made any serious mistakes,' he said. 'They've nothing solid against me, only hearsay. But I'd very much like to know who put them on my track. By no means all of the other ex-Communists were transferred, so why me? There may be a turncoat or a mole at the bottom of it. If you've got someone of that nature in your services, you'd do well to smoke him out.'

At the moment of parting, I handed him the envelope with the cash in it. He slipped it into his coat without a word, and I left him sitting quietly in the half-darkness. We never saw each other again.

A couple of years ago I read, in a series of documents about the Carelian, that he had been tailed by the British Secret Service ever since June 1951, the month he and I had our aborted meeting at Ealing Common station. So we had a close call that day, after all. My intuition had not failed me.

Later, I heard that John Cairncross had been interrogated several times more, before he left the Treasury altogether and went abroad.

Some people say he was finally exposed by MI5 in 1964. I think he confessed, but well before that date, in 1951 or possibly 1952, during interrogation by the famous investigator William Skardon, the same who broke Klaus Fuchs, the atomic spy. There is evidence for this, albeit indirect. Personally I am convinced that Cairncross told everything he knew in the early 1950s, in exchange for a promise of immunity.

If John Cairncross was never brought to trial, the reason must be that there was insufficient evidence to convict him. In other words, our side had done a first-rate job from beginning to end.

I lost track of Cairncross in the years immediately following his expulsion. Apparently he travelled to the United States and Asia, before returning to Rome, where he worked for the UN Food and Agriculture Organization's Agriculture Section. This, at any rate, is the story that emerges from the KGB files.

Cairncross's absence from British territory did not prevent MI5 from pursuing its investigation of his activities. In 1967, when he was in Rome, they discovered he had been recruited long ago by James Klugman at Cambridge. So they brought him back to England and made him attempt a ploy that most intelligence services are familiar with: that of recruiting the man who recruited him, i.e. Klugman. Cairncross duly called on his old friend, who was still a leading member of the Communist Party, and suggested he work for British intelligence. Klugman roared with laughter and told Cairncross the people who had sent him must be dismally ill-informed: he had already acted as a British intelligence officer during the war. There the matter rested and Cairncross stumped back to the Eternal City. I won't say where I obtained this information, but I do know that Klugman (whom I never met) found the whole incident deeply distasteful.

In Rome, Cairncross and his wife, Gabriella, separated, and by the 1970s he had moved on to France. He is still alive today and living in France, like many another retired Englishman. He's about eighty now, but his passion for French literature still burns as brightly as ever: in 1988, he even published a monograph entitled *The Humanity of Molière*. His days are spent peacefully with his books, his young American companion, Gayle, and his dogs. One of these is called Blackmail, I've heard. I don't think at this stage it would be altogether kind to disturb this old gentleman, who saved the lives of thousands of Russian soldiers, but I'd be glad to see him again.

Much of what I have written in this book will be news to British intelligence, but they do know a lot about Cairncross. Both the British and the French press focused heavily on him after the October 1990 publication of *KGB: The Inside Story* by Christopher Andrew and Oleg Gordievsky. Journalists tracked him down in his retreat, and he agreed to talk to them. He seems to have handled the interview with consummate skill: 'I'm not the fifth man, only a private soldier, second class,' he claimed, and again, 'I'm duty bound to exercise discretion . . . Even to set the record straight, there are certain areas of my experience which I may not reveal.' In a French newspaper, he was a trifle more explicit when he made the following comment, which to me has implications that are both clear and far-reaching: 'Perhaps the day will come when we can attempt to understand the truth that lies concealed behind the facts, and to explain the complex processes by which a young intellectual becomes embroiled in such machinations as these.'

Had British justice deemed it worthwhile to pursue John Cairncross, it would have done so long ago. But it did not. For this reason I have decided that it would do no harm for me to discuss this agent, of whom I was especially fond, and with whom I used to feel I had much in common.

In June 1951, Melinda Maclean had her baby (also called Melinda) and let it be known that she wished to leave England for a while to get away from the hordes of journalists besetting her. The house at Tatsfield was virtually under siege; Mrs Maclean dared not go outside, and her sons, Fergus and Donald, no longer went to school.

Before moving to her sister's villa at Beauvallon on the Côte d'Azur, Melinda was closely interrogated by William Skardon. She came through this with flying colours, clearly convincing Skardon that she had been in no way involved in her husband's activities. Skardon, who seems to have suspected nothing despite his enormous experience, even asked Melinda to let him know if Donald attempted to make contact with her.

In July, shortly before the Maclean family was due to go abroad, Mrs Dunbar (Melinda's mother) received a note in the post informing her that two thousand pounds had been deposited in a Swiss bank account in her daughter's name. The Centre had decided to help out Melinda, who had been effectively penniless since her husband's defection.

At about the same time, Dick White, the head of MI5, interviewed Kim Philby on his return from Washington. White opened the proceedings by declaring straight out that he suspected Kim of being the third Soviet agent in the ring; he then accused him of alerting Burgess to Maclean's imminent discovery. He was, of course, quite correct in both suppositions.

Mentally, Philby had rehearsed this scene so often that he was not in the least disconcerted. He defended himself vigorously.

'I freely admit that Burgess was a friend of mine, but I told him nothing of the sort. I have never allowed my professional affairs to get mixed up with my friendships. If you think otherwise, then you'll have to prove it.' He was to stick to this position for years, come what may.

The FBI agent I met in 1993 confirmed that his organization suspected that Philby was a Soviet agent well before Maclean's flight. The Americans insisted in 1951 that he be brought to trial, but MI5 flatly refused. Moreover, against the advice of the FBI, Philby was allowed to remain at liberty – though his freedom was largely relative, since he was subjected to one interrogation after another. For years he was called in regularly by MI5 agents, notably two highly competent and tenacious experts, Skardon and Helemus Milmó, who seemed to take a perverse pleasure in plying him with insidious questions.

From time to time Philby would be summoned for a weekend in the country by his tormentors, where the two men would walk with him in the woods talking of various subjects – only incidentally including the one that really interested them. During these conversations Milmó and Skardon asked him questions carefully prepared in advance, to which Philby had to produce extempore answers. Their method, one well-known to specialists in interrogation, was aimed at extracting different responses to what was basically the same question.

Much later, when I knew Philby in Moscow, we spoke often of this wretched period of his life. He always said that it required a gigantic, draining effort of concentration to avoid slips and contradictions. Nevertheless he hung on for years. I think that very few men under pressure from two such extraordinary specialists could have resisted them as well as Philby did.

During the autumn of 1951, MI5 formally notified Philby that his relations with Burgess had made him a prime suspect. In anticipation of his prosecution he was advised to claim forthwith the retirement benefit to which he was legally entitled. He jibbed at this for form's sake, then agreed to do so. He was given two thousand pounds on his severance from the secret service, and was allotted two thousand more to be paid in monthly instalments for a period of three years thereafter. Philby thought this procedure distasteful in the extreme, since he was clearly given to understand that the Foreign Office would probably have very few instalments to pay if he were prosecuted and sent to prison.

In December 1951, MI5 called Philby to its headquarters to appear before a panel of officers who had investigated him. He was nervous before he went in, but nevertheless felt reasonably confident, since to his knowledge there was no conclusive evidence. A set of suspicions, after all, is not enough to incriminate a man. In the event he came through the barrage of detail unscathed because at the very first question he realized that the inquisitors had found nothing conclusive – only odds and ends of documents which could as easily be traced to other MI6 agents as to him. Furthermore, he was braced by the attitude of some of his former colleagues, who still believed in his innocence and were waging a skilful campaign on his behalf.

After the defection of Burgess and Maclean we were obliged to act with redoubled discretion in our dealings with Anthony Blunt. MI5 knew that he was Burgess's closest friend, and he was thus bound to be closely watched. When he was questioned about Guy's disappearance, his initial tactic was to shrug and say he hadn't a clue why or how all this had happened. But this would only do for a short while, as the Centre understood only too well when it gave me orders to persuade Blunt to defect.

I met him in Normand Park, a small square in West London. He appeared neither worried nor anxious: his gentlemanly mask was as usual impenetrable. I told him how the others' escape had worked out, then let him know that the Centre believed he, too, should join them in Moscow.

We talked for a long time. I explained that he was more than likely to be interrogated and then arrested in the months to come; MI5 would go after him tirelessly. But Blunt had already drawn his own conclusions. He knew he was about to enter a phase of interrogation. When I suggested that his escape could be accomplished very quickly and safely, with every assurance of a comfortable life in Moscow, he began to smile.

'No doubt,' he murmured. 'No doubt you can also guarantee total access to the Château de Versailles, whenever I need to go there for my work.'

It was my turn to smile.

'You have to understand,' continued Blunt, 'that I simply couldn't live in the Soviet Union under the conditions you are offering. I know perfectly well how your people live, and I can assure you it would be very hard, almost unbearable, for me to do likewise.' This left me speechless.

'I've worked for many years for the British counter-espionage services and I'm well aware of what's in store for me,' he went on. 'I'm convinced that they can't bring me to confess if I don't feel like it, and I don't in the least feel like it. If you want to know why I don't feel like it, I can tell you that, too. I have deep respect and affection for Guy Burgess and I'd rather die than do anything that might place him in danger. He may have left the country, but still no proof exists that he is a Soviet agent. Therefore it's quite possible he'll come back here one day. As long as that possibility depends on me, there will be no proof against him, nor will I ever denounce him. That's why I categorically refuse to leave.'

Both of us knew it would be difficult to mount any case against him. Blunt hadn't even been a card-carrying Communist in his youth. I therefore accepted his decision to remain in England as a *fait accompli*; once again I had failed to bring him round to my point of view, and there was nothing left to do but settle on ways of staying in touch should we need to see one another.

We were walking side by side under the trees when Blunt was suddenly taken ill. He clawed at his chest, choking and sweating profusely. I steered him to a park bench. The incident had attracted a small group of people; a man asked if he should telephone for an ambulance. Blunt, slowly recovering, declined politely.

Within ten minutes or so he was much better, but I was thoroughly shaken and reluctant to let him go home alone.

'Peter,' he said, 'this isn't the first time this has happened. Don't worry, I'll just go back quietly in a taxi. And here's another good reason why I shouldn't scurry off to Russia. If I have to die of a heart attack, I'd rather do it here.'

With this he stood up, shook my hand and walked slowly away. I followed him at a distance till I saw him climb safely into a taxi, then made my own way back to the Soviet Embassy. Korovin quickly grasped that there was no point in pursuing the matter, especially when I described Blunt's precarious state of health. The Centre reacted by first abandoning the idea of his defection, then ordering me to cut off all communication with Blunt, at least until the storm blew over.

No suspicion could possibly be attached to me, and yet in the last four years I had carried out literally hundreds of contacts with Burgess, Blunt, Cairncross and other agents. I was sure I had left no clue to my activities. From the intelligence standpoint, the work I did was 'clean', as we say in the trade. It had allowed our side to obtain many hundreds of important documents which my government had duly exploited. Moreover, I had gained a certain reputation in the corridors of Soviet power. My wife received an unmistakeable confirmation of this while she was on holiday in Moscow in 1949. For administrative reasons she had to call on a senior Foreign Ministry official, who was intrigued to discover who she was.

'So you're Modin's wife!' he said. 'Everyone here knows his work and admires it. He's sent us such a mass of interesting intelligence and documentation about England that if it were bound into volumes it would make more books than the poet Lermontov ever wrote!'

Korovin asked me to interview Blunt one last time to confirm that we were terminating the relationship. Blunt seemed perfectly happy about Moscow's decision. I also told him we planned to break off all contact with Philby for two or three years. He refused my offer of money, and then we parted, after agreeing on a system for getting in touch if it became necessary to do so.

Provided we made no serious blunders, the risk to Blunt at this point was minimal. MI5 had proceeded so far with its investigations that if there was any solid evidence against him it would by now have emerged. The only thing I really dreaded was that some defecting Soviet agent might torpedo our network.

Indirect damage had already been caused by Anatoli Golitsyn, who turned over a certain amount of information on our agents, though not enough to cripple the ring. Golitsyn had no names or biographical data on the Cambridge Five. Even in Moscow, very few people knew who they were, outside the top echelons of the KGB, certain officers who had worked with them, and a smattering of politicians. Obviously, anything might still happen, but I was at least sure of one thing: both Blunt and Philby were sufficiently strong to endure interrogation without breaking.

In London we took maximum precautions. Nobody on the embassy staff had the slightest inkling of my work with the Cambridge Five. Some of them did know I was in touch with certain agents, but the only people who knew their identities were myself, the ambassador and Korovin.

Maclean and Burgess disappeared on 25 May 1951, and thereafter there was no official intelligence as to their whereabouts. After a crescendo of newspaper coverage towards the end of June, the topic gradually faded from the front pages, eclipsed by the final Nuremberg executions, the Korean War, and the October general election in Britain, which swept the Conservatives and the seventy-seven-year-old Winston Churchill back into power.

In the summer of 1952, the Soviet ambassador to the United Kingdom, Georgi Mikhailovich Zaroubin, was recalled to Moscow. My wife Anna and I were saddened by this: we both liked Zaroubin, a fatherly figure who had succeeded in creating an excellent atmosphere in the legation. The man who replaced him, Andrei Gromyko, was an altogether different animal. With the cessation of my work with the Cambridge Five, my energies had been redirected to the press section of the embassy, where I was delegated to receive visiting Soviet personalities. One day the *chargé d'affaires*, whose name was

Bielokhvostikov, called me in a panic to say that Gromyko was due to arrive at Southampton that very evening and he'd forgotten to send someone to meet him. I made a snap decision to go myself, and after a hair-raising drive in which the embassy chauffeur ran a few red lights, we arrived on the dock to find the ship already at the quayside and the gangway lowered. The official zone was cordoned off; diplomats from other countries were inside it waiting for their VIPs, but there was nobody there for Gromyko, whom I spotted sitting alone in the reception room. The police would let nobody through.

In the end, like the secret agent I was, I quietly climbed over a barrier when no one was looking, to welcome Russia's new ambassador.

On the road back to London we quickly warmed to one another, and before long Gromyko and I fell into the habit of taking walks together in north-west London, an area I knew well, having been there on many occasions to meet my agents. As a rule we chatted at length about politics, literature, economic theory and intelligence, though sometimes Gromyko would prefer to walk in silence, deep in thought. All this happened during the lull in my activities. Our walks abruptly ceased in the autumn of 1952, when I again had my hands full with urgent intelligence matters.

Part of our plan for the defection of Maclean was that Melinda Maclean – then about to give birth – should stay in England with her children till the scandal blew over, and would then take her family to rejoin him in Moscow.

Eighteen months after Donald's departure, the moment seemed to have come to make good our promise, and I was given the job of re-establishing contact with Melinda. I was concerned that she was still under surveillance, so I went down to Tatsfield and observed her from a distance, noting that she took her children to school by car every morning, the school being some distance away. Agents from our residence then shadowed her for several weeks without encountering the least sign of MI5 surveillance.

We finally decided to intercept her on her way home from the school, just after she dropped the boys. The road was a narrow lane through wooded country, with hedges either side: just the place to waylay someone. All we needed to do was drive ahead of her, pull up in a suitable spot – and show Melinda half of a postcard. The other half had been handed to Melinda by her husband a year and a half before, with orders that she should trust nobody who did not produce its match. I had this second half in my possession.

We rented a fast car under a false name and took it down to the country, where we picked up Melinda's Rover as she drove home, eventually passing her in the woods. Then our driver gently pulled up on the verge, signalling the young woman behind to do likewise. This she did, but not quite in the way we had expected. She burst out of her car like a deer breaking cover, yelling abuse at us for our bad driving. I was stunned by the speed of her reaction and by her sure reflexes – this woman, whom I had never seen before, was certainly not one to be pushed around.

She was very attractive, a handsome woman in a simple skirt and white blouse. I recovered my wits and drew the half postcard from my pocket. She calmed down instantly, reached across for a bag on the passenger seat of her car and produced the other half. In less than a minute we had agreed on a rendezvous in town and had gone our separate ways.

In London, another officer was sent to negotiate with Melinda, while I watched unobtrusively from a distance. I had noticed nothing untoward, but my fellow KGB agent was sweating with nerves. After leaving Melinda (who had appeared in an extremely elegant light beige suit), he veered off on a protracted *parcours de sécurité* which lasted well over two hours.

Back at the residence, he claimed that Melinda had been followed and that someone had observed them throughout their interview. Having noticed nothing myself, I wasn't sure if this was the truth or a figment of his imagination, and to this day I still don't know. At any rate, he reported that Melinda was eager to join her husband in Moscow but believed, as we did, that it would be just about impossible to slip out of England with three noisy children in tow. She therefore expected us to find a solution to this problem, and incidentally refused point-blank, should we find one, to accept any money for her travel expenses. My terrified colleague then had the presence of mind to establish a time and place for the next meeting – and two provisional ones in case of trouble.

Melinda failed to appear either at the prearranged rendezvous or at the provisional ones. I was anxious: perhaps our agent had upset her. He was an efficient operative, sure enough, but a trifle disconcerting in his manner.

A fortnight passed. Then one morning I read in the newspaper that Melinda Maclean and her children had moved to the house of her mother, Mrs Dunbar, at Montreux-Terrilet in Switzerland. She had gone about this so openly that the British press located her without the slightest trouble. One or two journalists had even contrived to speak to Melinda. She had left England, she said, to escape the spotlight of publicity for good and all.

The message came through to me loud and clear. All we needed to do was wait till the newspapers forgot about unobtrusive Melinda Maclean, living contentedly with her family in Switzerland.

In May 1953, I returned to Moscow, my tour of duty in London ended. A few months later, in September, the Centre decided to contact Melinda once again and, if she were still willing, to mount a simple operation to bring her out of Switzerland.

On Friday 11 September, Melinda told her mother she was off to spend a few days in France with close friends who lived in the Massif des Maures. Mrs Dunbar was delighted with this idea, which she felt would do her grandchildren – the two boys and the little girl, by then aged two – a power of good. So Melinda duly packed her family into her black Chevrolet and set off. But instead of heading for France she went straight to the Lausanne railway station, where at 6.30 p.m. she left her car at a garage, telling the attendant she had a train to catch and would be back in a week's time.

Carrying no suitcases whatever, she and her children boarded the night express to Austria. At the frontier, they got off the train, climbed into a taxi and passed through a customs checkpoint a few miles from Bregenz. Nobody asked any questions: she was just a woman with three kids coming back from a day trip. The taxi then carried them to Vienna, where the KGB's agents were waiting. From here on, the rest of the trip was simplicity itself; at that time our system for moving people out of Austria to the USSR functioned very nicely.

Mrs Dunbar didn't sound the alert till the following Monday evening, at which time she called the Foreign Office to announce that her daughter and her three grandchildren had vanished into thin air. By the time MI5's agents had arrived in Switzerland and begun to investigate, Melinda had been in the Soviet-occupied zone of Vienna for over twenty-four hours. MI5 managed to dig up a few witnesses – the man at the garage, the taxi driver who had taken Melinda and her children to Vienna – but discovered nothing which could possibly link a foreign intelligence service with the departure of the Maclean family. The papers immediately seized on the story, speculating freely on Melinda's likely destination. There had been no shortage of rumours about Maclean himself, who had been sighted in outlandish locations from Prague to Manchuria by way of the Middle East.

The guessing game began all over again. Some journalists even wondered, in print, whether Mrs Maclean's American origin might encourage Senator Joseph McCarthy to launch another of the Communist witch-hunts which were by then his speciality.

Meanwhile, the plane carrying Melinda and her three children had landed safely in Moscow.

In the first months of 1954, the Centre suffered a series of heavy setbacks. Two intelligence officers, one based in Tokyo, the other in Vienna, defected to the CIA. More ominous for the British section of the KGB, two of our agents in Australia, Vladimir and Evdokia Petrov, went over to the West. Both had worked for years at the Lubyanka and were familiar with the backgrounds of our organizations in France, England and Germany. They knew we had had a structured network of British agents in London since the early days of the war; they had heard the code names of these shadowy figures once or twice, but fortunately they had forgotten them, a fact we were able to ascertain fairly quickly. Nevertheless, the Petrovs were able to confirm that other moles, whose existence had been suspected ever since the defection of Burgess and Maclean, were definitely lodged either in the Foreign Office or in MI5.

It wasn't much, but it was a start for the opposition. More worrisome to us was the Petrovs' claim that Burgess and Maclean were living comfortably in the suburbs of Moscow, and that Melinda had known about her husband's spying activities from the first. Luckily for her, the British Secret Service refused to credit this last assertion.

During the same period, our English residence became aware that Philby was desperately short of cash. The sum allotted to him by the Foreign Office had been swallowed up long since by the needs of his family. He could find no work, and the monthly instalments provided by his ex-employers had ceased altogether. His mother, whom I knew to be far from wealthy, could not help.

The KGB's British section put together a report on the subject, specifically asking our masters what they planned to do about this agent, who had rendered us immense services – and who might need to be reactivated in the future, after a few years of lying low. Moscow's foreign intelligence bureau responded promptly enough, with a directive that Kim Philby – still known in our service as Stanley – should be presented with a large sum of money. Our problem was how to get this money to him, because all contacts were fraught with danger. Philby was under constant watch; several times our counter-surveillance teams had reported the presence of MI5 agents hovering in his vicinity.

The Centre sent me back to London to work out a solution. I went over the difficulties at some length with Korovin, finally giving it as my opinion that we should first of all re-contact Yan, the code name of Anthony Blunt, with whom I had never had any security problem. I was reasonably certain Blunt and I would not be entrapped, given that our system of mutual observation had worked very reliably in the past: once you acquire reflexes of the kind he and I shared, you never lose them.

Accordingly, I reverted to my old undercover habits to trigger the contact procedure we had devised at our last meeting in 1951. I went to Blunt's block of flats one dark evening and crushed a piece of chalk in front of the entrance. Though the street sweepers would certainly clean the asphalt at some stage, I could be certain that traces of white would remain, and that Blunt would catch sight of them sooner or later.

Nothing happened. Blunt did not appear at our agreed rendez-vous, nor at the contingency meeting-places we had planned. It was therefore up to me to waylay him. I knew the places he frequented, but the risks involved in an open encounter were far too great.

Anthony Blunt was already a man of some importance in England, director of the Courtauld Institute and a respected professor and journalist who was often to be seen at exhibitions and artists' gatherings. He was also a familiar speaker at conferences.

Every day I checked the cultural section of *The Times* for any exhibition or meeting which he might conceivably attend, and over a period of three months I went to a mind-scrambling series of exhibitions, sat through hours of lectures on the Etruscans, Upper Egypt, sixteenth-century Italian Renaissance painting, and more. I remember this as one of the more pleasurable interludes in my career as a spy, during which my general knowledge of art, which had hitherto not amounted to much, was randomly enriched.

Finally I spotted a notice in the paper inviting art-lovers to a meeting at the Courtauld Institute. The purpose of it was to protest a decision by the Italian authorities to pull down a Roman triumphal arch, which had got in the way of some modern housing project. The art world was up in arms, and the list of speakers prominently featured the name of Anthony Blunt.

At the appointed hour I drifted into the Courtauld and signed the book at the entrance in the name of Greenglass, nationality Norwegian. At that time I was still fairly lean, with a full head of fair hair, very much the stereotype of a Scandinavian male: no doubt these looks were the legacy of my ancestor Cherychov, who was expelled from Novgorod by the infuriated citizenry because he had married a Swede.

I sat down in the front row, in hopes that Blunt would notice me, realize why I had come and find a moment to speak to me after the meeting.

Blunt duly arrived, slightly older and more haggard, but still his elegant, cadaverous self. The meeting's organizer invited him to the rostrum just in front of me, where he delivered an impassioned speech.

For the first time I was seeing Blunt speaking on a subject, history of art, which he held dear. He brandished photographs of the triumphal arch we had all come to defend, and excoriated the villainous Italian authorities in a most convincing manner.

Our speaker could hardly fail to notice me, I thought, seated where I was. But strange to relate, he didn't recognize me. Fortunately, I had taken even this possibility into account, and had bought a postcard of a Renaissance painting. On the margin of this postcard I had clearly written the words *Tomorrow, 8 p.m., Ruislip*. Not far from the Ruislip tube station was a pub Blunt knew well, in which we had met from time to time in the past.

When the speeches were over, some of the audience filed out, leaving the usual rump of enthusiasts milling around the people who had spoken and peppering them with questions. Blunt in particular had attracted something of a crowd. I wandered about on the fringes, biding my time. Three young women, more zealous than the rest, blocked all the approaches to him, leaving no possibility for anyone else to slip a word in edgewise. They were obviously enchanted with Blunt and vied with one another in showing off their knowledge. I began to worry when they started steering him in the direction of the door, chattering all the way. Once the group got there, they were bound to separate all at once – and I wasn't about to jump on Blunt in the open street, which would have been perilous in the extreme. So before he could go any further I battered my way purposefully through his admirers, postcard in hand, elbowing one of the women hard in the ribs as I did so.

'Excuse me,' I grunted. 'Do you know where I can find this picture in the museum?'

Blunt took the card, looked at it closely and gave me a long stare.

'Yes, yes, yes,' he said, answering all three of my written instructions with commendable brevity.

I turned on my heel and left. I knew he had recognized me this time and would be as good as his word.

The next day we were face to face at last. He told me he'd been questioned on a number of occasions since 1951, that MI5 was sure he was involved with us but had no hard evidence against him. I could see Blunt was still as tough-minded as ever and was in no danger of caving in. We talked of Kim Philby, who was still holding up heroically under complex and repeated interrogation, and Blunt mentioned that his friend's financial difficulties were far worse even than we had imagined. He and his family were living in conditions of real poverty, but Kim was steadfastly uncomplaining.

I told Blunt the Centre would like to help Philby out if it could, and suggested he serve as an intermediary for our payment, which he agreed to do. We settled on another meeting after I had reported back to Moscow. Just as we were about to part, Blunt wondered aloud if it wouldn't be better for me to confront Philby directly. I rejected this idea for two reasons: first, it was far too risky for all concerned, and second, I had been given formal orders to contact Blunt, and Blunt only.

'Philby isn't being properly tailed,' he persisted. 'That I can tell you for certain, as an old hand at counter-espionage. But if you don't want to do it, it's all the same to me.'

When I next saw Blunt, in a small square just off the Caledonian Road, I handed him five thousand pounds sterling, in cash, and told him to keep us regularly informed of Kim's circumstances. I also gave him a brief account of how Burgess and Maclean were doing, and discussed new ways of keeping our lines of communication open.

As always with Blunt, I knew I was working in complete security: there was no fear that we were under observation, because our mutual antennae were all but infallible. But on this occasion I suddenly felt my hackles rise. Somebody was watching us. I quietly indicated the fact to Blunt.

He burst out laughing. 'My dear Peter,' he said, 'the man watching us is Kim Philby himself. You said you didn't want to meet him, but all the same, the two of us felt you might be induced to change your mind. So he's here, and quite prepared to join us if you see fit.'

I stared hard at the figure in the near distance. So this was the legendary Kim, the man whose adventures and exploits had been a part of my life for nearly a decade, but whom I had never seen in the flesh. The dark silhouette kept pace with us along the tree-lined path: a solid, four-square figure, hatless, shrouded in an overcoat.

Philby's features etched themselves so strongly on my mind that evening that I was to recognize him instantly when I saw him again in Moscow over ten years later. I remember saying to myself, with absolute conviction: 'That man is very strong. That man is a rock.'

Philby came no closer. It was my choice whether I wanted to meet him, but I could not bring myself to do so, despite my overwhelming curiosity.

I had to acknowledge that in itself the initiative had been a wise one, since had I indeed changed my approach and demanded to see Philby face to face it would have spared us yet another complicated assignation and a further set of risks.

For a moment I hesitated. Then I told myself that if by a thousand-to-one chance we had been followed, the simple fact of our having spoken to one another would establish incontrovertible proof of our connection. Professional caution won the day, and I refused the contact. Blunt was visibly disappointed. As we watched Philby striding away through the trees, I wondered what thoughts must now be passing through the mind of that solitary man.

I think our gift must have heartened him. Shortly afterwards he was to need all the moral support he could summon, when a huge press campaign broke over him without warning.

On 26 October 1955, every newspaper in Great Britain carried banner headlines on his case: 'Is Harold Philby the Third Man?'

The offensive had been launched in the House of Commons the night before by the Labour MP Marcus Lipton, who stated flatly that Harold 'Kim' Philby was the Soviet mole who had arranged the defection of Burgess and Maclean. The charge was a serious one, but the newspapers remained cautious in their wording. For one thing, the same story had appeared, somewhat ignominiously, in an American scandal sheet two weeks earlier. The editors of Britain's national newspapers therefore confined themselves to reporting Lipton's words more or less verbatim, for fear of a libel suit.

On the other hand, the hapless Roger Makins, Britain's ambassador in the United States, was loaded with ridicule. Makins had at one time been suspected of being Homer by the FBI; later he was given the task of organizing a tight security cordon around Maclean. Unfortunately for him, he had written somewhere in black and white that there were 'no grounds whatever' for any charges against the incriminated diplomat. The newspapers also skewered Lord Reading, who had recently told the House of Lords that it was 'to protect the public interest' that he had declared at the time of their flight that neither Burgess nor Maclean 'had ever been the object of any suspicion'.

One or two national newspapers cast doubts on Lipton's charges, noting that it would be peculiar indeed if Philby should turn out to be a Soviet agent, given that he had been decorated in 1938 by the arch-Fascist Franco.

Kim, with a sang-froid and an impudence that were truly breathtaking, decided to meet his adversaries head on. For a short while he refused to speak to journalists: then he held a full-scale press conference in his mother's flat on 8 November. Mischievous, ironical, beautifully dressed, he began by denouncing the charges against him as mere gossip and hearsay. Then, with his most predatory smile, he moved smoothly on to the offensive. First he challenged Lipton to repeat his slanders outside the House of Commons, where he would be liable to a civil suit under the Libel Act. Naturally, said Kim, he expected his opponent to produce evidence to back his assertions, and as a proof of goodwill proposed that should this evidence be too secret for public repetition, it should be communicated instead to a member of the Privy Council. Having thrown down this spectacular gauntlet, he went on to speak of his own political convictions. With unbelievable effrontery he made the following declaration:

'The last occasion on which I knowingly spoke to a Communist was in 1934, and the last time I did so unknowingly was in April 1951, when Guy Burgess was staying at my home.'

After this virtuoso demonstration, Lipton backed down. He made no reference whatever to Philby outside the House of Commons.

Kim had played his cards with consummate cunning. We concluded, just as he had, that the British Government had no serious evidence against him, and that a secret enquiry into his activities had been ordered and had found nothing. Harold Macmillan, the Foreign Secretary, was eventually forced to admit in public that Her Majesty's Government had no evidence to show that Harold Philby had infringed the laws of the country.

Philby's friends, who had supported him loyally since 1951, were overjoyed. They knew there was no question of reinstating him in his old job; instead, in 1956, a position was found for him as correspondent in Beirut for *The Observer* and *The Economist*.

In the same year the presence of Burgess and Maclean in Soviet territory was officially revealed by Khruschev, who announced that the two men had become Soviet citizens.

In Beirut, Philby excelled in his new role as a journalist, not only because he was a naturally gifted writer, but also because of his many contacts in the area. He reported briskly and stylishly, and his well-informed articles on the Middle East were highly influential in England. He continued to do occasional work for the KGB, whose Beirut residence was a hive of activity at that time, and the information he supplied on British policies in the region proved invaluable to our government in its relations with Arab countries. Philby's contribution came more in the form of political analysis than straightforward intelligence; I myself read several of his reports, noting with satisfaction that he had not lost his brilliant touch.

From time to time Philby also passed on news of Anthony Blunt, whom he saw regularly in London when he was home on leave. According to Philby, Blunt was still enduring regular interrogations by MI5 agents – who would call him in without warning, attempt to trap him in contradictions, then abruptly change their method of questioning to throw him off balance. As they had done with Philby himself, they asked the same questions over and over again, hundreds, even thousands of times. They were convinced that Blunt had worked for the KGB because he had been so close to Burgess.

Philby thought – and I agreed with him – that in its dealings with Blunt MI5 was consistently thwarted by two vital factors. The first was that Blunt was not only Burgess's friend: he had also been his lover, and for this reason alone neither man would ever have betrayed the other. The second factor was that Blunt was a man of honour, who simply did not choose to renounce the ideals of his youth.

Did he later regret his involvement with us? Neither Kim nor I would ever know. Whatever he may have felt, the news came back through Philby that Anthony Blunt was standing firm.

Aileen Philby and her five children, John, Josephine, Tommy, Miranda and Harry, had stayed behind in England, mainly because Kim thought life in Beirut was likely to prove too difficult for them. Shortly after her husband's departure, Aileen Philby's health began to deteriorate alarmingly, from a lethal combination of respiratory problems, heart trouble and the early symptoms of tuberculosis. All the more reason, thought Philby, why she should not join him in the Lebanon.

Yet Kim was not alone in Beirut. His father, Harry St John Philby, with his Saudi wife, Rosie, and their two sons, Khalid and Farid – half-brothers to Kim – were already living in the city. The family had temporarily retreated to the Levant, following Harry St John's quarrel with the Saudi princes who had succeeded the great Ibn Saud.

Harry and his family were established on the Maronite mountain of Ajaltoun, and there Kim joined them. From time to time he went down into the capital for his work, but otherwise he stayed close to his father. For the first time in his life he was able to have long conversations with that fiercely eccentric old man, but all the same Kim never admitted to Harry St John Philby that he was working for the Soviets.

The situation of Aileen and her children, who were established at

Crowborough in East Sussex, proved a constant worry to Kim, who was barely able to send them sufficient money to live decently. Then, in November 1956, Harry St John was reconciled with the Saudi royal family and returned to Arabia with his wife and boys.

Now Philby was on his own and lonely. In 1957, he was stunned by the death of his mother, Dora, a woman who had been in love with his father all her life, and had never stopped hoping he would come back to her. After this massive blow, Kim began to drink heavily.

At about this time he renewed an old friendship with Sam Pope Brewer, the *New York Times* Middle East correspondent, and his wife, Eleanor. Before long Philby had seduced Eleanor, whose husband adopted a complaisant attitude towards their affair. Eleanor went home to the States to spend some time with her family, and in her absence news reached Kim that his wife Aileen had died, on 11 December 1957. Aileen was only forty-seven.

The following year Eleanor returned to Beirut, where Kim asked her to divorce her husband and become his wife. She agreed, and the couple were eventually married in London on 24 January 1959, with two of Kim's former Secret Service colleagues as witnesses. Eight years after the departure of Burgess and Maclean, MI5 seemed to have forgotten its suspicions of Philby. Had they finally decided to leave him alone? Philby was soon to realize that this was far from the case.

He introduced his children to their new stepmother and then returned to Beirut with Eleanor. But on 30 September 1960, Harry St John Philby, aged seventy-five, died suddenly of a heart attack while staying with his son. This was a staggering blow to Kim, who organized a huge funeral at the Muslim cemetery in Beirut.

Now Kim began to drink really heavily, and his new wife matched him glass for glass. Within two years, he was a shadow of his former self.

MI5 chose this moment to administer the *coup de grâce*.

Nicholas Elliott, a former MI6 resident in Beirut and an old friend, paid Philby a visit just after the New Year in 1963; curiously enough, he appeared to have made the journey from London especially to see Philby, though the latter had heard no word from him in years. But Kim was by now so pickled in alcohol that he failed to register the warning signs and let his guard fall.

At the end of a long, hard-drinking evening, Elliott struck without warning. 'We now have irrefutable proof,' he told Philby, 'that you are a Soviet agent.'

Kim confidently denied the charge, as he had done so many times before. Then Elliott told him about Flora Solomon's testimony.

Philby had long been a close friend of Flora Solomon's, a brilliant woman fascinated by politics, who was linked to the Rothschild banking family. According to Elliott, Flora had confessed that Kim Philby had not only told her he was a Soviet agent, but also attempted to recruit her on behalf of the KGB.

At that moment the man who had held up through scores of complex interrogations, who had lived for over a decade with the spectre of betrayal, suddenly broke.

Later, in Moscow, when we had become friends, we often spoke of this cataclysmic instant, when Philby's whole world collapsed in ruins. His explanations never seemed quite to make sense: to this day I still don't know if Flora Solomon had revealed the secret, or if the story was a fabrication, or even if she had heard a similar tale from someone else. Perhaps her friend Aileen Philby had talked. Nobody will ever know.

After this conversation, the two men agreed that Philby would write a complete confession for MI5, which Philby said would take several days. Elliott went back to his hotel and, oddly, was neither seen nor heard of for forty-eight hours. Philby, having had time to gather his wits and analyse the situation, contacted us and told us about the colossal blunder he had made. When the KGB's Beirut resident asked him what he planned to do next, he replied without hesitation that only one course was open to him – immediate defection to the Soviet Union.

Spiriting Philby out of the Lebanon was child's play. All he had to do was pack his bags and go aboard the Soviet cargo ship *Dolmatova*, which happened to be lying in the port of Beirut. On 23 January the ship weighed anchor and steamed out of Juniyeh. Philby, standing at the rail as the magnificent bay slowly receded in the wake of the *Dolmatova*, knew that his last link with England had been severed for ever. Apart from his family, henceforth his only ties to the past were Donald Maclean and Guy Burgess, who had been living in Moscow for twelve years and whom he was soon to join.

Meanwhile the KGB was taking the usual measures to cover his tracks. Letters were sent to Eleanor from a number of different Arab capitals, as though Kim were away on a reporting assignment: but this time the British newspapers weren't fooled. To them it was evident that Philby had gone to the Soviet Union, like Burgess and Maclean before him. Eleanor Philby stayed on in Beirut for a while, and when it became painfully obvious that her husband was never going to reappear she quietly made her way home to the United States. There she learned the full truth when Kim wrote to her from Moscow, and before long she had promised to join him there.

The attitude of Nicholas Elliott throughout this affair has always been something of a riddle to me. I quickly formed the impression that MI5 had no plans whatever to arrest Philby – all they wanted from him was some kind of verbal confession, and afterwards it was as if the secret service had actively encouraged him to slip away. There was no dearth of means to detain him in Beirut, or even to have him taken into custody. It would also have been a comparatively simple matter to bring him to London on some family pretext, or even to arrest him during his holidays, which he invariably spent in England.

To my mind, the whole business was politically engineered. The British Government had nothing to gain by prosecuting Philby. A major trial, to the inevitable accompaniment of spectacular revelation and scandal, would have shaken the British establishment to its foundations; and the blundering incompetence of successive administrations from 1938 to 1963, not to mention the carelessness of the British Secret Service, would have been shockingly exposed.

After my first prolonged tour of duty in London came to an end in 1953, the Centre sent me back to England on a special mission the following year. I had no trouble entering the country, and the British authorities gave me a visa without difficulty. This was a clear indication, I thought, that neither Cairncross nor Blunt nor any of my other agents had betrayed my name. I confess that my heart was in my mouth as I walked through immigration, but thereafter I felt entirely secure as I once again immersed myself in this world I had come to know so well.

In 1955, I again returned to London, to help with our preparations for the state visit of Bulganin and Khruschev scheduled for 1956. This assignment, initially a temporary one, was to become a semi-permanent post at the embassy as interim KGB bureau chief for Great Britain. This was because Korovin had shrewdly anticipated that complications might arise during the state visit: he therefore judged it prudent to spend 1956 in Moscow, well out of harm's way, leaving me holding the baby. In May 1956, my wife and my daughter, Olga, joined me in the British capital. This second and last tour of duty in England was to last until May 1958.

In 1956, the Burgess–Maclean affair was already half forgotten, and newspapers were concentrating on other more important events, such as Khruschev's de-Stalinization campaign, the Hungarian uprising and the Suez crisis. The British public's deep disapproval of and even hostility towards our country's policies was unpleasantly obvious to the embassy staff. The fighting in Budapest, in particular, cut a swathe through the ranks of the British Communist Party, hundreds of whose militants tore up their Party membership cards in protest.

It was not until the following year that the West's attitude in general, and that of the British in particular, showed signs of softening. That was the year of *Sputnik*, which to some extent repaired the appalling impression left by Budapest.

On 4 October 1957, the USSR stunned the world by sending an object into orbit for the first time in human history. This was followed a month later by a second experiment, when a dog called Laika was kept alive in space for six days, thereby proving that living creatures could survive under conditions of weightlessness. These missions caused a sensation in Britain; their clear implication was that the Americans were not the only people on earth who could master the intricacies of modern technology. British public opinion began to view us with more favour. The crushing of the Hungarian uprising, as well as the outrages committed by Stalin and denounced by Khruschev, were to some extent mitigated.

In the midst of this slight but perceptible thaw in Soviet–British relations, I arrived at my office one November morning in 1957 to find the embassy surrounded by an angry crowd. There were slightly fewer protesters than in 1956, when Russian tanks were reducing the Hungarian capital to piles of rubble, but nevertheless every street around the building was packed. Shrieking women brandished placards which read 'Red Bastards – No Dogs in Space'. Inside the embassy, there were scenes of deep dismay.

The demonstrators sent in a delegation to interview the ambassador. I received them in his place. Six or seven indignant men and women stalked through the entrance, each accompanied by a dog. I made them a speech about how we Russians also loved dogs; Russians, I claimed, were just as fond of their dogs as English people. Then I made the mistake of drifting into a homily on the triumphant advance of science. Scowls, black looks. I faltered, then instinctively, to prove my goodwill, grabbed a bulldog in the arms of one of the women and planted a kiss on its slobbering muzzle. This gesture was greeted with a storm of applause; my point was taken, the news was carried to the crowd outside and the satisfied demonstrators melted away.

In 1963, the Burgess–Maclean affair was resurrected, Philby left Beirut and on 19 August Burgess died in Moscow. Soon after this last event, Anthony Blunt made his confession to the British authorities, in early 1964.

Until the death of his friend and lover, Blunt continued to hope against hope that one day Burgess would return to England. In the twelve years following Burgess's departure, he had steadfastly resisted every effort to undermine him. But now that Guy was gone for ever he felt justified in seeking some relief from the heavy burden that had poisoned his life for so long. All the same, he prepared and refined the actual content of his confession with the greatest care, and delivered it only when he had received the assurance of the Attorney-General that he would be immune to prosecution if he revealed the truth about his dealings with the Soviets.

Thus it was that Anthony Blunt revealed my own name to MI5; luckily, I had already been out of London for over five years by then. The British already knew that the last KGB contact of Burgess, Blunt, Philby and Maclean in London was code-named Peter. Then came Blunt's avowal that Peter was Modin, an unobtrusive staff member of the press section at the Soviet Embassy.

My name was duly mentioned in the press, but no newspaper made reference to Blunt, whose statement was kept a close secret by MI5. Blunt also gave some other vague items of information to Martin, his MI5 interrogator, who concluded in his report that 'Blunt still had Communist ideals; he had worked with the Soviet intelligence services during the war but ceased altogether to furnish them with information in 1945.'

Of course, what Blunt omitted to say was that after the war and until 1951, he served as the liaison between Burgess and myself. His tactic was very simple: he confessed only to things which could not be used in the courts against him. This proved by far the best approach. When George Blake, another of our agents, was caught in 1961, he behaved in a very different fashion, signing a complete confession which landed him with a very heavy prison sentence.

I believe that everything concerning Blunt was kept secret because Queen Elizabeth wished it so. It should not be forgotten that she had knighted Blunt in 1956, awarding him the KCVO; and that he had been a good friend to the Queen's father, George VI, who liked to visit art galleries and exhibitions in his company. The two men shared a deep love of painting. Blunt was among the world's greatest experts on seventeenth-century art and the King loved to hear him talk about it. I think it was because of this that the Queen turned a blind eye to his Communism and gave Blunt a *de facto* secret pardon.

It was not until 1979 that the then Prime Minister, Margaret Thatcher, took up the topic again following the appearance of several new books on the Secret Service (notably Andrew Boyle's *The Climate of Treason*). Blunt's name was never actually mentioned, but it could easily be inferred from the authors' allusions. When Margaret Thatcher finally revealed that he had indeed been a Soviet agent, Blunt immediately renounced his knighthood and offered to resign from his official post with the Art History Association. However, his fellow members refused to accept his withdrawal, and another eminent art historian, Professor Steinberg, made a speech to the effect that Sir Anthony Blunt's contribution to the discipline had been of inestimable value, and that he, Steinberg, had no intention of abandoning him in his time of trial.

Shortly afterwards Blunt gave a press conference which was a model of its kind.

Before a carefully selected group of journalists, he acknowledged that he had worked for the Russians. 'In the mid-1930s,' he proclaimed, 'it was a question of conscience; not to struggle against Fascism was to betray your country.' He then firmly denied having warned Burgess and Maclean that they were about to be taken into custody, and when asked what kind of information he had given to the Russians, if any, he replied that he had indeed done so, 'but only during the war; it was bound to be minor intelligence, given my position with MI5. What I told the Russians concerned the German services only, never the British ones.' This, of course, was the literal truth as far as the war years were concerned. Finally, when one of the journalists questioned him about his recruitment of Soviet agents at Cambridge, he retorted that he 'could not answer this, being bound by the Official Secrets Act'.

When I read the press reports in Moscow, I was lost in admiration for Blunt's extraordinary adroitness.

Naturally, the exposure of Blunt triggered more speculation in the British press about the identity of the 'Fifth Man'. Andrew Boyle went so far as to claim that 'twenty-five living British citizens, including a peer of the realm, have at one time or another served as agents for the Soviet Union'.

He went on to state that all of these individuals had been questioned by the British counter-intelligence services, but that their identities had never been revealed for lack of hard evidence against them. Among the welter of names, certain journalists advanced that of Maurice Oldfield, the head of MI6 from 1973 to 1978, who according to them had tipped off Philby that Burgess's network had been blown open. In my view this was not to be credited.

Once again the fuss gradually subsided and Anthony Blunt was able to continue his work in peace. He remained a familiar figure at universities and learned societies, giving lectures on seventeenth-century art. His particular speciality was the French master Poussin, on whose work he had published a monumental study in 1966–67. Experts still use Blunt's book as a reference.

Anthony Blunt died on 26 March 1983, brilliant, aloof and enigmatic to the last.

Chapter 8

THREE SOVIET CITIZENS

When Guy Burgess and Donald Maclean arrived in the Soviet Union, I remained in London. I did not return with my family to Moscow until May 1953, having completed my first tour of duty in Great Britain.

During that summer I was reunited with Burgess in Moscow. He now bore the name of Jim Andreievich Eliot, out of cock-eyed respect for the novelist George Eliot. He had just arrived back from Kuibyshev (now called Samara) where the Soviet authorities had obliged him to remain for over a year.

Burgess was convinced that Maclean and he had been removed from Moscow in case he should meet with foreigners there, and he was quite right. I didn't go to see Donald Maclean at that point: first, because I didn't know him personally, and second, for the very good reason that he refused to see any KGB officers. He was learning Russian, he said, and wanted to be left alone.

I found Burgess living in a small village near the river port then on Moscow's outskirts, on the road to Sheremetyevo Airport. (Today the place is completely built up and unrecognizable.) The Centre had authorized me to visit him whenever I wished.

The Burgess abode was small and attractive, a wooden, typically Russian structure. He had put in a special request to be lodged in old buildings dating from before the Revolution, and this was easily granted. A woman was employed to do the housework, and otherwise Burgess was assigned a KGB bodyguard to help him in his day-to-day existence. He seemed to like his lodging, which had five well-furnished rooms and a fully equipped kitchen. It seemed to suit him, a real intellectual's retreat with a large tidy garden planted with fruit trees.

Guy Burgess greeted me warmly, and we settled down to talk over a bottle of wine.

It is a curious fact about my profession that you know the people you work with much better and more thoroughly than ordinary individuals. When you meet them in the line of duty, you are invariably under stress, alert to the slightest gesture or change of expression. You get to know a man very quickly that way. The body feels threatened; everything about it is strained to the utmost; and as a result you are super-receptive.

Immediately following his arrival in the USSR and the first months of his new life at Kuibyshev, things had not been easy for Guy Burgess. But his relations with the KGB were good and he had been debriefed in the normal way, meaning that several discussions had taken place over dinner with officers from the Lubyanka. Guy was not suspected of being a double agent, and there was no question of exerting any kind of pressure on him. Philby, who of course was still in the West, was now a source of deep concern to the Centre, and KGB agents often came out to consult Burgess on what he thought could be done to assist his fellow agent.

Though Guy had not suffered in the least from these interviews, he wondered why he wasn't simply allowed to go home to England. He told me he was sure the British had no proof of anything against him. He also told me – as if I had the power to decide anything at all about his fate – that he felt capable of facing any amount of MI5 interrogation without turning a hair. So his spell at Kuibyshev, a dreary industrial city on the Volga some five hundred miles from Moscow, had not amused him in the least, and without his having to say so I felt that he was more than a little resentful on that score. He felt that the Soviets might have spared him this purgatory of exile, after all he had done for them: and for Guy Burgess boredom was the worst torment of all.

Fellow homosexuals were very hard to come by, for one thing, in the highly provincial, conservative city of Kuibyshev, and even Guy's contacts with Donald Maclean (who was living there, too) were kept to a minimum. The two men met from time to time, but they were quartered in different parts of town. It may seem strange, given the loneliness they must have endured during that year, that they did not seek one another's company more often. Neither spoke Russian, and they were certainly the only two Englishmen in the whole of that vast region. Yet if one analyses their behaviour from a psychological standpoint one understands very well. It is a common syndrome with people who have been through dramatic events together, such as imprisonment under terrible conditions or being taken hostage, that the last thing they want is to see anyone involved, ever again. They effectively blot out the memory of it, for the very sight of somebody connected with a past horror can only reawaken an old pain.

From the day they arrived at Kuibyshev, the paths of Burgess and Maclean inexorably diverged. Burgess refused point blank to learn Russian, and since he was given no work to do he spent his time reading and walking. He also learned to appreciate Georgian wine.

Maclean, whose new name was Mark Petrovich Frazer, in homage to the Scottish anthropologist James Frazer, had positively decided to build a new life in the USSR. He set himself to study the Russian language and continued to interest himself in political questions as seriously as was possible in a town like Kuibyshev. He cannot have been very happy, either, but in contrast to Burgess he at least exerted himself to join in Soviet life. In the end he was the only one of the three Cambridge agents who came to the USSR ever to speak decent Russian.

I asked Burgess a question which had been nagging at me ever since his departure in 1951. Why hadn't he turned back at Prague?

By then, I reasoned, Maclean was home and dry. Guy had carried out his mission, and he could quite easily have slipped back to London at that juncture. He could give me no coherent answer, but I had a clear impression that at the time he hadn't been fully aware of what he was doing when he accompanied Maclean all the way to Moscow. I concluded that he came along for the fun of it, expecting some kind of party at the Kremlin in his honour, and he was genuinely stunned when they forbade his return to England. He bitterly resented this treatment at the hands of the KGB, and he included me in his resentment, believing I was more influential within the organization than was the case.

After 1953, I made a point of dropping in to visit Guy Burgess whenever I could find the time. Every time I saw him it was only too painfully obvious that he was incapable of reconciling himself to life in the USSR. His impossible dream was to return some day to

England. The only bright spot for him in those years was a visit from his mother, in early 1954.

As to Donald Maclean, whom I had never met, I was to encounter him face to face on only one occasion, in September 1953. I had been detailed to join the welcome committee which turned out to greet Melinda Maclean and her children in Moscow, following their dramatic defection. This did not take place at the airport, for fear that some journalist or foreigner might recognize the family, but at the Sovetskaya Hotel near the Dynamo Stadium on the road to Sheremetyevo Airport.

A sizeable drove of KGB officers was present, and I was hurriedly introduced to Donald Maclean in the hotel foyer while we were waiting for his family to make their appearance. We shook hands. He was just as I had imagined: cold, distant, supercilious and thoroughly aristocratic. The weight of his presence was overwhelming. We had nothing whatever to say to each other, probably because of the occasion. We chatted about nothing in particular, and then Melinda arrived with her sons, Donald Junior and Fergus, and her little daughter, Melinda, whom Maclean had never seen before. I moved discreetly away. The meeting was curiously unemotional; Donald remained distant, even with his sons, and barely embraced his wife. At that moment it was clear to me that their marriage was doomed. I had no reason to hang around, so I slipped out of the hotel and went back to work. I never saw Donald Maclean again.

The Maclean family were temporarily housed in a small apartment, before being moved in 1955 to a splendid six-room home on Bolshaya Dorogomilovskaya Street in the centre of Moscow. The building was in the purest Stalin-era style, brand-new, with windows facing the Ukraine Hotel and the Moskva. There was a market just below. Fergus and Donald Junior, who were aged ten and eight, went to school in the normal way and quickly learned to speak Russian perfectly; later the older boy, Fergus, spent several holidays in a camp and the younger became a Pioneer. They had no difficulty blending into Soviet life.

In 1954, despite the revelations of the Petrovs, who among other things defected to the West with the news that Burgess and Maclean had come to roost in Moscow, the KGB still felt that it would serve no purpose either to confirm or to deny their presence in the USSR. They made this decision on the grounds that everyone knew anyway.

Stalin was dead, but the Cold War was far from over. In the United States, the doctrine of containment – the use of all possible means to block Soviet expansion – was more than ever the watchword. Joseph McCarthy's witch-hunt was in full swing, and his spotlight was now playing on the US Army, where the senator had claimed to discover a number of Soviet moles; and as a result the Soviet Union and the West were on very poor terms.

Our own government was little inclined to poison the atmosphere further by acknowledging the presence of the traitors Burgess and Maclean on our territory. Any official announcement was super-fluous, especially since the KGB had already drawn maximum profit from the situation; intelligence operatives all over the world who had to deal with KGB handlers on a regular basis were greatly heartened by the Centre's brilliant exploit in spiriting its foremost British agents back to Moscow. They were grateful to us for not leaving Maclean and Burgess high and dry, and they felt reassured about their own situations. They were aware that something very difficult had been accomplished for two fellow agents, and they were impressed. We might have chosen this moment for an all-out promotion of our secret services: personally, I am glad we did not, because it could have jeopardized our ability to keep the rest of the Cambridge network functioning for three more years.

So the presence of Burgess and Maclean in the USSR was an open secret, after the defection of the Petrovs and the visit to Russia of Guy Burgess's mother. Nonetheless, the official policy of silence did not prevent Melinda Maclean from meeting Sam Russell, the correspon-dent of the *Daily Worker*, in 1955, or from telling him that she had always known about her husband's spying activities. I never knew what devil possessed Melinda when she said this; but luckily very few people noticed Russell's article, even though the Burgess–Maclean affair was far from forgotten. In the autumn of 1955, as I have said, it once again made headlines when the MP Marcus Lipton accused Kim Philby of being the 'Third Man' who had organized the defections of his two fellow moles. The world press once again took up the cudgels.

Who exactly were the members of the Cambridge ring? I read much newsprint about the Third Man, the disappearance of Melinda, and the fourth and even the fifth Cambridge spy. The investigation of this last point has now been under way for forty years. Hundreds of books, articles and documents, some of which emanated from the governments involved, have been put out. Some of these have cast light on the affair, while others, more far-fetched, have only served to muddy the waters.

The fascination of the international press with the Cambridge network increased even further when, in 1956, Nikita Khruschev finally confirmed that Burgess and Maclean were living in the Soviet Union. He officially announced that the two men had, at their request, recently received Soviet citizenship. Guy Burgess's British passport had expired in 1954 and even he felt a certain delicacy about asking Her Majesty's Embassy in Moscow for a new one.

The Twentieth Party Congress, which was to endorse the de-Stalinization of the USSR, was only a few weeks away; 1,424 delegates were expected and droves of journalists were converging on Moscow. The KGB had refused to permit one-on-one interviews with the two British agents. A certain amount of time was allowed to pass; then a press conference was arranged at the National Hotel on Saturday 11 February 1956. One or two carefully screened representatives of the press were allowed to meet Burgess and Maclean, among them Richard Hughes, the *Sunday Times* foreign correspondent. The two men appeared relaxed, healthy, dressed in well-cut English suits and completely sure of themselves.

They stated baldly that they had never worked for the Soviet Secret Service. Then they embarked on a long digression about the merits of Communism, concluding with the claim that they had left England for fear of a third world war, which they had judged to be imminent in 1951. China had intervened in Korea; a state of emergency had been decreed in the United States; MacArthur was urging a second front against China. According to Burgess and Maclean, the risks of world-wide confrontation had never been as great as in 1951, and so, as pacifists, they had decided to take refuge in the only place where war could not reach them: the USSR.

I myself did not attend this press conference, being still in England at the time.

In Moscow, Donald Maclean continued to perfect his Russian. After four years he spoke and wrote the language fluently; he was also a member of the Communist Party, attempting as far as possible to live out his ideal. He sternly refused the official car and the luxury dacha which were the usual perquisites of the *apparatchik*. Instead he made use of a simple house in the vicinity of Moscow, where he took

his family for weekends. As he said, he preferred to live modestly. At various moments in his life Donald Maclean had been a heavy drinker, notably during his time in Cairo, but in Moscow he virtually gave up drinking altogether. On rare occasions he would pour himself a glass of scotch, but he was never drunk.

Above all, he insisted on working. His first job was with a newspaper specializing in the world economy. In political matters, Maclean's views were highly unorthodox; he was far from being a blinkered Party-line man, sticking to the rules laid down by the Supreme Soviet. He was friendly with a number of prominent dissidents, refused to hide his convictions, was ready at any moment to defend them, disagreed with Soviet foreign policy and said so openly.

Despite his dissident contacts – whom he would often invite to his home – Maclean remained a Communist. In 1956, he began a correspondence with the great British historian Arnold Toynbee, whom he had known before the war. The two men exchanged several letters, but Toynbee abruptly stopped writing after Maclean justified the Soviet intervention in Hungary. At that time the Maclean family was very much turned inward on itself, and Donald saw very few people apart from the ubiquitous Sam Russell of the *Daily Worker*.

He never realized the dream of his youth, which was to teach English in a Russian primary school. Instead, in 1961 he entered the Institute of World Economic and International Relations (IMEMO). Here he gave courses and conducted research, notably on the foreign policy of the first Labour government in Britain. He was the author of several books, one of which, *British Policy Since Suez (1956–68)*, was very well received.

As for Guy Burgess, he was eventually moved into an old apartment, furnished in the same style as the house he had lived in earlier. In a one-and-a-half-hour documentary film made by an English crew, he was shown living in a modern building in Moscow. This was misleading; he liked only old houses and apartments decorated with fine antique furniture.

After 1956, he began to meet more and more foreigners, with whom he took no pains to hide his identity. He telephoned England very frequently and gave a number of interviews to journalists and writers. Among these was Tom Driberg, the Labour MP and journalist who soon afterwards wrote a book about Burgess's life in the Soviet Union.

Guy saw so many foreigners because he was still unreconciled to Soviet Russia, uprooted and unable to find a place for himself in our society. He missed his pub, and he missed the freedom to indulge his homosexual leanings in a country where such behaviour was strictly against the law. Nevertheless, he managed to find partners by hook or by crook, chiefly because the KGB and the militia turned a blind eye. He had an official lover and a number of unofficial ones.

The Centre did what it could to make the lives of Burgess and Maclean as easy as possible. When they needed something, they had only to ask. While Maclean's requests were few and eminently reasonable, Burgess tended to go overboard. At one point, I found myself rummaging all over London for quantities of books destined for Burgess's new library in his Moscow apartment. Several times a year, he would demand made-to-measure suits, which we had to order from his Soho tailor. Since in his own eyes he could never have enough suits, he would sometimes obtain them by roundabout means.

One day he met a woman, a tourist, in the street. She was the Australian-born actress Coral Browne, then living in London, who was with a theatre company touring the Soviet Union. He went up to her immediately and offered to show her round.

'But I don't know who you are!'

'Oh, yes you do,' said Guy Burgess.

Coral was duly charmed and allowed him to walk her back to her hotel. Along the way they got to know each other, then had a drink and agreed to meet again for dinner next day. By the end of the meal she knew exactly who Burgess was, and didn't seem unduly put out by the knowledge; even better, she agreed to take his measurements herself and deliver them to a London tailor along with Guy's detailed order for a suit: I don't know if Guy gave his new friend the money to pay for it, though I'm sure that on this occasion he didn't ask the KGB for a single penny of the cost. Maybe his mother, who was then living in London, settled the bill.

True to her promise, Guy's new friend went to the tailor in question, and produced the measurements. The fitter looked at the figures quizzically.

'That's very odd, madam . . . Would you be good enough to tell me this gentleman's name?'

'Guy Burgess.'

The man's face cleared. 'I thought as much,' he said. 'These measurements are about the same as his used to be, but I wasn't quite sure. I'm afraid Mr Burgess must have gained a little weight since he was last in . . .'

The suit was duly made, and Coral eventually delivered it. The episode is immortalized in Alan Bennett's play *An Englishman Abroad*.

Burgess didn't have much to occupy his time. He read a lot, walked and occasionally picked up another man for sex. He would sometimes help the KGB on a consultative basis, if asked. To my way of thinking, Guy was hardly to blame if he did so little work in Russia – it was much more the fault of the KGB, which was incapable of exploiting his knowledge and great intelligence. He might have been very useful to it; but instead he did nothing because nothing was asked of him, and it was not in his nature to solicit work.

Burgess, it must be remembered, was still only in his forties. He was full of energy and wanted to live by his own lights, rather than by the rigid laws prevailing in Russia. An early retirement could hardly be a satisfactory solution for him. Nevertheless, he remained the man of conviction he had always been. Moreover he was a true friend, as he proved to me in 1958.

While I was still stationed in London, I ran into serious trouble with the heads of my department. By then I considered myself an experienced and competent agent: wrongly, perhaps, but I still believed it. I had maintained a reasonable relationship with Korovin, my resident, and we helped one another as best we could. For example, I perfected the rigorous system of liaison with agents in the field that he had initiated. This he was glad of, but although he insisted that everybody else observe it, he himself was lax in the extreme. As I have said before, he would sometimes turn up at a rendezvous in an embassy car, which I thought was little short of criminal.

The most serious problem of all, however, was Korovin's unpleasant habit of imputing blame to his juniors for faults a thousand times less consequential than his own. After a while I could bear it no longer, and while I was on leave in Moscow in 1958 I asked the Centre if I could give up my London post. I had a good pretext:

my daughter would shortly complete her fourth year at the school of the Soviet Embassy in London, which could offer no further education after that; hence I would be obliged to leave her on her own in Moscow when the next school year began – and there was nobody to look after her.

I explained this to Aleksandr Mikhailovich Sakharovsky, the head of the PDG (the First Directorate, or espionage section of the KGB). Sakharovsky was an efficient, intelligent officer who knew how to listen to his subordinates; indeed, he held a record for longevity in his post, fifteen years.

He heard me out in his big office at the Lubyanka. When I had finished, he said, 'Now tell me frankly, isn't there something else that's bothering you?'

I felt compelled to tell the truth.

'Yes,' I replied, 'I can't get on with Korovin any more. I know I owe him a lot; he taught me my job. But his methods of work are intolerable to me now. He's excessively demanding with everyone else, but won't stick to any of the rules himself.'

Sakharovsky didn't seem particularly surprised by this.

'Yes, we know all about that, Yuri, and we have nothing much to add.'

Unfortunately, this interview was attended by another section chief, who immediately afterwards wrote to Korovin and told him what I had said, distorting and exaggerating my words.

The result was that Korovin immediately riposted with a violently critical report on me, which he sent not to Sakharovsky but to Ivan Aleksandrovich Serov, President of the KGB. Serov had taken exception to me for personal reasons and he leapt at the chance to give me a hard time. He was a small man, built like an athlete, with a highly expressive, clever face. Yet he couldn't hide his deep mistrust and suspicion of everyone surrounding him.

In his harsh, grating voice, Serov berated me as a bad officer who had produced nothing but bad results for years.

My response was to enumerate everything I had achieved in London since 1948. I saw quite clearly that he wasn't even bothering to listen. After a while he called in one of his assistants and told him to arrange for me to be sent up north, or to somewhere in Siberia.

I was furious. 'In that case, here's my resignation,' I said hotly, and marched out of Serov's office.

When my Russian friends heard the news that I was to be fired or hustled off to Murmansk or Siberia, they melted away. Not one of them dared speak to me.

Only Guy Burgess was there to intercede on my behalf. When he heard about the incident, he wrote a forthright letter of protest to Serov. What he said in it about me was precisely true, and it was brought home to me with some force that though I had prided myself on knowing Guy inside out, he had observed me even more closely. By acting in this way, Guy strengthened my conviction that he genuinely saw himself as a totally committed KGB agent, who considered he had a right not only to his point of view, but also to contradict a man as formidable as the boss of bosses. His intervention on my behalf triggered a second display of support from my section chief, who pointed out my wide knowledge of Western intelligence methods and of international political problems. The upshot was that Serov withdrew his Siberian threat and I remained with the KGB; moreover, I was withdrawn from London, just as I had requested.

Once I was back in Moscow, my relations with Burgess evolved into a personal friendship, now that its professional context had lapsed. We met often and talked much, greatly enjoying one another's company. From time to time I would help him out when he was bored or had some problem; any problems I would usually hear about from the KGB men detailed to look after him.

Towards the end of the 1950s, he embarked on some research for the Centre, notably a study of British students in the 1930s, with a discussion of their behaviour and their political and social aspirations. This work included a brilliant analysis of the methods used by the Soviets to recruit young Britons at that time, in which Burgess showed quite clearly how and why the NKVD had succeeded in creating a network of absolutely crucial importance. The uniqueness of this study lay in the fact that it was the fruit of Burgess's own long experience, and that, for the first time, it offered an analysis, with the full benefit of hindsight, of the way Russia's intelligence networks in Great Britain had been built up.

Unfortunately for us, the KGB at the time was getting fat and lazy. Nobody bothered to read this fascinating report and act on it, and it was quietly shelved in the archives.

When Guy was asked to do something, he did it with speed and alacrity. He never refused a job. The result was always good, never banal and boring as so many experts' reports tend to be. It was a pity that the KGB failed to call on Burgess's great skills as often as it might have; and it was a shame that he himself never offered them as did Philby, who was always proposing his services to the Centre for one thing or another.

I always respected Guy Burgess, despite the constant slanders that appeared about him both in the Soviet Union and in England. His one effective defender was Anthony Blunt, who spoke only good of him in several newspaper interviews. To *The Sunday Times* he declared: 'People have heaped such abuse on Guy Burgess because of the last, terrible years of his life, that I think it only right to repeat that he was one of the most remarkable intellectuals I have ever met.' In *The Times* of 20 November 1979, he said, 'I first met Burgess when he was an undergraduate ... he was difficult, but his intelligence was such that he could go to the heart of any problem. He was interested in absolutely everything.'

It is also intriguing to note that Dick White, the head of MI5 and, later, MI6, stated on several occasions that it was thanks to the personal qualities of Guy Burgess that the group of five Cambridge agents was formed at all. I think he was correct, although Philby was the actual founder of the club. Philby found Burgess, but Burgess was the man who recruited Blunt, and so on down the line. Dick White was right: the real leader was Burgess. He held the group together, infused it with his energy and led it into battle, so to speak. In the 1930s, at the very start, it was he who took the initiatives and the risks, dragging the others along in his wake. He was the moral leader of the group.

This brilliant, difficult character could not adapt to Soviet conditions. His one desire was to return to England, and he never stopped harassing the heads of the KGB to let him do so. He begged to be released, swearing that he would never breathe a word of betrayal. My superiors refused to believe him. He was so physically and morally broken down that he would have collapsed at the first interrogation, as they knew only too well. In Moscow, he burned himself out like a torch, drinking more and more.

Sometimes I would drop by to see Burgess in the morning, to spend an hour or two talking over the latest news, or arguing about literature. He was a voracious reader, with an encyclopaedic knowledge of English literature and an insatiable appetite for the

English-language papers with which his bodyguard kept him supplied. He analysed everything he read and invariably produced
intelligent, balanced, unbiased judgements on world events and the
policies of the great powers.

Sadly, when I arrived at his house the first thing I usually saw was a
half-empty bottle of dry Georgian wine on the kitchen table. When I
told him it was against the unwritten laws of England to drink before
noon, he just laughed at me.

'I'm not in England, comrade.'

As time went by, being with him became more and more painful.
Other people found him impossible to get on with, though I myself
had no problem in this regard. Those detailed to look after Guy
Burgess suffered acutely, for he was unpredictable, aggressive and
provocative to them by turns. I remember one counter-espionage
agent who had been with Burgess in a KGB holiday camp in the
south, who told me how odious he had been. For example, he derived
a warped satisfaction from dragging an inflatable bed along the
beach, brushing past the people sunbathing and spraying them with
sand. He was roundly abused, of course, but he didn't give a damn.
Then, during a reception at the Chinese Embassy in Moscow, he is
said to have urinated into a fireplace, to the horror of Maclean, who
was also present. I don't know if this anecdote is true, but I'm sure he
was more than capable of such a thing.

In the early 1960s, the authorities chose to portray Guy Burgess as
a man in the pink, completely relaxed and good-humoured. He was
photographed strutting jauntily over one of the city's bridges in a
brand-new suit. I believe this was staged, for the Burgess I knew in
the last years of his life was a rather melancholy person, despite the
regular visits of his mother, who came to keep him company.

In 1962, he let it be known semi-officially that he wanted to return
to England. The press somehow got hold of this news and blew it out
of proportion. 'Burgess and Maclean to Fly to London' screamed the
headlines.

MI5 went into a paroxysm. The British knew very well that there
was insufficient evidence to convict the two men; nevertheless
Scotland Yard asked the Chief Metropolitan Magistrate in London,
Sir Robert Blundell, to issue a warrant for the arrest of Burgess (and
Maclean, who was for some reason expected to come too) the
moment they set foot in Britain. The authorities took the affair so

seriously that they called in Superintendent George Smith, the celebrated detective who had dismantled the Kroger–Lonsdale ring a year earlier. (The Krogers, a husband and wife team, and Lonsdale were both KGB agents, and Lonsdale was a KGB 'illegal'. They were jailed for twenty-five and twenty years respectively in 1961.)

The rumours grew to such an extent that on the evening of 17 April it was announced that the two former diplomats had boarded a plane for London via Amsterdam. All this was pure nonsense, but it gave the British press another chance to resurrect the affair. Certain journalists claimed they had spotted Burgess at the 1960 trial of Francis Gary Powers, the pilot of the American U-2 spy plane which was shot down over Soviet territory. I myself attended that trial throughout, and I never saw Burgess once. The frenzy increased when the news broke that Donald Maclean's mother had died: no fewer than seven plain-clothes police inspectors attended her funeral at Penn cemetery in July 1962 – no doubt they were there on the off chance of picking up Donald. Only the Labour MP Tom Driberg, who had seen Guy Burgess in Moscow, scoffed at the rumours, declaring that it was out of the question that either man would ever return to England alive.

Around that time I was sent on a protracted mission and consequently was away from Moscow when Guy suddenly came down with a severe liver complaint. Nor was I on the spot to welcome Kim Philby, who finally came across from the West in January 1963. Guy was in hospital when he heard this news, and he begged Philby to come and see him. The KGB, in the belief that the sight of Kim could only do Burgess good, passed the message on: but Kim categorically refused. He could never forgive Burgess for defecting with Maclean. He regarded him as an out-and-out traitor, who had broken his word in the full knowledge that by doing so he was leaving a friend in desperate danger.

Kim Philby was implacable. Despite Burgess's pleas, the two men never saw each other again.

Guy Burgess died on 19 August 1963 at the Botkin Hospital in Moscow. He bequeathed his library to Kim Philby, but Kim refused even to attend the funeral of his old friend and accomplice. I went to the brief cremation ceremony, along with a couple of KGB officers and a few homosexual friends of the dead man. Guy's ashes were then sent home to his family in England, as he had willed.

* * *

As for me, I had to wait until 1964 to meet Kim Philby, at which time I was detailed by the KGB to work with him on his autobiography. The idea was to write an official KGB version of his life, for distribution in Russia and the other Iron Curtain nations. The moment I had waited for so long had finally come.

Philby was quartered not far from the centre of Moscow, in a new, nondescript but well-maintained building. I climbed the three flights of stairs and rang the bell. A man in his fifties appeared at the door: he was of average height, slightly stout, but still handsome and distinguished-looking.

I introduced myself, and he grasped my hand, grinning.

'You and I are old friends, Peter. Come in!'

We sat down with a bottle of vodka and began to talk. It was a strange sensation to have so much in common with a man I had never spoken to in my life, and I believe he shared this feeling. As we talked on, an image rose up in my mind. I had the impression that together we were piecing together two halves of a puzzle. When he spoke of a given event or recounted an anecdote, I responded with my own version of it, drawing on memories of my times in Moscow (1944–47) and London (1947–55). Each of us could reveal to the other the part of the picture that had been hidden from him.

It didn't take me long to discover that Kim Philby believed me to be a very important figure within the KGB. He was highly deferential towards me, and I did nothing to disenchant him. I heard later that he had told his wife Eleanor, who rejoined him in Moscow a few months after his arrival, that she should stay out of the way when I was around. 'Peter is my chief,' he said. 'He doesn't care to be seen, so you don't need to see him.' And indeed Eleanor stayed in the kitchen throughout our lunches.

At this first interview we immediately set up a cordial relationship, as if we had been on familiar terms for a long time. Over a period of nearly twenty years I had read and translated so many notes and reports written by Kim Philby that I seemed to understand the innermost workings of his mind. Burgess, too, must have told him good things about me in the early days. Thus we chatted for hours about England, Beirut and, above all, Philby's arrival in Moscow on 27 January 1963. He told me he had walked off the *Dolmatova* in the port of Odessa after a few days' voyage, just like any other tourist.

There he was welcomed by three KGB officers in uniform and by a plain-clothes man named Sergei. After the customary formalities, Sergei accompanied him to Moscow, where he was lodged in a small apartment with a woman to do his housework and cooking. Sergei took care of everything else, notably his contacts with the KGB, his security and his transportation when required. Sergei spoke excellent English and had excellent manners; he also had a sense of humour which delighted Kim. The same Sergei remained in his service till the day he died.

Like Burgess and Maclean in their time, Kim had been extensively debriefed by KGB officers, a procedure to which he submitted with good grace. He was then shown a number of apartments in Moscow, and his choice had fallen on the one we were in now. A number of books and pieces of furniture had been taken by the KGB from his Beirut residence and brought by ship to the USSR, with the result that Kim Philby was now comfortably set up with familiar things around him. He had a car, a chauffeur and a dacha in the vicinity of Moscow, along with Soviet citizenship. He and Maclean quickly re-established contact: Melinda showed him round Moscow before Eleanor arrived in September 1963, nine months after his escape from Beirut.

Eleanor had never known about her husband's past, and was therefore not amused by his sudden disappearance and her own reception by hordes of news hounds when she got back to London. Kim had written a letter to reassure her, but the British and American secret services had naturally exerted pressure on her not to go to the Soviet Union, as her husband begged her to do. She was very angry, but nonetheless she decided to rejoin him, openly requesting a visa from the Soviet Embassy in London. The consulate arranged for her trip, which was closely monitored by MI5.

At our second meeting Philby and I began working seriously. He showed me the synopsis of his book, which I cleared with my superior before we settled down to the first chapter. Philby would write a batch of text and ask me what I thought of it. We were usually in agreement: he knew as well as I what he could say and what had to remain hidden. Sometimes my superior requested alterations; I would ask Kim, in a roundabout fashion, if he could find a different interpretation of the facts.

He was just as indirect as I was. He never answered right away. If he finally said, 'Yes, I think we can manage that,' everything would be all right. But if he said, 'I'll think about it,' that meant he refused point blank to alter a single word, and I would have to break the news to the KGB as best I could. We went through everything, down to the last points of detail, with the utmost care, and as a rule we would work out some kind of compromise.

Philby's reputation as a writer was entirely deserved. The book he produced about his life has much to recommend it, even though it has major gaps and is not always truthful.

As I got to know him better I saw that he was a master of winning the confidence of his interlocutors. He would never disagree with me head-on and he always gave me every opportunity to express my point of view. Then he temporized. Ultimately, he never conceded any point, and he could be completely inflexible when he thought it necessary. This side of his character was always veiled from me, but on several occasions I felt it close to the surface and backed off. On the other hand, the moment he saw he could get no further with me, he would take a half-step backward to avoid collision. Philby was a born secret agent, a man who knew how far to compromise.

We worked together for several months, and then I was sent away on a mission. Another KGB officer took over from me. Philby's book finally appeared in 1968, under the title *My Silent War*.

The mysterious Eleanor Philby, whom I had not seen once at their apartment, completely failed to adapt to life in Moscow. She hated the cold, which her husband loved. The couple had few friends, apart from one or two journalists and, from time to time, Donald and Melinda Maclean. Eleanor was very bored, though she didn't seem unhappy. Kim was kind and even sentimental: sometimes when she was busy in the kitchen cooking a meal she would find a note from him in one of the saucepans saying 'I love you'. She, too, was in love with her husband, but she could not quite forgive the fact that he had slipped out of Beirut without a word of explanation to her. She never recovered from that first shock of betrayal.

In 1964, Eleanor Philby went back to the United States for the summer to stay with her daughter. She needed, she said, a radical change. At the same time the Macleans, with their three children and

Kim Philby, went on an extended tour of the Baltic states. On their return in September, Eleanor wrote to Kim to say she was staying on a while longer in the United States. Philby continued to see a lot of the Macleans, and went skiing with them that winter, at which time he and Melinda embarked on a love affair. I never saw the Macleans, but I knew that Donald's relationship with his wife was somewhat cold and distant. I had assumed Melinda was resigned to this, but I was wrong.

Donald quickly realized what was happening and the two men quarrelled. When Eleanor returned to Moscow for Christmas, Kim welcomed her coolly. By then he was no longer speaking to Maclean, and Eleanor soon understood what had happened in her absence. She was shattered, though she said nothing, and in May 1965 she left Moscow for good. They separated on good terms, however. Three years later, Eleanor Philby died suddenly in the United States.

Shortly after Eleanor's departure, Kim Philby was given the Order of Lenin and the Order of the Red Banner, decorations of which he was very proud.

In the meantime Melinda had left her husband to move in with Kim. Donald didn't take kindly to this, of course, but still he managed to keep his life on an even keel. He continued working at IMEMO, studying Russian, writing books and seeing his tiny circle of friends – with the exception of Philby, naturally. Even in England, the two men had never had much in common.

As it turned out, Melinda's adventure with Kim was short-lived. In 1966, she left him, probably because he was drinking again. Now she was alone in Moscow with nowhere to go, and ultimately, partly because of the housing crisis, she was forced to return to her husband. She lived with him, rather amazingly, until 1979, in which year she left Russia for good to live in the United States. Those thirteen years cannot have been easy, especially since the Maclean children had all grown up and married Russians. Indeed Melinda and Donald were now grandparents. The two elder children, Fergus and Donald Junior, left the USSR with their families in 1973 and emigrated to London. Little Melinda, after a first failed marriage, became the wife of a Moscow painter named Aleksandr Driuchin; in 1979, she, too, left Russia with her husband and her daughter by her first marriage (yet another Melinda). This girl ended up living in the United States with her great-grandmother, Mrs Dunbar.

I heard that Donald Maclean – who was in poor health following an operation that he had had to undergo after an attack of pleurisy – was deeply depressed by the departure of little Melinda, whom he called 'Melindushka'.

For the last four years of his life, he lived alone in Moscow and fell back, I think, on alcohol. In early 1983, his much-loved brother Alan came to visit him; it was the first time they had spoken since 1951. In spite of everything, Alan was still full of admiration for his brother; the two spent several days together before Alan had to return to England.

Donald Maclean died shortly afterwards, on 9 March 1983. His remains were cremated at the Douskoi cemetery in the presence of a couple of KGB officers, his colleagues from IMEMO, some former students, Kim Philby and George Blake. Nobody from his family was present. The coffin, which was covered with a red flag, bore the words 'Bon Voyage, Donald Donaldovich'. Fergus Maclean, the elder son, arrived after the ceremony and took his father's ashes home to England, where they were placed in the family vault at Penn after a short service. Naturally, the death of Donald Maclean was an excuse for the Western press to resurrect the whole affair for the umpteenth time.

After I came back from a nine-month stint in India in 1967, my encounters with Kim Philby ceased to be professional in nature. We were now good friends. Kim had plenty of time on his hands: he and I were in much the same position, with less and less work coming our way from the KGB. Nevertheless I kept after the heads of the service to give him as much employment as possible, pointing out that in Philby we had something of a phenomenon, a brilliant analyst and an expert on international relations whose skills should be exploited. I even suggested he should teach at the KGB school: he was, after all, the most celebrated spy alive.

To begin with, these requests fell on deaf ears, but that didn't mean that Kim was left with nothing to occupy him. Although, like Burgess, he had refused to learn Russian, he remained a prominent KGB consultant. The First Directorate (foreign intelligence) called on him whenever they needed advice on the spying or counter-espionage activities of other nations, and when they did he helped them conscientiously and energetically. Détente was in the air, but this in no way abated the rivalry between the various secret services. The KGB would sometimes ask Philby for his views on purely political matters having to do with Britain or the United States, or on specific problems involving their secret services. For example, he produced a complete insider's report on the CIA, including a full analysis of its internal workings and charts of its secret structures both at home and abroad. He had a remarkable memory for names and his judgements of individuals were uncannily accurate. His early view of James Angleton, head of the CIA's counter-espionage service, was that he was 'off his head', and as it turned out he couldn't have been more right; likewise, he put together full biographies of Britain's SIS chiefs and most effective officers. Kim was certainly not idle, but his talents could and should have been put to far greater use.

Sometimes I would drop by to spend an hour or two in his company. We rarely talked about his life in England, because I understood that any reminder of home made him sad. When he talked about Burgess, I could see that his judgement of his former friend was still completely objective, despite their bitter quarrel at the end. In his heart of hearts I think Kim had an enduring respect for Guy Burgess. Unlike many others, we two had known Guy for what he truly was – a proud, complete man, who never did anything by halves.

Burgess may have been a heavy drinker, but he was also a heavy worker. He made some giant blunders, but these were often a consequence of bold initiatives. Once he had identified his goal, he could and would move mountains to attain it.

I tried to explain to Kim why Burgess had followed Maclean behind the Iron Curtain. I explained that he trusted Korovin, who had given him to understand that he would return to London. Philby scoffed at this. He thought that Guy was sufficiently bright to understand that if he went with Maclean there would be no return except to a very long spell in prison. Nothing could shake Kim in this view. Burgess had let him down, and that was that.

Again and again we went over the crucial moments in the history of our network, good and bad. It was Philby, for example, who gave me the hair-raising details of the Volkov affair, related earlier in this book.

When he asked me why we had put so much energy into getting him and the others out of the West, I replied that the Soviets had always made a point of doing everything possible to save agents who expressed a desire to cross over. In some cases, this couldn't be done, either for lack of time, or because the agents in question had quickly confessed and been locked up. This was the case of Allan Nunn May and Klaus Fuchs, the atomic spies, and then of George Blake in 1961, though Blake managed to escape and make his way to the USSR in 1966. We didn't care to leave our friends in the lurch.

A puzzling question for us both was this: had the British looked the other way, or even quietly assisted in the defections of our network members? We concluded that this could not have been the case in regard to Maclean, who was scheduled for interrogation by MI5. Perhaps the idea might have occurred to the heads of British counter-espionage, but the American involvement had to have ruled it out. The Americans would never have stood for any back-pedalling on the part of the British. But in his own case, Philby shared my view that the British services had all but ushered him through the door, because they knew very well that if he were brought to trial he would bring down the roof.

As he got older, Kim sank deeper into his memories. He would have loved to meet everyone, without exception, whom he had worked with on the Soviet side. But sadly, all his former handlers were now dead: there was only me. This was for the very simple reason that when I worked with the Cambridge Five in London I was only twenty-five, whereas my KGB predecessors in the job were considerably older.

Whenever Kim went to conferences or official ceremonies, he looked around the room for familiar faces. There were depressingly few.

In the main, he seemed to take day-to-day existence in the Soviet Union fairly well. He needed very little for himself, but it upset him terribly to see basic foods progressively disappearing from the shelves. The endless queues in front of the butcher's shops and bakeries horrified him – even though he himself lacked for nothing, because Sergei made sure he had what he wanted.

I think his happiness was something of a sham. He was too proud to betray any regrets, but, objectively speaking, the conditions of his life in England, the United States and even Turkey were very different to anything we could offer him in Moscow, even though he lived in a comfortable apartment and had no material worries. I believe he was resigned to his fate. In contrast to Burgess, he never expressed the wish to go back to England. It may have crossed his mind, but he never said a word because he knew full well the wish would never be fulfilled.

In 1966, when Melinda left him, Philby found himself completely alone since Donald and he were no longer on speaking terms. Kim was now drinking with a vengeance, and unfortunately the KGB people around him didn't notice it till the problem was well advanced. For several years he lived an empty, bored existence, dividing his time between his Moscow apartment, the holiday houses of the *nomenklatura* by the Black Sea, and the various countries of the Eastern Bloc. He drowned his sorrows in wine, or in whisky if he could get it. The only happy time during this period was a visit from his son Tommy in 1967. On his return to England, Tommy declared, 'My father is a hero.'

Kim was lost in depression when Ida, the wife of his fellow exile George Blake, introduced him to her best friend, a good-looking redhead called Rufina. Rufina was half-Russian, half-Polish. They saw each other several times at Blake's country dacha: Blake himself had just become the father of a small boy. (I would add, at this point, that I myself never worked with George Blake at any time and was never his handler in Britain.)

Philby took Rufina home several times, and shortly afterwards asked her to marry him. She hesitated: after all, he was much older than she was. Finally she accepted and they were married in Moscow on 19 December 1971, the KGB presenting the couple with a magnificent service of English china for the occasion. Rufina was Kim Philby's fourth wife.

I continued to see Kim and Rufina from time to time, and I was struck by the fact that she seemed to know very little about her husband's life. In contrast to Maclean, Kim never divulged any secrets to the women in his life. Neither Aileen, Eleanor, Melinda nor Rufina were told about his activities. During the seventeen years he worked as an active agent for the KGB, we never had a single problem on this score. It may seem cynical to say so, but in this way he avoided the possibility of blackmail or any other difficulty linked with his work, each time he divorced or was separated. It may be that he simply didn't trust women.

After their marriage, the lives of both Philby and his wife altered completely. Rufina, who up till then had lived with her mother, came to her husband's new apartment in the centre of Moscow, close to the Moskva, on the fifth floor of a building reserved for high-ranking government officials. The rooms were huge, well lit and comfortably furnished, with books lining every shelf. Rufina had her own chauffeur-driven car, and the Blakes and Philbys continued to see a lot of one another. George Blake's son Misha, who was born the same year that the Philbys were married, remained very close to the man he always knew as 'Uncle Kim'.

Kim stopped drinking and took up his consulting activities where he had left off. He continued to do occasional work for the Centre on international questions, mainly dealing with the Near East, a region he knew exceedingly well. Nor did he hesitate to tackle purely operational problems. On several occasions he spent many hours identifying agents from photographs shown to him. He was given a new lease on life when the Centre finally suggested that he take part in the training of a new generation of agents at the KGB spy school, a job he accepted with great enthusiasm. He proved an excellent teacher, imparting what he knew with pleasure, patience and devotion. He loved the work.

During their holidays, Philby and his wife travelled widely around the Soviet Union, notably in the Baltic states and around the resorts of the Black Sea. They stayed in the best hotels and never had the slightest problem moving about the nation's interior. They also visited Eastern Bloc countries such as Poland, Bulgaria and East Berlin, and even travelled to Cuba. This last trip was fairly risky, and we pulled out all the stops to ensure their complete security. They were asked not to travel by plane – what would happen if their aircraft had engine problems and was forced to land in the United States? So they went by sea, even though the trip took longer. For the first time in many years, Kim came close to his native country, as his ship passed along the English Channel. Standing at the rail, he watched the coasts of Kent and Sussex fade away astern. He never told anyone what he felt at that moment. In Cuba, he was awarded a decoration by the government, though Castro was unable to receive him.

The KGB was all in favour of Rufina even though she had strictly no connection with the secret services. Eleanor, who had almost certainly been contacted by MI5 and the CIA, had been a liability, while the Kim–Melinda liaison had been voted a terrible idea.

Rufina, by contrast, was an intelligent, highly educated woman, and above all, she had succeeded in dragging Philby out of the morass of alcoholism.

I saw Kim again a few times in the mid-1980s. At that point I was very busy with my own job at the Andropov Institute, the KGB training unit. I derived a lot of pleasure from our meetings, even though they weren't as frequent as I could have wished. We invariably talked politics, the one subject that passionately interested us both; and in particular we discussed Afghanistan, on which the KGB had several times requested Kim's views. Like a number of other specialists working at the Centre, he had strongly advised that the Russians should not set so much as the tips of their toes in the Afghan quagmire, recalling how the British had come hopelessly adrift there. The British had waged no fewer than three Afghan wars, the last of which was concluded with the liberation of Afghanistan from foreign interference.

In 1983, two events took place which hit Kim Philby hard. The first was the death of Donald Maclean, with whom he had quarrelled, but whom he still held in sincere respect. Then, barely a month later, Anthony Blunt died. Apropos of Blunt, Philby could never understand what possible interest the British Government can have had in officially recognizing in 1979 that Anthony Blunt was a Soviet agent.

I paid another visit to Kim after the introduction of Gorbachev's *perestroika* programme. He was violently against Gorbachev and all his works, particularly the endless and absurd Party Congresses that were taking place at the time. According to him, the leaders of the Soviet Union had ceased to be Communists many years before. Their only goal was to stay in power by any means that came to hand. He was fully aware that the *apparatchik* system was rotten from top to bottom and that everyone within it who had any power at all was out for himself, for his family and most of all for bribes. Philby had always detested Brezhnev, whom he viewed as an utterly corrupt individual. Now, with Gorbachev in charge, he was profoundly disillusioned and anxious for the future of the Soviet Union.

I knew that Kim Philby remained faithful to his ideals right to the end; above all, he never went back on the commitment he had made as a young man. He often told me that Stalin, like Khruschev, Brezhnev and the rest, had passed into history, but the shining ideal of Communism would never die. Even though it was wrongly put into practice almost from the first, he said, it still held out the best hope for mankind.

In September 1986, Kim was visited by an old acquaintance, a man with whom he had worked during the war. This was the novelist Graham Greene. When he was SIS resident in Sierra Leone, Greene's immediate boss in London had been Kim Philby. The two men weren't really friends at that time but became so later: from 1969, they corresponded intermittently. Greene visited Moscow on four separate occasions, and the two men saw a lot of each other. Greene, the voluntary exile living in Antibes, and Philby, the involuntary Muscovite, had one point in common – an indelible Britishness. They shared the distinction, detachment and edge of cynicism that characterized gentlemen of the old school. I know that Philby didn't much care for the character in *The Human Factor* who is supposed to be modelled on him, a whining fool who ekes out his days in a Moscow hovel. His own circumstances were totally different, what with his huge apartment, his magnificent view, the copies of *The Times*, *Le Monde* and the *Herald Tribune* to which he had subscribed, the videotapes of cricket test matches and the pots of Cooper's Oxford marmalade sent from London. Kim Philby listened to the BBC and the Voice of America, read the spy novels of John le Carré and even learned to cook like a chef, a far cry from the Greene character. I was amused, after one of Greene's visits, to read Kim's remark to the *Sunday Telegraph*: 'Change in the USSR can come only from the KGB, which recruits all the best and the brightest.'

Since the 1960s, Kim had experienced several minor cardiac alerts. In the spring of 1988, he had his first real heart attack. After this, I badly wanted to see him again. I was, after all, the only survivor of his fabulous adventure. I applied to my KGB colleagues, who passed the message on to Rufina. Kim replied that he would be more than happy, indeed he badly wanted to speak to me. Almost immediately afterwards he was taken to hospital. His state was not deemed critical, and when Rufina left him on the evening of 10 May she wasn't unduly concerned. But in the night the hospital called to tell her that Kim had died at 2 a.m. precisely.

I went to Kim's funeral, which was held on 13 May, a fine spring day. His coffin, draped with a red flag, lay in state at the Lubyanka, so that his KGB friends could pay their last respects. A cushion bearing his decorations lay on top of it. He was then buried at the Kuntsevo cemetery west of Moscow, in the plot reserved for generals. Although Kim Philby was never given the rank of general (contrary to what has been said), a detachment of KGB guards in full regalia paid him the last honours, firing three salvoes over his grave and playing the Soviet anthem. One of his sons, John Philby, was present, along with his daughter Josephine and a sizeable crowd of well-wishers, which included KGB officers of every rank and even the head of the Centre, Vladimir Aleksandrovich Kryuchkov, later one of the leaders of the 1991 coup. I considered it a great honour that I was chosen to read the funeral oration.

Kim Philby was the last and greatest actor in what has been called – correctly, I believe – the most spectacular espionage network of the twentieth century. For the first time in history, a secret service had contrived to recruit men who reached the highest levels of a foreign government, and to have them operate for years on its behalf without their being killed, arrested or even accused of any crime, for lack of proof. Luck and professionalism in equal measure were behind this brilliant success. At no time was there any major incident within the network, though we routinely organized meetings that were fraught with every conceivable danger over a period of many years.

For more than four decades the world has been mesmerized by the story of the Cambridge Five; and with good reason, for it is an extraordinary tale which will remain in the collective memory long after we who took part in it are all dead.

I sometimes go to Kim's grave in Moscow and stop there for a while. I cannot do the same for the others, whose ashes are in England, but I often think of them with regret, because with all their faults and qualities they were in a way dear to me. They were men who were ready to give their lives for a cause, and that is something I must admire. I would, I hope, have been ready to do the same had it been necessary.

With Melinda, John Cairncross, perhaps Litzi, and one or two others, I am one of the last living protagonists of this adventure, and probably the only one who had a chance to view it from all angles. With the benefit of hindsight, I am in a position to give a balanced judgement of the men and the events involved.

In my view, Somerset Maugham – himself a secret agent during the First World War – was close to the mark when he wrote that only a man's actions bear witness to his true nature. When a man must face the world around him he shows only what he wants to show. He composes an outward personality for himself so that others will accept the image that he wishes to project. To understand his true nature, it is possible to analyse his unconscious gestures and the expressions which pass across his face without his knowing; sometimes a man gets so accustomed to the mask he is wearing that he becomes in reality exactly what he is pretending to be. On the other hand, in the book he writes, the painting he composes and the tasks he undertakes, a man has no defence. Nothing can hide the mediocrity of his work. If one observes his actions carefully, one can uncover the profoundest secrets of his soul.

What a man says has no importance whatever: it is what he does that matters. Even so, I realize I shall never know the full personalities of all the agents I worked with, and one of them – Kim Philby – will always be a mystery to me.

In his operative career he committed scarcely any errors, and as time went by he acquired huge experience. He knew the traps that might be set for him and he knew how to circumvent them, but he was no genius for all that. He wasn't as brilliant as Burgess, Blunt, Maclean or even Cairncross. I do not think he was a remarkable student, or even particularly highly cultivated. He had intellectual qualities, it is true, but in all of them Guy Burgess far surpassed him.

On the other hand, Kim Philby possessed a rare faculty which the others lacked, that of assessing the real meaning of events. Most men judge facts only from their own standpoint; hence there is often a great difference between their assessment and reality. Philby always considered problems from every angle and tried to guess at whatever was hidden from him. He had a remarkable grasp of complex issues, along with an instinct about how they would unfold. That is what made him such a consummate secret operative. You had only to explain a practical problem to him and he would come straight back with a rapid, effective, irreproachable and infallible solution to it. Burgess, who as a rule recognized no superior authority and listened to no advice whatsoever because he was so sure of himself, respected Philby. When he was in trouble he went to Kim and did as he suggested. Even so, Philby's knowledge was far less extensive than his own, which embraced virtually every subject from politics to music, theatre and art.

I think that in spite of his faults Kim Philby was truly the greatest spy of the century, although I have often wondered whether Maclean wasn't even greater. If the criterion for judging an agent is the quantity and quality of the information he supplies, I can attest that what Philby produced was invariably flawless and immediately exploitable, concerning the activities of the other side, the locations of their agents and their attempts to mount sabotage operations.

On the other hand, if one considers that the aim of espionage is to furnish governments and heads of state with information that will assist them in their decisions, then the spy of the century has to be Donald Maclean. He gathered the political, economic and scientific intelligence that guided the strategy of our leaders for over ten years – and what years. During that period, the planet passed from a World War to a Cold War. What could be more crucial to the KGB at that time than to be fully informed of Anglo–American strategy *vis-à-vis* the Eastern Bloc?

The situation at the time was an odd one. The Centre's admiration for Philby was boundless. Nobody paid much attention to Maclean; his intelligence held little interest for the KGB hierarchy, which was more concerned with secret work in the field than with politics. I believe that only Molotov and his entourage, who were virtually the sole recipients of Maclean's information, could say with any authority which of the two men was the more devastating spy.

Whether he was the spy of the century or not, as far as I am concerned, Philby will always be a conundrum. I never knew him as well as I knew Burgess, Cairncross or Blunt, even though Blunt, too, was impenetrable to a degree.

Despite my admiration for him, despite everything I know about the extraordinary work he did for us, I never really felt close to Kim Philby. He never revealed his true self. Neither the British, nor the women he lived with, nor ourselves ever managed to pierce the armour of mystery that clad him. His great achievement in espionage was his life's work, and it fully occupied him until the day he died. But in the end I suspect that Philby made a mockery of everyone, particularly ourselves.

It may be that my restraint concerning Philby, Burgess and Blunt derived in some sort from a feeling of inferiority. From the moment I met them, I was aware that their intellects were superior to my own. They were all intellectuals of the very first rank, superbly educated at home and in the best schools their country could provide. By comparison, I was not only very young and callow, but also painfully aware of my own ordinariness. The Leningrad Naval Academy is not a bad school, but it can hardly be compared with Cambridge.

I was young, proud, courageous and bright: yet I soon understood that if we were to work well together it was best not to try to match these men's brilliance, but to listen to them, understand them and gain their confidence through respect. We differed in everything, even in the nature of our devotion to the cause. I was devoted because my superiors expected me to be so, because the system I lived in required it and because I was a member of the Communist Party. It was the right way to behave, even though my loyalty to Communism was purely formal. It was not until many years had passed and I was an old man that I understood the full extent of the impasse into which Marxism had led my country.

For the Cambridge Five the choice was altogether different. There was nothing bureaucratic or agreed about their commitment. Their certainty sprang from a comprehensive analysis of theory and reality. In the 1930s, when they were young men, the political and economic situation of Great Britain left a lot to be desired. Poverty and unemployment existed side by side with the most ostentatious luxury. Generosity, a craving for justice and sympathy for others motivated all their actions. They foresaw and dreaded the rise of Fascism in Germany and the rest of Europe, in Italy, France and even in Great Britain. The crisis of the capitalist system and the discontent of the workers also influenced their commitment. They arrived at the conclusion that the Soviet Union should be given all the help that could be mustered.

This was in the early 1930s. With time, their ideas altered, but by then they couldn't go back, nor could they think of betraying their ideals.

As a rule, the work of the secret agent is dismissed as immoral, and agents themselves as amoral. In the case of the Cambridge Five, nothing could have been further from the truth. If secret agents are amoral, how much more so are the bosses and the political leaders who send them on missions for reasons of state?

Today I believe that the Cambridge Five were truly remarkable men. I still find it hard to comprehend that I worked with these people, who so excelled in culture, education and commitment, who forecast the decline of the USSR at a time when everything seemed to be going perfectly well for us, yet continued to serve the cause.

I have often been asked, and sometimes with real spitefulness, how they could have dedicated their lives to a task which could in no way profit them. If the KGB heads couldn't understand this, how much harder it must have been for the British . . .

The British have a preconceived view of the Five. They cannot work out how a group of aristocrats could have renounced wealth, ambition and love in exchange for risk and danger; how they could have held to the illusion that all this was to serve a great idea. They cannot see how these men could have climbed so high in the social hierarchy of their country, why they were not arrested in time, why, finally, they were allowed to flee to the Soviet Union and thus escape justice. In an era of betrayal and inconstancy, the British cannot understand how the Cambridge Five remained true to their ideals.

The most baffling part of all was that the Five were typical representatives of their nation and their class.

But I think I understand behaviour which might seem inconceivable to some in the West. First of all, I admire their patriotism. All of them, but particularly Guy Burgess, nourished a profound and passionate love of England. Most people view them as traitors, but I don't. I don't think it is an exaggeration for me to say that I know more than anyone about the material they supplied to the Soviets, and I can affirm that not one of the Five ever felt that he was in any way doing harm to his country by supplying it. They worked tirelessly against the Americans, of course. They passed on to us whatever information they could lay their hands on, sometimes to excess. But never once did they knowingly deliver up any secret in the belief that it would damage Great Britain.

In their Cambridge days they unknowingly became caught up in a giant process. They were subscribers to the Communist movement; it never crossed their minds that they were betraying Great Britain. First of all they fought for the triumph of world revolution. The rest came later. What lay behind that revolution, how much cruelty and perfidy would it breed? These, for them, were not the issues. They were above all loyal to an ideal, to the creation of a just, egalitarian society to combat Fascism. For this they made common cause with

Russia. They weren't simply Communists or fellow-travellers; they saw themselves as true revolutionaries, ready to sacrifice other people as well as themselves for the cause. Nor can they be faulted on account of their trust in Stalin: the same error was made by an entire generation of honest men and women all over the world.

In hindsight, it is clear that they were naïve – but in the 1930s, that was the way it was.

When I think of them now, I see them as Don Quixote figures who spent their lives tilting at windmills, while history was inexorably destroying their ideal. Scorning the other illusions of humanity – power, wealth, love, ambition, serenity and glory – they chose to follow the greatest illusion of all, which is politics. They swore an oath of loyalty to the revolution. They did not break faith.

INDEX